THE ATMAN PROJECT

Ken Wilber is also the author of
The Spectrum of Consciousness

THE
ATMAN
PROJECT
A Transpersonal View
of Human Development

By Ken Wilber

*This publication made possible
with the assistance of the Kern Foundation*

The Theosophical Publishing House
Wheaton, Ill. U.S.A.
Madras, India/London, England

Quest books are published by The Theosophical Publishing House, a department of The Theosophical Society in America which is a branch of a world organization dedicated to the promotion of brotherhood and the encouragement of the study of religion, philosophy, and science, to the end that man may better understand himself and his place in the universe. The Society stands for complete freedom of individual search and belief. In the Theosophical Classics Series well-known occult works are made available in popular editions.

Library of Congress Cataloging in Publication Data

Wilber, Ken.
    The atman project.

    (A Quest book)
    Bibliography: p. Includes index.
    1. Genetic psychology. 2. Consciousness.
    3. Spiritualism (Philosophy) I. Title.
    BF701.W5   158'.1   79-3662.   ISBN 0-8356-0532-9

Printed in the United States of America

TO

Roger Walsh,

Whom I am proud to call

friend.

Contents

Preface

The theme of this book is basically simple: development is evolution; evolution is transcendence (Erich Janstch's marvelous phrase: "Evolution as self-realization through self-transcendence");[199] and transcendence has as its final goal Atman, or ultimate Unity Consciousness in only God. All drives are a subset of that Drive, all wants a subset of that Want, all pushes a subset of that Pull—and that whole movement is what we call the Atman-project: the drive of God towards God, Buddha towards Buddha, Brahman towards Brahman, but carried out initially through the intermediary of the human psyche, with results that range from ecstatic to catastrophic. As *Up From Eden*[427] tries to demonstrate, if men and women have ultimately come up from amoebas, then they are ultimately on their way towards God, but in the meantime they are under sway of the incredible half-way house known as the Atman-project. And this entire movement of evolution simply continues from unity to unity until there is only Unity, and the Atman-project finally dissolves in the impact of very Atman.

This book began as a series of articles for the journal RE-VISION, articles which eventually appeared, as a matter of course, in the first four issues of that publication.[412, 415, 416, 424] That overall period of publication, however, stretched out over a year and a half, almost two, and during that time my own thoughts on the subject matter had naturally progressed and matured. This present book, then, while it began as a series of articles for RE-VISION, now bears only a mild resemblance to those articles. To all who read and followed with interest those long articles, I therefore owe the following.

The RE-VISION series took as its major starting-point the suggestion of several Western researchers that the earliest period of infancy, when the neonate is inseparably *fused* with the mother and the environment at large, becomes the model for all adult states of perfect transcendent union and ecstatic oneness. If that is so, then it naturally appeared that the necessary development of the child out of this early fusion-unity represented a fundamental deprivation, not just of an extremely pleasant state, but of a metaphysically *higher* state—a loss of "paradise," or an "alienation from the Self," as Jungians put it. However, as many further suggested, this "higher paradise" could be *recaptured*, by the adult, in a mature and healthy form. This view, or something very like it, has been held in whole or part by the Jungians, by Neumann,[279] by Norman O. Brown,[67] by Mahler and Kaplan,[218] by Loewald and the neo-psychoanalysts,[246] by Watts,[390] by Koestler and Campbell.[66] And while I otherwise hold the views of those researchers in the highest regard, upon further reflection, that particular notion seemed more and more untenable. Not only did it incorrectly invite odious comparisons of the transpersonal realm with the infantile, it seemed to be based on a lack of appreciation of the profound differences between what we (following Wescott[395]) will call "pre-" states and "trans-" states.

The infantile fusion-state is indeed a type of "paradise," as we will see, but it is one of pre-personal ignorance, not transpersonal awakening. The true nature of the pre-personal, infantile fusion state did not acutely dawn on me until I ran across Piaget's description of it: "The self at this stage is *material*, so to speak...."[297] And *material union* is, as we will see, the lowest possible unity of all—there is nothing metaphysically "high" about it; the fact that it *is* a unity structure, prior to subject-object differentiation, erroneously invites its identification with the truly higher unity structures which are trans-subject/object. At the point that became obvious to me, the whole schema that I had presented in RE-VISION re-arranged itself slightly in just the right spots, and this whole book more or less fell into place of its own accord. Although little of the actual data I presented in RE-VISION have changed, my new understanding of a different context for that data (*pre* and *trans*) has necessitated a few changes in terminology.

I have reserved "uroboros" for the pre-personal state of infantile material fusion (along with "pleroma"); "centaur" is now reserved strictly for the mature integration of body and ego-mind, and "typhon" is introduced for the infantile period of pre-differentiation of body and ego (Freud's "body-ego" stages); "transpersonal" refers strictly to the mature, adult forms of transcendence of the ego-mind and body; my use of the terms "evolution" and "involution" has been brought into accord with that of Hinduism (e.g., Aurobindo), and my original use of those terms (based on Coomaraswamy) has been replaced by the terms "Outward Arc" and "Inward Arc." The notion of the Atman-project remains precisely unchanged; however, since the ideal state of ecstatic union is not even slightly the pre-personal fusion of "infantile cosmic consciousness" but rather the transpersonal unity of the causal-ultimate realm, the context of the Atman-project has naturally shifted towards that state, much more explicitly than it was in my original formulations. All of the above could, I believe, be understood by reading every now and then between the lines of the original articles; in this book, it is presented *in* the lines, as straightforwardly as I can put it.

There follows, then, the story of the Atman-project. It is a sharing of what I have seen; it is a small offering of what I have remembered; it is also the zen dust which you should shake from your sandals; and it is finally a lie in the face of that Mystery which only alone is.

Ken Wilber
Lincoln, Nebraska
Winter, 1978

Know that, by nature, every creature seeks to become like God.

Meister Eckhart

All creatures seek after unity; all multiplicity struggles toward it—the universal aim of all life is always this unity.

Johann Tauler

Being one with the universe, one with God—that is what we wish for most whether we know it or not.

Fritz Kunkel

1

Prologue

Everywhere we look in nature, said the philosopher Jan Smuts, we see nothing but *wholes*.[354] And not just simple wholes, but hierarchical ones: each whole is a part of a larger whole which is itself a part of a larger whole. Fields within fields within fields, stretching through the cosmos, interlacing each and every thing with each and every other.

Further, said Smuts, the universe is not a thoughtlessly static and inert whole—the cosmos is not lazy, but energetically dynamic and even creative. It tends (we would now say teleonomically, not teleologically) to produce higher- and higher-level wholes, evermore inclusive and organized. This overall cosmic process, as it unfolds in time, is nothing other than *evolution*. And the drive to ever-higher unities, Smuts called *holism*.

If we continued this line of thinking, we might say that because the human mind or psyche is an aspect of the cosmos, we would expect to find, in the psyche itself, the same hierarchical arrangement of wholes within wholes, reaching from the simplest and most rudimentary to the most complex and inclusive. In general, such is exactly the discovery of modern psychology. As Werner put it, "Wherever development occurs it proceeds from a state of relative globality and lack of differentiation to a state of increasing differentiation, articulation, and hierarchical integration."[394] Jakobson speaks of "those stratified phenomena which modern psychology uncovers in the different areas of the realm of the mind,"[196] where each stratified layer is more integrated and more encompassing than its predecessor. Bateson points out that even learning itself is hierarchical, involving several major levels, each of which is "meta-" to its predecessor.[23] As a general approximation, then, we may conclude that the psyche—like the cosmos at large—is many-layered ("pluridimensional"), composed of successively higher-order wholes and unities and integrations.

The holistic evolution of nature—which produces everywhere higher and higher wholes—shows up in the human psyche as *develop-*

1

ment or *growth*. The same force that produced man from amoebas produces adults from infants. That is, a person's growth, from infancy to adulthood, is simply a miniature version of cosmic evolution. Or, we might say, psychological growth or development in humans is simply a microcosmic reflection of universal growth on the whole, and has the same goal: the unfolding of ever higher-order unities and integrations. And this is one of the major reasons that the psyche is, indeed, stratified. Very like the geological formation of the earth, psychological development proceeds, stratum by stratum, level by level, stage by stage, with each successive level superimposed upon its predecessor in such a way that it includes but transcends it ("envelops it," as Werner would say).

Now in psychological development, the *whole* of any level becomes merely a *part* of the whole of the next level, which in turn becomes a part of the next whole, and so on throughout the evolution of consciousness. Take, as but one example, the development of language: the child first learns babbling sounds, then wider vowel and consonant sounds, then simple words, then small phrases, then simple sentences, and then extended sentences. At each stage, simple parts (e.g., words) are integrated into higher wholes (e.g., sentences), and, as Jakobson points out, "new additions are superimposed on earlier ones and dissolution begins with the higher strata."[196]

Modern developmental psychology has, on the whole, simply devoted itself to the exploration and explanation of the various levels, stages, and strata of the human constitution—mind, personality, psychosexuality, character, consciousness. The cognitive studies of Piaget[294] and Werner,[393] the works of Loevinger[243] and Arieti[7] and Maslow[262] and Jakobson,[196] the moral development studies of Kohlberg[229]—all subscribe, in whole or part, to the concept of stratified stages of increasing differentiation, integration, and unity.

Having said that much, we are at once entitled to ask, "What, then, is the *highest* stage of unity to which one may aspire?" Or perhaps we should not phrase the question in such ultimate terms, but simply ask instead, "What is the nature of some of the higher and highest stages of development? What forms of unity are disclosed in the most developed souls of the human species?"

We all know what the "lower" stages and levels of the psyche are like (I am speaking in simple, general terms): they are instinctual, impulsive, libidinous, id-ish, animal, ape-like. And we all know what some of the "middle" stages are like: socially adapted, mentally adjusted, egoically integrated, syntaxically organized, conceptually advanced. But are there no higher stages? Is an "integrated ego" or "autonomous individual" the highest reach of consciousness in human beings? The individual ego is a marvelously high-order unity, but compared with the Unity of the cosmos at large, it is a pitiful slice of holistic reality. Has nature labored these billions of years just to bring forth this egoic mouse?

The problem with that type of question lies in *finding* examples of truly higher-order personalities—and in deciding exactly *what* constitutes a higher-order personality in the first place. My own feeling is that as humanity continues its collective evolution, this will become very easy to decide, because more and more "enlightened" personalities will show up in data populations, and psychologists will be forced, by their statistical analyses, to include higher-order profiles in their developmental stages. In the meantime, one's idea of "higher-order" or "highly developed" remains rather philosophic. Nonetheless, those few gifted souls who have bothered to look at this problem have suggested that the world's great mystics and sages represent some of the very highest, if not the highest, of all stages of human development. Bergson said exactly that; and so did Toynbee, and Tolstoy and James and Schopenhauer and Nietzsche and Maslow.

The point is that we *might* have an excellent population of extremely evolved and developed personalities in the form of the world's great mystic-sages (a point which is supported by Maslow's studies). Let us, then, simply *assume* that the authentic mystic-sage represents the very highest stages of human development—as far beyond normal-and-average humanity as humanity itself is beyond apes. This, in effect, would give us a sample which approximates "the highest state of consciousness"—a type of "superconscious state." Furthermore, most of the mystic-sages have left rather detailed records of the stages and steps of their own transformations into the superconscious realms. That is, they tell us not only of the highest level of consciousness and superconsciousness, but also of all the intermediate levels leading up to it. If we take all these higher stages and add them to the lower and middle stages/levels which have been so carefully described and studied by Western psychology, we would then arrive at a fairly well-balanced and comprehensive model of the spectrum of consciousness. That, exactly, is the nature and aim of this volume.

The Outward and Inward Arc

Once we put all the stages and levels of consciousness evolution together, we arrive at something that resembles an *overall life cycle.* Further, we will find that—if all the higher stages reported by the mystics are real—this life cycle moves from subconsciousness (instinctual, impulsive, id-ish) to self-consciousness (egoic, conceptual, syntaxical) to superconsciousness (transcendent, transpersonal, transtemporal), as shown in Fig. 1. Further, we can divide this cycle, for convenience, into two halves: the Outward Arc, or the movement from subconsciousness to self-consciousness, and the Inward Arc, or movement from self-consciousness to superconsciousness (see Fig. 1). The overall cycle is nicely described by Ananda Coomaraswamy:

> The life or lives of man may be regarded as constituting a curve—an arc of time-experience subtended by the duration of the individual Will to Life. The outward movement of this curve...—the Path of Pursuit—the *Pravritti Marga*—is characterized by self-assertion. The

inward movement—...the Path of Return—the *Nivritti Marga*—is characterized by increasing Self-realization. The religion of men on the outward path is the Religion of Time; the religion of those who return is the Religion of Eternity.[86]

The story of the Outward Arc is the story of the Hero—the story of the terrible battle to break free of the sleep in the subconscious, the immersion in the primal matrix of pre-differentiation. The story of the Outward Arc is also the story of the ego, for the ego *is* the Hero; the story of its emergence from unconsciousness—the conflicts, the growths, the terrors, the rewards, the anxieties. It occurs in the arena of differentiation, separation, and possible alienation; of growth, individuation, and emergence.

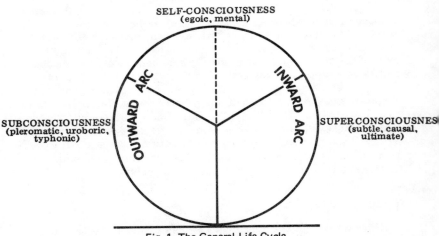

Fig. 1. The General Life Cycle

But the Outward Arc, the move from subconsciousness to self-consciousness, is only half of the story of the evolution of consciousness—a necessary half to be sure, but a half nonetheless. Beyond the self-conscious ego, according to mystic-sages, lies the path of return and the psychology of eternity—the Inward Arc. Our job, then, is to try to set forth the entire story of the evolution of consciousness, including not only the Outward swing from sub- to self-consciousness, but also the Inward swing from self- to superconsciousness (a complete map of which is offered in Fig. 2 for future reference). We will find that the subconscious is a type of pre-personal unity; the superconscious is a transpersonal unity—and the incredible voyage between these two terminals is the story of this volume.

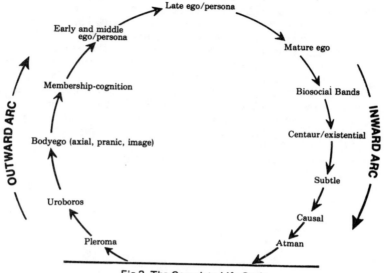

Fig 2. The Complete Life Cycle

The Approach

The psychological evolution of men and women from infancy to adulthood—that is, the whole process of ontogeny—has generally been investigated in the West under the very broad heading of "developmental psychology." Historically, the field as a whole has included such diverse elements as cognitive development, moral maturation, learning theory, psychosexual stages, motivational and affective and intellectual development, role appropriation—all of it, however, being more-or-less confined to just the Outward Arc.

But even that study of the Outward Arc alone is today so vast, and embodies so many different theoretical and methodological approaches, that only the broadest and most general conclusions can, at this time, be drawn. We have, at the very least, the major works of Baldwin, Dewey, Tufts, G. H. Mead, Broughton, Jung, Piaget, Sullivan, Freud, Ferenczi, Erikson, Werner, Hartmann, Arieti, Loevinger, Kohlberg, etc. I mention all those names only so I can say that it is not my intention to argue the merits of any of them over the others, but merely to discuss the significance of the Outward Arc as a whole in light of the Inward Arc. Thus, I will simply present a working outline of some of the generally accepted stages of the development of the self sense, drawing freely from the major developmental schools in what might appear at times a rather indiscriminate fashion.

Further, I will not absolutely distinguish the different lines of development, such as cognitive, moral, affective, conative, motivational, emotional, and intellectual, since whether any or all of these sequences are parallel, independent, or equivalent, or whether they represent one source or many cannot yet be decided in all cases, and I wish from the start to avoid such intricate debate.

The same thing holds, in essence, for the Inward Arc as well: I will take the same type of general over-view approach, drawing freely from the mystical schools East and West, Hinduism, Buddhism, Taoism, Sufism, Christianity, Platonism, etc. I am aware that in assuming this friendly and neutral approach to each of the various schools, high or low, psychological or religious, I am apt to be disowned by them all—but no other approach will give us the necessary data for a well-rounded and completed model.

We begin, then, at the beginning. Or rather, at the moment of birth....

2

The Primitive Roots of Awareness

The Pleromatic Self

By almost all accounts, neither the fetus in the womb nor the infant at birth possesses a developed self sense. For the neonate there is no real separation whatsoever between inside and outside, subject and object, body and environment. It is not exactly that the baby is born into a world of material objects which he cannot recognize, but that—from the infant's view—there literally are as yet no *objects* whatsoever. Events, yes; objective events, no. That is, the infant is indeed aware of certain events, but not as "objective," not as separate from himself. The objective world and the infant's subjective awareness are completely undifferentiated—the neonate cannot differentiate the material world from his actions on it. And thus, in a special sense, his self and his physical environment are one and the same.

The self is "pleromatic," as the alchemists and gnostics would put it, which essentially means that the self and the *material* cosmos are undifferentiated. Piaget himself says precisely as much: "During the early stages the world and the self are one; neither term is distinguished from the other...the *self is material*, so to speak," (my italics).²⁹⁷ The self is embedded in the *materia prima*, which is both the primal chaos of physical matter and the maternal matrix or Prakriti from whence all creation was fashioned.

"The baby at birth," concludes Loevinger, "cannot be said to have an ego. His first task is to learn to differentiate himself from his surroundings."²⁴³ Or, as von Bertalanffy puts it, "The most primitive stage [of consciousness] apparently is one where a difference between outside world and ego is not experienced.... The baby does not yet distinguish between himself and things outside; only slowly does he learn to do so."³⁴ And Koestler summarizes it all very nicely: "Freud and Piaget, among others, have emphasized the fact that the new-born infant does not differentiate between ego and environment. It is aware of events, but not of itself as a separate entity.... The universe is focused on the self, and the self is the universe—a condition which Piaget called 'protoplasmic' or 'symbiotic' consciousness."

Because this stage is one of absolute adualism, oceanic and autistic, it also tends to be pre-spatial and pre-temporal. There is no real space for the neonate in the sense that there is no gap, distance, or separation between the pleromatic self and the environment. And thus, there is likewise no time, since a succession of objects in space cannot be recognized. The neonate's awareness is spaceless, timeless, objectless (but not event-less). And for all these reasons, analysts (such as Ferenczi) are fond of referring to this stage as one of "unconditional omnipotence," which "persists as long as no conception of objects exists" (Fenichel).[120] That is, since there is no real conception of space, time, and objects, there are no perceived limitations. Hence, the omnipotence of ignorance. As the Jungian researcher Neumann put it, this is "the pleromatic stage of paradisal perfection in the unborn, the embryonic stage of the ego, which a later consciousness will contrast with the sufferings of the nonautarchic ego in the world."[279]

Notice that this is a *pre*-personal perfection, not a trans-personal one. It is indeed a type of primal paradise, but a paradise of innocence and ignorance, the state before the Fall into self-consciousness. And, as we will see, it should not be confused with the trans-personal paradise of superconsciousness. The one is pre-, the other trans-, and the difference between them is simply the entire life cycle of consciousness.

PLEROMATIC SELF	
• cognitive style—	absolute adualism; objectless, spaceless, protoplasmic
• affective atmosphere—	total oceanic, unconditional omnipotence, pleromatic paradise
• conative or motivational factors—	almost entirely absent; desireless, choiceless
• temporal mode—	timeless as pre-temporal (not trans-temporal)
• mode of self—	oceanic, protoplasmic, pleromatic, *materia prima*

The Alimentary Uroboros

One of the first tasks of the infant is to construct some sort of objective world apart from himself, an act which simultaneously begins to structure his subjective self-sense. But this task is by no means an immediate success, and between the stage of complete adualism and that of a rudimentary self sense localized as the individual body, the infant's awareness floats in what Neumann called an "extrapersonal, uroboric realm." As he words it, "I think of this stratum of the archetypal field as something 'extra-personal,' as well as 'beyond' the opposites of psychical and physical determined by consciousness." I would prefer "prepersonal," wherein psychical and physical have not yet been differentiated, but the point is that in the "development of the individual there is an initial preponderance of [uroboric] factors, [pre-personal or extra-personal], and only in the course of development does the personal realm come into view and achieve independence."[279] The uroboros is collective, archaic, still mostly oceanic: the word "uroboros" itself is taken from the mythical serpent that, eating its own tail, forms a self-contained, pre-differentiated mass, "in the round," ignorant unto itself.

"The initial stage symbolized by the uroboros," writes Neumann, "corresponds to a pre-ego stage; the stage of earliest childhood when an ego germ is just beginning to be.... Naturally, then, the first phases of man's evolving ego consciousness are under the dominance of the uroboros. They are the phases of an infantile ego consciousness which, although no longer entirely embryonic [that is, no longer entirely pleromatic] and already possessing an existence of its own, still lives in the round [the uroboros], not yet detached from it and only just beginning to differentiate itself from it."[279] As Neumann points out, there is a difference between the pleromatic and the uroboric self. As we are explaining it, the pleromatic self is absolutely adual, with no significant boundaries whatsoever; but the uroboric self already possesses some sort of self-boundary—it is already beginning to break the old oceanic state into two global terms, namely the uroboric self versus some sort of "uroboric other" or "uroboric environ." Both are prepersonal.

At this point, then, the infant's self no longer *is* the material chaos, for he is beginning to recognize something *outside* of himself, something other than his self, and this global, undifferentiated, prepersonal environ we call the *uroboric other*. This stage, therefore, is marked by pervasive adualism, but not (like the previous stage) an absolute adualism. But this also means that, although to a lesser degree than in the pleromatic stage, there exists in the infant's awareness "only momentary states, with no distinctions of time and place," which Sullivan called the "prototaxic mode" of experience, where all that the infant knows are "momentary states, and his experiences are 'cosmic' in the sense that they are undefined and unlimited."[46] Uroboric.

Because this stage occurs towards the beginning of the extended oral phase of infancy—where the infant's major connection with the world is an *oral* connection—Neumann also calls the self at this point the "alimentary uroboros," and, in some few ways, this corresponds with the pre-ambivalent (pre-personal) oral stage of psychoanalysis.

It is also called "alimentary" because the entire uroboros is dominated by "visceral psychology"—by unconscious nature, by physiology, by instincts, by reptilian perception and the most rudimentary emotional discharges. As Neumann puts it, in the uroboric state the organism still "swims about in its instincts like an animal. Enfolded and upborne by great Mother Nature, rocked in her arms, he is delivered over to her for good or ill. Nothing is himself; everything is world [the self is still more-or-less material and pleromatic]. The world shelters and nourishes him, while he scarcely wills and acts at all. Doing nothing, lying inert in the unconscious, merely being there in the inexhaustible twilight world, all needs effortlessly supplied by the great nourisher— such is that early, beatific state."[279] And it is beatific because it is pre-personal, almost pre-existence—the self does not yet suffer much because there is not yet much of a self.

In some ways, then, this uroboric state is still one of blissful ignorance and pre-Fall awareness. "The ego germ still dwells in the pleroma..., and, as consciousness unborn, slumbers in the primordial egg, in the bliss of paradise."[279] According to psychoanalysis, this is the stage of "magical hallucinatory omnipotence," which is the "period immediately after birth when the infant feels that all he has to do is wish for something and it will appear."[120] Eventually, we will see this pre-personal blissfulness—the euphoria of not yet being an ego— give way to *ananda* and *mahasukha*, the supreme bliss of no longer being an ego: the bliss of transcendence.

Of course, to agree that the uroboros "slumbers in paradise" is not to say that it is without its fears, or rudimentary tensions, or "unpleasures." As blissfully ignorant as some researchers maintain this stage to be, we must not overlook the fact that here also exist the roots of a primordial fear. The Upanishads put it, "Wherever there is other, there is fear." The uroboric self of the infant begins to sense the oppressive and primal mood of fear for the simple reason that it now recognizes an *other*—the uroboric other. We might note that the Jungians, the Freudians, and the Kleinians all agree that this primal fear is best interpreted as an *oral* one—that is, the primal fear is a fear of being swallowed, engulfed, and annihilated by the uroboric other (often in the form of the "bad breast").[279, 120, 225] Since the uroboros can "swallow" the other, it likewise fears the same fate.[120] And this whole state of affairs, this primal fear of being annihilated at the hands of the uroboric other, Neumann calls *uroboric castration*.

To round out this survey of the uroboros, we might note that the organism's cognitive development is only in the earliest stages of the sensorimotor realm (stages 1, 2, and 3, which altogether we call the "uroboric forms" or uroboric "schemes", following Piaget's work).[297] The state is said to be completely acausal,[7] dominated by reflexes and reflex elaboration,[46] and still exhibiting a pre-temporal orientation.[97]

The alimentary uroboros, while experienced in its "purest" form at this pre-ambivalent oral stage, nevertheless will exert a profound influence at least through—to temporarily adopt the psychoanalytic viewpoint—the subsequent oral-sadistic and anal stages, although it is gradually transcended in favor of an increasingly personal and individual awareness. The alimentary uroboros itself, however, remains strictly pre-personal, collective, archaic, reptilian. It is surely one of the most primitive structures of the human psyche, and, together with the base pleroma, might reach back through lower life forms to the very beginning of the cosmos itself.

THE UROBORIC SELF	
• cognitive style—	first subject-object differentiation; acausality; prototaxic mode; hallucinatory wish-fulfillment; uroboric forms (early sensorimotor)
• affective atmosphere—	oceanic-euphoria, primordial fear
• motivational or conative factors—	primitive urge to survival (of uroboric self), physiological needs (hunger)
• temporal mode—	pre-temporal
• mode of self—	uroboric, archaic, pre-personal, reptilian, reflex, alimentary

3

The Typhonic Self

As the infant's sense of self begins to shift from the pre-personal uroboros to the individual organism, we see the emergence and creation of the organic or bodyego self. The bodyself or bodyego is, in a sense, the transition from the serpent stage of the uroboros to the truly human stage of the mental-ego, and therefore we often refer to this entire realm (with all its stages and sub-stages) as the realm of the "typhon"—the typhon, in mythology, is half human, half serpent.

I will divide this phase of typhonic development into three major sub-stages: the axial-body, the pranic-body, and the image-body, recognizing always that these sub-stages greatly overlap in several areas.

The Axial-Body and Pranic-Body

By "axial-body" I mean essentially the physical body felt as distinct from the physical environment. The infant from birth has a physical body, but the infant does not recognize an axial-body until around age 4 to 6 months (and does not finally differentiate self and not-self until around age 15 to 18 months).[218] "Axial-image" is simply a general term for the first stable images which help differentiate the perceiving subject from the perceived or felt object. Axial-images participate in present sensations and perceptions. All of the objects in your field of awareness right now are axial-objects or axial-images: objects "out there" (as well as sensations "in here"). Thus, axial-images recognize *objects* (items somehow different from self), but only *present* objects. Axials dominate the third, fourth, and fifth stages of sensorimotor intelligence. "At stage 5," as Gardner summarizes it, "the child has already achieved an effective, supple commerce with the world of objects. Yet, he remains restricted to the world of objects present; when things disappear from view (or when he looks away), he

12

has difficulty incorporating them into his domain of thought."[149] His world is still largely (but not totally) *axial*—it is limited to the simple, the immediate, and the still rather vague present. At any rate, under the influence of systems of axial-images, the infant constructs both a type of external reality as well as a physical or bodily sense of inward self.[218]

Because a definite organic self is starting to emerge, the basic emotions of this self likewise begin to emerge. This basic emotional component (as opposed to the cruder reflex-instincts of the uroboros) we call the pranic level or the pranic-body (after the Hindus and Buddhists.) But at this stage, the emotions are still rather primitive and elementary. As authors such as Werner[393] and Arieti[7] have pointed out, the cognitive constructs of this early level (that is, the axial-images) are so elementary and skeletal in nature that they cannot elicit or sustain any of the higher or more complex emotions. Rather, the basic emotions present at this stage are what Arieti, in a careful survey of the literature, calls elementary emotions or "proto-emotions," such as rage, fear, tension, appetite, and satisfaction or simple pleasure.[7]

Since, as we have seen, the characteristic time-component of the axial level is nothing but the immediate present, it is not surprising that Arieti also calls these emotions "quick" or "short-circuited." That is, short-circuited emotions are the only emotions that can be floated or carried by the axial-image in the quick and immediate present; no other emotions can be sustained in this simple temporal mode, and thus no others are elicited. Cognitive constructs more elaborate than the axial-image will have to develop before more complex or sustained emotions can emerge. All in all, the emotions characteristic of this early stage are—as general psychoanalytic thought also maintains—very quick, short-circuited, and thus they tend towards immediate and undiluted discharge, there being nothing in time to prevent them.[120, 243]

We might note, in passing, that according to psychoanalysis, and especially the Kleinians, the most significant axial-images are those of the breast, "the mother regarded as part object." This breast-image tends to emerge out of the "projective identification" wherein the mother, the self, and the breast are all initially one and undifferentiated. The corresponding fear at this stage is "loss of breast." This fear is said to lead to a splitting of the breast-image into a "good breast" and a "bad breast," the former promising life (Eros), the latter threatening death (Thanatos).[226, 46]

The axial-image and the quickness of the temporal mode of this level are also intimately related to the two broad motivational aspects of this level; (for convenience, I am combining the axial and pranic levels as one) the pleasure-unpleasure principle and the drive for immediate survival. Take the survival drive first: Insofar as the self sense of the infant has begun to center and focus on his individual organism, he apprehends the vague and as yet unarticulated threat of extinction more keenly than he did in the uroboric state. Being more aware of his separate self sense on this axial-body level, the infant is more keenly attuned to its possible extinction. Thus simple and "quick" survival, or more precisely, the moment-to-moment continuation of the separate self sense, becomes paramount on this level.

The second of the two broad motivational atmospheres of this level is the pleasure-unpleasure principle. I use this phrase, as Freud not always did, in both its positive and negative senses: the search for bodily pleasure and satisfaction as well as the avoidance of tension, unpleasure, and discomfort. For at this stage—the axial-pranic, or physical-emotional—"motivation as a tendency to search for pleasure and avoid unpleasure, thus becomes a fundamental psychological force."[7] Neumann would agree with that appraisal and would further point out the reason why the pleasure-unpleasure or pleasure-pain principle is not so prominent in the previous uroboric and pleromatic stages, but truly blossoms on this axial-body level: "When the ego begins to emerge from its identity with the uroboros, and the embryonic connection with the womb ceases, the ego wakes up to a new attitude to the world. The individual's view of the world changes with every stage of his development, and the variation of archetypes and symbols, gods and myths, is the expression, but also the instrument, of this change [he is, as we will see, talking about "symbols of transformation"]. Detachment from the uroboros means being born and descending into the...world of reality, full of dangers and discomforts. The nascent ego becomes aware of pleasure-pain qualities, and from them it experiences its own pleasure and pain. Consequently, the world becomes ambivalent."[279] So where "oceanic blissfulness" rules over the pleromatic and uroboric states, the pleasure principle reigns over the bodily. The latter, we will see, is a *transformation* of the former.

According to psychoanalysis, bodily pleasure is initially "polymorphously perverse," which is to say, the infant is capable of securing pleasurable sensations from all activities, surfaces, and organs of the body. The pleasure principle, in this sense, is a bodily principle, for, to be more precise, the whole body at this stage is "full of a still undifferentiated total sexuality which contains all the latter 'partial instincts' in one."[120] Further, "the pleasure-fulfilling movement occurs spontaneously and unhesitatingly as 'an averting movement away from something disagreeable, or an approach towards something agreeable.'"[7] Thus, quick or short-circuited seeking and quick or short-circuited avoidance mark the two closely interrelated and almost inseparable motivational tones of this axial/pranic level: survival and pleasure.

Dr. Arieti gives a finely balanced and penetrating summary of the major aspects of this level of the self sense:

> Is it possible at this sensorimotor...or exoceptual pleasure-principle level [that is, the overall axial/pranic body] to experience a sense or awareness of the self, which includes and integrates the functions that we

have studied? If by "self" we mean a living subject, then
of course we can state that at this stage the self is an
organism operating at a protoemotional-exoceptual
level ["exocept" is roughly similar to what we have
called the "axial-image"]. If by self we mean the individual as he is known to himself, then we must say that
this state of consciousness is rudimentary. It probably
consists of a bundle of simple relations between physiostates, perceptions, protoemotions, and exocepts—
relations which at first involve some parts of the body,
particularly the mouth [oral stage]. However, as patterns of motor behavior develop in relation to external
objects, a kind of primitive motor identity, as well as
awareness of the totality of one's body, probably evolves
even in subhuman animals.[7]

Finally, as suggested above in brackets, the overall typhonic
stage(s)— axial, pranic, and image—is in some ways similar to the
whole oral (and especially oral-sadistic) period described by psychoanalysis. The typhonic realm itself, however, reaches back to the
alimentary uroboros, and will reach forward to the anal and phallic
aspects of the subsequent stages of development.

THE AXIAL and PRANIC SELF

- cognitive style —   feeling; sensorimotor; acausal-
                                 ity; axial-images; exoceptual

- affective elements —   elementary emotions (fear,
                                 greed, rage, pleasure); pranic
                                 level

- motivational/conative factors— immediate survival; the pleas-
                                 ure-unpleasure principle

- temporal mode —   concrete, momentary, passing
                                 present

- mode of self —   axial-body, pranic, sensori-
                                 motor, narcissistic

The Image-Body

The emergence of the infant's ability to create extensive imagery
marks a decisive point in development. Most significantly, the image
allows the infant to eventually construct an extended world of objects
and an expanded mode of time, both of which contribute greatly to the
establishment of "object constancy."[294] By means of the concrete
image, inexact and diffuse and adual at first, but increasingly more

definite, the infant begins the grand construction of a new type of
environment and a new sense of self, a construction which, in Piaget's
system, leads to the final completion of the sensorimotor realms,
and—at the same time—starts to reach far beyond them.

As the first significant axial-image is said to be of the breast, the
first significant concrete image is of the "mothering one" (Sullivan),[259]
for "the first object of every individual is the mother."[46] According to
Sullivan, "This is a very vague image [the mothering one] which,
gradually gets distinguished as not being a part of himself."[46] Furthermore, as a type of continuation and transformation of the split
between the good and bad breast, "the mothering one who contributes
to a feeling of well-being or euphoria is characterized as the 'Good
Mother.' When she disturbs him in some way, another 'complexus of
impressions' becomes the 'Bad Mother.'"[46] The infant thus enters the
decisive but rather prolonged relationship with the Great Mother, a
relationship played out on the bodily plane as an existential (life or
death) drama between the individual organism and its mothering environ.[25] This debate is so significant that, according to Erik Erikson,
it involves nothing less than a conflict between basic trust and basic
mistrust.[108]

We may further note that this whole stage of development (reaching back to the axial/pranic level and forward to the anal and even
phallic stage) has been intensely studied by Jung and his followers as
the "realm of maternal symbolism",[279] and by Freudians as the stages
of the pre-Oedipal mother.[57] Both of these investigations were spurred
on by Bachofen's monumental discovery of the religion of the Great
Mother (underlying, as it were, the patriarchal religions).[17] But by all
accounts, "the wicked, devouring mother and the good mother lavish-
ing affection are two sides of the great...Mother Goddess who reigns
over this psychic stage."[279]

Just as the infant creates and organizes a nexus of images and
impressions of the mothering one, as well as other significant environ-
mental objects, he likewise begins the correlative construction of
non-reflexive self-images, commonly called, at this stage, "body
images." Body-images are simply "image pictures" of the physical or
axial-body, and the "closer" the body-image is to the physical or axial-
body the more "accurate" it is said to be.[339] "Due to the simultaneous
occurrence of both outer tactile and inner sensory data, one's own body
[the axial-body] becomes something apart from the rest of the world
and thus the discerning of self from nonself is made possible. The sum
of the mental representations of the [axial] body and its organs, the
so-called body image [the image-body], constitutes the idea of I [at
this stage] and is of basic importance for the further formation of
the ego."[120]

According to Sullivan, the initial self-images themselves are simply
the "good-me," the "bad-me," and the "not-me"—which, we might
add, are usually correlative of the Good Mother, the Bad Mother, and
the Devouring Mother, with the entire "nexus of impressions" reflect-

ing the status of the being vs. nullity debate so acutely felt on this bodyself level.[359] We might also note, in connection with the basically undifferentiated organism at this point, that this stage is, not surprisingly, said to be bisexual, with sense organs overlapping.[120, 279, 135]

But let us now turn to the image itself, for it is most significant that at this stage of development many objects which are not immediately at hand can, by virtue of the image, be *imagined*. That is, the infant can begin to imagine or picture the existence of those objects not immediately present (this differentiates the image proper from the axial-image; the axial-image can picture only present objects, the image proper can picture non-present objects). Thus the infant's present matrix of experience is to some extent *expanded* through time in a symbolic and representative fashion.[7] The infant begins to enter the world of an extended, but as yet random, series of moments. He moves in an *extended present* through which float the unorganized images of past events and the random images of future possibilities.[359]

Now at this point, these images seem to operate in what Sullivan called the "parataxic mode," where the "undifferentiated wholeness of experience is broken down into parts, which are still not connected in any logical way. They 'just happen' together or not, depending on circumstances. The process is analogous to the grammatical term 'parataxic', which refers to the placing of clauses one after another without any connectives ('and,' 'or,' 'since,' etc.) to show logical relations between them. What the child experiences he implicitly, without reflection, accepts as the natural way. There is no step-by-step process of symbolic activity, and inferences cannot be made. Experience is undergone as momentary, unconnected organismic (bodyself) states."[46]

Further, the parataxic mode is roughly equivalent to what Freud termed the prelogical "primary process," for in "cases of parataxic (cognition), a response takes place which follows a primary-process type of organization."[7] This type of organization was codified by von Domarus as "predicate-identity" or "part-identity": objects are perceived as identical if they share outstanding predicates or parts, and thus classes are confused with members of the class, and each member confused with each other.[7, 23] Thus, to give a simple example, the primary process cannot easily distinguish between a cave, a box, a womb, and a cup, because all share the predicate "hollowness" and the part "opening." All of these objects belong to the class of "hollow objects with one opening," and thus each object is viewed as identical with each other object, and one object can *be* the whole of the class and the whole of the class can *be* entirely in one object alone. At any rate, "in their purest forms images belong to the primary process,"[7] and it is mostly this fact which accounts for the phenomena of "displacement" (one object "becomes" another) and "condensation" (a whole class of objects collapses entirely onto one member of the class).[135]

I will later be at pains to differentiate the infantile primary process from the higher forms of phantasy (which we will call vision-image).

The lower-phantasy—the primary process—can be an endless source of trouble, whereas the higher-phantasy process is an endless source of creativity. The lower phantasy, the primary process, is actually a type of magical cognition that confuses the subject and the predicate as well as the whole and the part (that is, cannot distinguish a member of the class from the class itself).[28] In the same way, the primary process tends to confuse subject and object—it might best be thought of as a "blurring" of the subjective psyche with the material world. Since the subject and the object are just starting to differentiate at this stage, the cognitive mode of this stage tends likewise to be "confused," or undifferentiated. Piaget explains it this way:

> During the early stages the world and the self are one; neither term is distinguished from the other [the pleromatic-uroboric stages]. But when they become distinct, these two terms begin by remaining very close to each other: the world is still conscious and full of intentions, the self is still material, so to speak. At each step in the process of dissociation these two terms evolve in the sense of the greatest divergence, but they are never in the child (nor in the adult for that matter) entirely separate.... At every stage there remain in the conception of nature what we might call 'adherences', fragments of internal experience which still cling to the external world.[297]

This basic and magical confusion of inner and outer, psyche and material environment, is one of the characteristics of the pre-verbal primary process (a point Arieti also makes).[7] It is as if this most primitive of cognitive forms, which develops as the psyche crystallizes out of the material pleroma, partakes of both the mental subject and the material object, belonging to neither exclusively, but reflecting the first rudimentary spark of knowledge that occurs when subject and object first begin to differentiate.

The image proper does not emerge until around the third stage of sensorimotor development; prior to that time, the infant has only uroboric forms, axial-images, motor schemes, etc. "It is only toward the seventh month that the child starts to experience images. For instance, if he is able to look for a rattle when the rattle has been hidden under a pillow, presumably he can carry in his mind the image of the rattle."[7] But from that period onward, images begin to enter decisively in awareness, and by the sixth stage of sensorimotor development (toward the end of the second year), the child can so accurately imagine absent objects that he can form a correct "picture" of object-permanence, "the knowledge that the world is composed of substantial, permanently existing objects which can be manipulated and transformed in diverse ways while still maintaining their identity."[149] And he does this essentially through the power of "picturing" absent objects, however otherwise feeble this imagining process is at this stage.

The presence of the image also greatly extends the infant's emotional and motivational life, for now he can respond not only to present events, persons, and objects, but also to the mere *image* of these entities, which themselves may or may not be present.[116, 120] For the image can *evoke* the same types of emotions and feelings as the actual object or person. Further, the infant can for the first time experience *prolonged* emotions, for not only can the image evoke feeling-tones, it can sustain and prolong them. Thus, as Arieti so clearly shows, the infant can experience anxiety, which is nothing but *imagined*, and thus sustained, fear. Likewise, he can *wish*, since a wish is simply an *imagined* pleasure.[7] No longer just present fear, but imagined fear; no longer just present bodily pleasure, but wished-for pleasure. Thus the image gives rise to *wish-fulfillment* as well as *anxiety-reduction*, and these are extended transformations of the simpler pleasure-unpleasure principle which operated on the previous level.[7] Wish-fulfillment and anxiety-avoidance thus become significant motivations of this level—and both reach beyond the present or axial moment to future possibilities. However, since there are still as yet no strong or effective inhibitions, these emotions tend still to find immediate discharge.[120] Because of this "unruly" immediacy, this stage is often referred to as one of "impulse predominance."[243]

Be that as it may, the infant has now stepped out of his initial material and pleromatic embeddedness, and so awakens to find a world apart from himself, and a world of which he is no longer the prime mover. The pleromatic paradise is gone forever.

THE IMAGE-BODY SELF

- cognitive style—
  parataxic, magical primary process, multivalent images; sensorimotor completion

- affective elements—
  sustained emotions, wishes, anxiety, rudimentary desires

- motivational/conative elements—
  wish-fulfillment, anxiety-reduction, prolonged survival and safety

- temporal mode—
  extended present

- mode of self—
  non-reflexive body-image

The Nature of the Typhon: A Summary

I would like to conclude this section by emphasizing that it is generally agreed, by Eastern and Western psychology alike, that the lowest levels of development involve simple biological functions and processes. That is, the lowest levels involve somatic processes, instincts, simple sensations and perceptions, and emotional-sexual impulses. We have seen the Western evidence: in Piaget's system, this is the sensorimotor realms; Arieti refers to them as instinctual, exoceptual, and protoemotional; Loevinger calls them presocial, impulsive, and symbiotic; this is the id-realms of Freud and the uroboric realms of Neumann; and it is Maslow's lowest two needs, the physiological and the safety.

Eastern psychology agrees perfectly with that assessment. To Vedanta Hinduism, this is the realm of the anna- and prana-mayakosa, the levels of hunger and emotional-sexuality (those are precise translations).[94] The Buddhist calls them the lower five vijnanas, or the realm of the five senses.[107] The chakra psychology (of Yoga) refers to them as the lower three chakras: the muladhara, or root material and pleromatic level; svadhisthana, or emotional-sexual level; and manipura, or aggressive-power level.[329] This is also the lower three skandhas in the Hinayana Buddhist system of psychology: the physical body, perception-feeling, and emotion-impulse.[107] In the Kabbalah, or Hebrew-mystic school, this is the malkuth (the physical plane) and the yesod (the vital-emotional).[338] And all in all, this simply points up one of Freud's major ideas: "The ego," he said, "*is first and foremost a body-ego.*"[140]

We saw that the bodyego—the typhon or bodyself—tends to develop in the following way: It is generally agreed that the infant initially cannot distinguish self from not-self, subject from object, body from environment. That is, the self at this earliest of stages is literally one with the physical world. "During the early stages," we heard Piaget say, "the world and the self are one—the self is still material, so to speak." That initial stage of *material oneness*, which Piaget calls "protoplasmic," we have been calling pleromatic and uroboric (if I may, by way of summary, lump these two stages together). "Pleromatic" is an old gnostic term meaning the material universe—the materia prima and virgo mater. "Uroboros" is the mythic image of the serpent eating its own tail, and signifies "wholly self-contained" (autistic) and "not able to recognize an other" (narcissistic).

It is out of this primordial fusion state (or rather, out of what we will eventually introduce as the "ground-unconscious") that the separate self emerges and, as Freud said, the self emerges first and foremost as a body, a bodyself. That is, the mind—itself very fledgling and undeveloped—is almost *totally undifferentiated from the body*, so that the self's approach to the world is almost totally through *bodily categories* and schemes (biting, sucking, chewing, hitting, pushing, pulling, pleasure, sensory, feeling, oral, anal, phallic, etc.). The self, then, is one of an undeveloped mind—operating only with images—which is undifferentiated from the body: thus, the bodyself. It is, in Neumann's words, a rudimentary self "still identified with the functioning of the body as a whole and with the unity of its organs."[279]

The infant bites a blanket, and it does not hurt; he bites his thumb, and it hurts. There is a difference, he learns, between the body and the not-body, and he gradually learns to focus his awareness *from* the pleroma *to* the body. Thus, out of primitive material unity emerges the first real self sense: the bodyego (I am, in this summary, speaking of the axial, the pranic, and the image body as one). The infant *identifies* with the newly-emergent body, with its sensations and emotions, and gradually learns to differentiate them from the material cosmos at large.

Notice that the bodyego, by differentiating itself from the material environment, actually *transcends* that primitive state of fusion and embeddedness. The bodyego transcends the material environment, and thus can perform physical *operations* upon that environment. Towards the end of the sensorimotor period (around age 2), the child has differentiated the self and the not-self to such a degree that he has a fairly stable image of "object constancy" and so he can *muscularly* coordinate physical operations *on* those objects. He can coordinate a physical movement of various objects in the environment, something he could not easily do as long as he could not differentiate himself *from* those objects.

Let us note that triad: by *differentiating* the self from an object, the self *transcends* that object and thus can *operate* upon it (using *as tools* the *structures* of the level of that self—at this stage, the sensorimotor body).

At this bodyego stage(s), then, the self no longer is bound to the pleromatic environment—but it *is* bound to, or identified with, the biological body. The self, as bodyego, is dominated by instinctual urges, impulsiveness, the pleasure principle, involuntary urges and discharges—all the id-like primary processes and drives described so well by Freud *et al*. This is why we also call the bodyego the "typhonic self"—the typhon, in mythology, is half human, half serpent (uroboros). In physiological terms, the reptilian complex and the limbic system dominate the self at this stage.

The typhon, then, however primitive and lowly it may be, represents a transcendence of the old pleromatic and uroboric embeddedness. The typhon is therefore actually a higher-order unity, since "the body stands for wholeness and unity in general, and its total reaction represents a genuine and creative totality."[279] Thus, finally, we must look upon the typhon, the bodyself, as "a generalized body feeling in which the unity of the body is the first expression of individuality."[279]

4

The Membership Self

The emergence and acquisition of language is very likely the single most significant process on the Outward Arc of the individual's life cycle. It brings in its broad wake a complex of interrelated and intermeshed phenomena, not the least of which are new and higher cognitive styles,[337] an extended notion of time,[120] a new and more unified mode of self,[243] a vastly extended emotional life,[7] elementary forms of reflexive self-control,[267] and the beginnings of—in Castaneda's sense—*membership*.[70]

Now the deep structure of any given language embodies a particular syntax of perception, and to the extent an individual develops the deep structure of his native language, he simultaneously learns to construct, and thus perceive, a particular type of descriptive reality, embedded, as it were, in the language structure itself.[70] From that momentous point on, as far as that Outward Arc goes, the structure of his language is the structure of his self and the "limits of his world."[428]

The matured and calibrated form of this membership cognition, elaborated into its more logical and conceptual forms, is known by many names: the secondary process by Freud,[135] the syntaxical mode by Sullivan,[359] realistic thinking by Piaget,[297] Aristotelean thinking by Arieti.[7] But—and this is what we must carefully explore at this particular stage of evolution—this syntaxical cognition, this verbal-logical thinking, does not develop fully-blown and all at once. In the previous stage of evolution, that of the image-body, we found the infant's awareness dominated by parataxic, magical imagery, along with some remnants from the uroboric, prototaxic modes of cognition. And obviously, the child does not move from this magical primary process, the multi-faceted imagery of the parataxic mode, to the secondary process of verbal, linear, syntaxical thinking all at once. There is a vast gap between the world of paratax (magic images) and the world of syntax (linear, verbal thinking). Between these two worlds lies an intermediate series of cognitive modes, representing something of transition hybrids generated when syntax collides with magic.

Neither purely alogical nor purely logical, this overall intermediate stage(s) has been termed precausal (Piaget),[297] prelogical (Freud),[185] animistic (Ferenczi), magic words and thoughts (Ferenczi),[121] paleological (Arieti),[7] autistic language (Sullivan)[359]—and it has been extensively investigated by Lacan as the "forgotten language of childhood," a language that creates the most prominent structures of the unconscious (according to Lacan's view, which is one I accept when placed in context).[236] Like the magical primary process, this paleologic thinking frequently operates on the basis of a whole/part equivalency and predicate-identity; but unlike the pure primary process, which is strictly composed of non-verbal images, precausal thinking is largely verbal and auditory—it is constructed through linear word-and-name, with abstract and auditory symbols. Unlike the image of the primary process, it is a true type of thinking-proper, operating with proto-concepts, verbal abstraction, and elementary class formation. We might say it is language informed by the magic primary process. This is precisely why Sullivan said that this precausal thinking, which he called "autistic thinking or language", is the *verbal manifestation of the parataxic*.[46] Arieti reports a striking example given by Levy-Bruhl:

> "A Congo native says to a European: 'During the day you drank palm wine with a man, unaware that in him there was an evil spirit. In the evening you heard a crocodile devouring some poor fellow. A wildcat, during the night, ate up all your chickens. Now, the man with whom you drank, the crocodile who ate a man and the wildcat are all one and the same person.'" Obviously [writes Arieti] a common characteristic or predicate (having an evil spirit) led to the identification.... In my view, the logical process is arrested at a stage where a common characteristic...leads to the identification of different subjects. The different subjects (the man, the crocodile, and the wildcat) become equivalent.... At this level of organization, the individual tends to register identical segments of experience and to build a conceptual organization upon the identical segments.[7]

The whole/part equivalency and predicate-identity of this type of thinking places it squarely in a type of mythical and magical atmosphere—and, indeed, Ferenczi (among many others) speaks of this stage as one of "magic words and thoughts".[121] Von Bertalanffy explains:

> Meanwhile, the specific human faculty of speech, and symbolic activities in general, have developed. Here we come to a magical phase, where the animistic experience still persists, but with an important addition: the human being has gained the power of language and other symbols. However, no clear distinction is yet made

between the symbol and the thing designated. Hence, in some way the symbol (e.g., the name or other image) *is* the thing, and manipulation of the symbolic image— such as uttering the name of a thing with appropriate ceremony, depicting the beasts to be hunted, and the like—gives power over the objects concerned. The savage, the infant, and the regressed neurotic have no end of rituals for exerting such magic control.[34]

It might be obvious that many investigators use the terms "magical" and "mythical" somewhat interchangeably, which is perfectly acceptable. I, however, am reserving "magical" for the previous stage of "magic images" and the pure primary process. "Mythical," on the other hand, seems best to describe this present stage of paleologic— more refined than magic, but not quite capable of logical clarity: there is our mythic-membership stage. But I would like to add that mythic-thinking, *in its mature forms*, is not at all pathological or distortive, but rather joins with the higher phantasy (of vision-image) to disclose depths of reality and high modes of archetypal being quite beyond ordinary logic. Nonetheless, the immature paleologic is an unending source of psychic confusion for the child, and leads to a host of unfortunate results—many of them finally pathological.

It is fair to say, then, that this precausal thinking is more-or-less abstract, but it is of rudimentary abstractions shot-through with mythical elements: "At the paleologic level, contrary to the phantasmic level [the previous stage of pure images only], man has the capacity to abstract. He can separate similar data from the manifold of objects and can build up categories or classes of objects. The process of abstraction, however, is far from complete. Either the abstracted part is confused with the whole, or else different wholes to which the similar parts belong are misidentified."'

Thus, rudimentary language formation and precausal thinking infuse the entire consciousness of this early membership level. But the more language itself develops, the more paleologic sinks into the background, for "the growth of speech gradually transforms prelogical thinking into logical, organized, and adjusted thinking, which is a decisive step toward the reality principle."[46] Paratax gives way to syntax.

Of great importance at this stage is the fact that as the child develops the syntax of those around him—a process beginning at this stage—he starts to reconstruct the perceived world of those around him. Through language, grammar, and syntax, he learns a particular description of the world which he will be taught to call reality. This, surely, is the penetrating message of don Juan:

> For a sorcerer, reality, or the world we all know, is only a description.
>
> For the sake of validating this premise don Juan concentrated the best of his efforts into leading me to a genuine conviction that what I held in mind as the world

at hand was merely a description of the world; a description that had been pounded into me from the moment I was born.

He pointed out that everyone who comes into contact with a child is a teacher who incessantly describes the world to him, until the moment when the child is capable of perceiving the world as it is described. According to don Juan, we have no memory of that portentous moment, simply because none of us could possibly have had any point of reference to compare it to anything else...

For don Juan, then, the reality of our day-to-day life consists of an endless flow of perceptual interpretations which we, the individuals who share a specific *membership*, have learned to make in common.[70]

The child learns, then, to transform and thus *create* his perceptual flow according to his membership description.[403] At first he can only *recognize* his new membership reality, but eventually he will be able to *recall* it, moment to moment, whereupon the world-as-described becomes his higher reality and he effectively enters the linguistic realm of being. This is a decisive growth experience, but naturally tends to render the previous stages more-or-less inaccessible. The greatest reason that most childhood experiences are forgotten is not so much that they are violently repressed (some indeed are), as that they do not *fit* the structure of membership-description and thus one doesn't have the *terms* with which to recall them.

This is not, of course, to condemn language, only to point out that the increasing growth and evolution of consciousness also brings many difficulties and potential conflicts. For evolution—on the Outward as well as the Inward Arc—is marked by a hierarchical series of *emergent* structures, running in general from the lower to the higher, and each newly-emergent structure has to be integrated and consolidated with its predecessors—a task of no easy proportions. Not only can the higher structures tend to repress the lower ones, the lower structures can rebelliously disrupt and overwhelm the higher ones. The emergence of the verbal mind is simply a classic example of a higher structure which has the potential to suppress all lower ones, and this can lead to the most unfortunate consequences.

But, as we said, the emergence of language itself—the lower or verbal mind—marks a decisive growth in consciousness, particularly in comparison with the previous bodyself of simple physiostates, perceptions, and simple emotions. In particular, we note that through the use of language the child can, for the first time, construct a representation of a *series* or *sequence* of events, and thus he begins to construct a world of vast emporal extension. He constructs a solid notion of *time*—not just an extended present of imaged objects (as in the previous stage), but a linear chain of abstract representations, running from past to future. "Since a verbal representation of a *sequence* of events is now possible, a temporal dimension is added: man acquires his first understanding of the past and the future. Although long periods of time cannot yet be measured exactly, the past and non-immediate future emerge as full temporal dimensions."[7] Or, as Blum puts the psychoanalytical view, "Speech introduces an extended function of anticipation, since events can be planned in the world of words,"[46] so that, as Fenichel puts it, "time and anticipation become incomparably more adequate through the development of words. The faculty of speech changes...prethinking into a logical, organized, and more adjusted thinking."[120]

All of the above can be quickly summarized: in actuality, the emergence of the verbal mind marks a significant transcendence of the typhonic body, the present-bound body of simple moment-to-moment feelings and impressions. The mind, in fact, is beginning (but only beginning) to crystallize out and differentiate from the body, just as in the previous stage the body crystallized out of the material environment. With the verbal or lower mind, the self is no longer bound and chained to the present, myopic in its vision and confined in its perception. Consciousness is, as it were, expanded through the vehicle of symbolic language, which *creates* for the mind a perceptual space quite beyond mere sensory input.

This is, of course, a monumental advance along the evolutionary curve of consciousness, and a step taken, to date, only by mankind. But, as I tried to demonstrate in *Up from Eden*,[427] there is a price to be paid for every increase in consciousness—as the child himself soon discovers. For notice immediately that language itself carries some sort of *tense*, in its verbs, and as the child looks at the world through the eyes of language, he not surprisingly sees a temporal or *tensed world*—and thus a world of tension, time and anxiety being synonymous (as Kierkegaard knew). Likewise, he learns to construct and identify with a *tensed-self sense*—he gains a past and looks to a future. The price he pays for this growth in consciousness is an increased recognition of his own separateness and thus his own vulnerability. For the child is, to a greater and greater degree, beginning to awaken from his slumber in the subconscious—he is, so to speak, being ejected from that paradisical state of ignorance and thrust into the world of separation, isolation, and mortality.

And so, shortly after the acquisition of language, and rarely before, every child goes through an extended period of nightmares—awakened from sleep screaming bloody murder, alive to the inherent terror of being a separate self, shaken by that primal mood of terror which always lurks beneath the surface of the separate self.

On the positive side, however, as verbal seriality allows the binding of time and the construction of a tensed-membership world, so does it participate in the child's increasing ability to delay, control, channel, and postpone his otherwise impulsive and uncontrollable activities. According to Ferenczi, "Speech...accelerates conscious thinking and the consequent capacity for delay of motor discharge."[46]

The child must conceive and recall the world of time—understand the past and future in abstract terms—if he is to actively gear his responses to that world. That is, "active mastery" and "self-control" depend intimately upon tense and time, as well as upon the growing mastery of the body's musculature.[108, 243] Further, this development of active mastery is a "gradual substituting of actions for mere discharge reactions. This is achieved through the interposing of a *time* period between stimulus and response."[120]

According to the Jungian view, this "delayed-reaction and de-emotionalization runs parallel to the splitting of the archetype into groups of symbols."[194, 279] That is, the self at this stage learns to "break up a large content into partial aspects, experiencing them piecemeal, one after the other," which is to say, experiencing them in linear succession, in time. But, says Neumann, this differentiation is "far from being a negative process," because it is the only way uncontrollable emotional reactivity can be replaced by a growth in consciousness. "For this reason," he says, "there is sound sense in the tendency to separate the [immediate and instinctual] reaction from the perceptual image which releases it [i.e., to insert *time* between the instinctual-response and the image-stimulus]. If the emergence of an archetype is not immediately following by an instinctive reflex action, so much the better for conscious development, because the effect of the emotional-dynamic components is to disturb or even prevent...consciousness."[279]

Not only does language help establish a higher-order membership reality and a higher-order self, it also serves as a major vehicle through which actions acceptable to this membership world may be communicated, generally by the parents. By means of word-and-thought, the child internalizes the early parental prohibitions and demands, and thus creates what has variously been called the "preconscience" (Fenichel), "sphincter morality" (Ferenczi), the "early moral superego" (Rank), "pre-superego," "forerunners of superego," "visceral ethics," or the "inner mother." Note, however, that at this stage the "inner mother" is no longer just a nexus of images—as was the Great Mother of the image-body stage—but a nexus of *verbal* representations as well. It is not just an implicit formation, it carries explicit information. It is not highly organized nor tightly bound, however, and thus tends to degenerate if the corresponding authority figure is not actually present.[120, 243, 343]

Language and the emergent function of abstract thinking immensely extend the child's affective and conative world, for emotions are now freed to run through the world of time, and to be evoked by time—specific temporal desires, as well as concrete temporal dislikes, can for the first time be entertained and vaguely articulated. Choices are also presented to the child's awareness, for in a tensed world things no longer "just happen" (as in the typhonic realms), but display multiple possibilities which can be selectively engaged. Only in language can you say the word "or...". "Should I do this, OR should I do that?"

So we find here the roots of proto-volition and will-power, transformations of the more diffuse and global wishing of the previous level.

In some few ways this stage corresponds with the anal-sadistic period described by psychoanalysis. (Strictly speaking, the anal stage *per se* refers only to libido or pranic or emotional-sexual development, and that cannot be equated with either ego or cognitive development. However, since in this book I am not differentiating the various lines of development, the anal stage is included at this point since it tends to develop at this point. In the same fashion, I will include the phallic stage in the discussion of the mental-ego level, next chapter.) The specific fears of this stage are said to be the fear of loss of body (feces), and the fear of body mutilation.[120] We will be closely examining this fear of body mutilation when we look into the dynamic of evolution, for it plays an extremely important role. Finally, Erik Erikson, representing psychoanalysis, adds that the struggles of this stage concern a sense of autonomy vs. one of doubt and shame—in other words, how the child is going to feel in this new world of membership and choice.[108]

All in all, the self sense at this stage is still somewhat typhonic, but less so; that is, the self is starting—but only starting—to differentiate from the body. The fleeting images of the "good-me" and "bad-me" of the previous stage are organized into a rudimentary, linguistic self-sense—a membership-self, a tensed-self, a name-and-word self.

THE VERBAL-MEMBERSHIP SELF

• cognitive style—	autistic language; paleologic and mythic thinking; membership cognition
• affective elements—	temporal desires, extended and specific likes and dislikes
• motivational/conative factors—	proto-volition, roots of will-power and autonomous choice, belongingness
• temporal mode—	time binding, time structuring, past and future
• mode of self—	verbal, tensed-membership self

The Verbal Mind: Summary

What we have seen is that true mental or conceptual functions are *beginning* to emerge out of, and differentiate from, the simple body-ego. As language develops, the child is ushered into the world of symbols and ideas and concepts, and thus gradually rises above the fluctuations of the simple, instinctual, immediate and impulsive body-ego. Among other things, language carries the extended ability to picture sequences of things and events which are *not immediately* present to the body senses. "Language," as Robert Hall said, "is the means of dealing with the non-present world," and, to a degree, infinitely beyond that of simple images.[176]

By the same token, then, language is the means of *transcending* the simply present world. (Language, in the higher realms of consciousness, is itself transcended, but one must go from the pre-verbal to the verbal in order to get to the trans-verbal; here we are talking of the transcendence of the pre-verbal by the verbal, which, although only half the story, is an extraordinary achievement). Through language, one can anticipate the future, plan for it, and gear one's present activities in accordance with tomorrow. That is, one can delay or control one's present bodily desires and activities. This is, we saw, "a gradual substituting of actions for mere discharge reactions. This is achieved through the interposing of a time period between stimulus and response."[120] Through language and its symbolic, tensed structures, one can postpone the immediate and impulsive discharges of simple biological drives. One is no longer totally dominated by instinctual demands, but can to a certain degree *transcend* them. And this simply means that the self is starting to differentiate from the body and emerge as a *mental* or verbal or syntaxical being.

Notice again that triad which we introduced in the last chapter: as the mental-self emerges and *differentiates* from the body (with the help of language), it *transcends* the body and thus can *operate* upon it using its own mental structures as tools (it can delay the body's immediate discharges and postpone its instinctual gratifications using verbal insertions). At the same time, this allows the *beginning* of the sublimation of the body's emotional-sexual energies into more subtle, complex, and evolved activities. This triad of differentiation, transcendence, and operation is, as we will see, the single most basic *form of development*, repeated at every stage of growth, and leading—for all we know—right to the Ultimate itself.

5

Mental-Egoic Realms

For a variety of reasons, the child's self sense gradually centers around his syntaxical-membership cognition and the affects, motivations, and phantasies intimately associated with membership cognition. The child switches its central *identity* from the typhonic realms to the verbal and mental realms. Paratax dies down, and the syntaxical or secondary process burgeons—linear, conceptual, abstract, consensus-verbal thinking decisively enters every element of awareness. As a final result, the self is no longer just a fleeting, amorphous self-image or constellation of self-images, nor merely a word or name, but a higher-order unity of auditory, verbal, dialoging, and syntaxical self-concepts, very rudimentary and tenuous at first, but rapidly consolidated.

> Except in the earliest phases of development, the individual's state of cognition determines most of the changes which occur in his psychodynamic life. It is his state of cognition that re-elaborates past and present experience and, to a large extent, alters their emotional associations. Among the powerful and emotional forces which motivate or disturb men are many which are sustained or actually engendered by complicated symbolic processes. The individual's concept-feelings of personal significance, of self-identity, of his role in life, of self-esteem, could not exist without these complex cognitive constructs.... Concepts enter into and to a large extent constitute the image of the self. Man at the [syntaxical] conceptual level no longer sees himself as a physical entity or as a name, but as a repository of concepts which refer to his own person.... In thinking, feeling, and even in acting, man becomes more concerned with concepts than with things.[7]

Fenichel puts it thus: "The decisive step toward the consolidation of the conscious part of the ego is taken when the auditory conception of words is added to the more archaic orientations."[120] This auditory, conceptual, syntaxical self is the egoic level proper, with nearly all aspects of the self sense, including affective and conative factors, inextricably embedded in membership thinking and conceptual cognition.

Now the ego—as I am using this term—differs from the other forms of the self sense in important ways. Where the uroboros was a pre-personal self, where the typhon was a vegetal self, where the membership-self was a name-and-word self, the core of the ego is a thought-self, a self-*concept*. The ego is a self-concept, or constellation of self-concepts, along with the images, phantasies, identifications, memories, sub-personalities, motivations, ideas and information related or bound to the separate self-concept. Thus a "healthy ego," as psychoanalysis puts it, is a more-or-less "correct self-concept," one which adequately takes account of the various and frequently discordant trends of the ego.[119] Further, the ego—although differentiated from the body—is rooted in the *voluntary* musculature of the body, so that pathological ego states tend to show a corresponding muscular dysfunction.[249] The egoic-syntaxical level, then, is dominated by conceptual cognition and marked by a transcendence of the typhonic body.

The ego-concept stage, whose beginning is similar to the phallic (or locomotor-genital) stage of psychoanalysis, also marks the final emergence of the super-ego proper.[46,108] (As I earlier pointed out, the phallic stage *per se* refers to the typhonic or body realms, but it generally occurs in conjunction with the emergence of the early ego and the super-ego proper. Since I am not differentiating various lines of development, throughout the book I will treat the early egoic period as the egoic-genital.) Now the super-ego is an internalized or introjected auditory, verbal-conceptual set of suggestions, commands, injunctions, and prohibitions generally absorbed from the parents.[120] Actually, the internalized idea or concept of the Parent includes the parent's attitudes, feelings, and thoughts about the child himself (or rather, what the child understands them to be). In other words, it is not so much the parent alone that is internalized as it is the *relationship between the parent and child,*[244] so that, to use the convenient terms of transactional analysis, the Parent and Child are correlative intra-egoic structures. In the psyche, they lean against each other (a fact generally overlooked by classical analysis—which prompted Fritz Perls to say that Freud was "half-right, as usual": he got the super-ego, but forgot the "infra-ego").[291] For as the child conceptually internalizes the parents, he at the same time *fixes* and *binds* the relationships that he *as child* has with the parents and that the parents *as parents* have with him. Thus, the relationship—part conventional, part imaginative—between parent and child becomes a stabilized intra-egoic relation.[243] This is a distinctive feature of the ego level.

To put it differently, at this stage the previous *inter*-personal relationships become *intra*-psychic structures—and this is allowed because of verbal-conceptualization. That is to say, the development of even rudimentary conceptual or syntaxical thinking carries with it the ability to take on abstract roles, and this is decisive in ego development. Baldwin's "dialectic of personal growth,"[20] Lacan's "the Other" and the "mirror-stage,"[236] Cooley's "looking-glass self,"[82] Kohlberg's "taking the role of others,"[229] Mead's "particularized other" and "generalized other"[267]—all point to "the internalized dialogue of roles as the social origin of the self."[243] Most importantly, "the dialogue of roles is child versus parent, impulse versus control, dependence versus mastery, all at once. Each time the role of alter or object is appropriated, the child's ego and hence his alter or object is correspondingly complicated."[243]

Thus there comes about that decisive "internal differentiation of ego structure"—basically into a Parent and Child, a super-ego and infra-ego, a topdog and underdog (along with other sub-personalities too various to detail). Further, the internalized Parent-and-Child is a relationship rooted in specific retroflections.[418] This is so because the child takes the role of the Parent towards himself by retroflecting, or turning back on himself, those concept-affects not permissible to the Parent. For example, when the parent repeatedly scolds the child for getting angry, eventually the child will identify with the role of the Parent and scold himself for his outbursts. Thus, instead of the parent physically controlling which impulses are permissible, the child begins to control himself.[292] He can both praise himself, which results in feelings of pride, or he can condemn himself, which results in feelings of guilt.[120] The point is that by taking the role of the Parent towards himself, he is able to differentiate his ego into various segments, all of which are *initially* (but only initially) based on the original inter-personal relations of the child with the parent. The external relation between parent and child thus becomes an internal relation between two different sub-personalities of the ego. Inter-personal has become intra-personal, so that the Parent and Child ego states are networks of criss-crossed retroflections and internalized dialogues.[418]

The super-ego or Parent may be sub-divided into the Nuturing Parent or ego-ideal, and the Controlling Parent or conscience; and the Child ego state into the Adapted Child, the Rebellious Child, and the Natural Child.[33] All of these, however, are—as I see them—*intra-ego-ic thought structures*, of one degree of conceptual complexity or another. That is, they all possess dominant syntaxical-dialogue elements, along with the corresponding affects, images, and feeling-tones. So it is not that affects and phantasies and images do not occur on this conceptual-egoic level—indeed they do, but they are largely related or bound to conceptual forms of membership-reality.

Further, it is this syntaxical-dialogue nature of the Parent-Child ego (what we will be calling the P-A-C ego, for Parent-Adult-Child sub-personalities) that *allows* script programming, so admirably dealt with by transactional analysis.[33] You cannot program the uroboric self nor the typhonic self (they are, as it were, programmed by nature) but you can to some extent program dialogue-thinking, for you can insinuate yourself (as parent, brain-washer, hypnotist, or therapist), into one of the significant roles of the individual's internal dialogues. To the extent the individual is identified with his ego (conceptual-dialogue self) he will then be "script-bound," or programmed by the internalized directives. And it is to Berne's credit,[33] following Perl's discovery,[291] to detail how almost every aspect of ego states can be discovered as "internal dialogue"—syntaxical trains of auditory signs with accompanying affects and images, so that even the typhonic id, on this level, is experienced as a "living voice."[33]

Very few individuals survive childhood with an ego intact in consciousness, or even largely intact, for "after the super-ego is established, it decides which drives or needs will be permitted and which suppressed."[46, 120] That is to say, under the influence of the super-ego, and dependent upon the whole history of the prior developmental levels of the self, certain concept-affects are split off, or alienated (May),[266] remain undifferentiated or forgotten (Jung),[209] are projected (Perls),[291] repressed (Freud),[137] or selectively screened out of awareness (Sullivan).[359] The individual is left with, not a realistic or reasonably accurate and flexible self-concept, but a fraudulent self-concept, an idealized self (Horney),[190] a weak ego (Freud),[140] a persona (Jung).[210]

For simple convenience, I divide the overall ego realm into three major chronological stages: the early ego (ages 4 to 7), the middle ego (7 to 12), and the late ego (age 12 to the beginning of the Inward Arc, when and if the individual begins it—rarely earlier than age 21). At any point of the ego's development, any aspect of the self that, if represented in consciousness would be perceived as over-threatening, can be suppressed. These suppressed aspects we call the "shadow," and the resultant fraudulent self we call the "persona" (after Jung). For us, the shadow represents aspects of the personal self which could just as well be in consciousness, but are not for dynamic reasons (described by Freud and Jung). This can occur at any point of the ego's emergence (although the decisive points occur during the early egoic period), and so in general we sometimes refer to all the ego stages as the ego/persona realm.

But let us note that persona *per se* is not necessarily a pathological structure, but something of a "good face" or "social mask" that one can don to facilitate social interaction. It is a particular role engineered to help facilitate different tasks, so that one may, and should, possess several different personae—a father persona, a doctor persona, a husband persona, a wife persona, and so on. The sum of all one's possible personae is the total ego (in my definition), and the ego itself is built and constructed by the learning and combining of various personae into an integrated self-concept. Just as the "particularized other" precedes the "generalized other," the persona precedes the ego.

The difficulty arises when one particular persona (such as the "non-aggressive good boy") capitalizes and dominates the field of awareness, so that other legitimate personae (such as the "healthy-aggression" or "assertiveness" persona) cannot enter consciousness. These split-off facets of the ego-self thus become shadow, or submerged personae. Our general and somewhat simplistic formula is thus: persona + shadow = ego. Note that all of the shadow is unconscious, but not all of the unconscious is shadow. That is, there are all sorts of levels to the unconscious, only a few of which are "personal" or "submerged personae-shadow"; large tracts of the unconscious are pre-personal (uroboric, archaic, collective and low-archetypal); large tracts are transpersonal (the subtle, the casual, the transcendent, the high-archetypal—as we will see).

Finally, I see the late ego/persona period (ages 12-21), as being crucial in regard to all forms of personae. That is, the individual up to that point has been learning to create and *identify with* several appropriate personae, and at this point, the late ego stage, not only does he normally master his various personae (Erikson's "identity vs. role confusion" stage),[108] he starts to transcend them, to dis-identify with them. Now by "dis-identify" I do not mean "dissociate" or "alienate"—I use it in the most positive sense of letting-go of an *exclusive* and restrictive identification, so as to create a *higher-order* identification. The infant dis-identified with the pleroma, or differentiated itself from that restrictive identity. Likewise, the ego dis-identifies with the typhonic body, which means that it is no longer *exclusively* attached to or identified with the pranic realm. There can be no higher identifications unless the lower-order identities are broken in their exclusivity—and that is how I use "dis-identification." Once the self dis-identifies with the lower-order structures, it can then *integrate* them with the newly-emergent higher-order structures.

THE MENTAL-EGOIC SELF	
• cognitive style—	syntaxical-membership; secondary process; verbal-dialogue thinking; concrete and formal operational thinking
• affective elements—	concept-affects, dialogue-emotions, esp. guilt, desire, pride, love, hatred
• motivational/conative factors—	will-power, self-control, temporal goals and desires, self-esteem needs
• temporal mode—	linear, historical, extended past and future
• mode of self—	egoic-syntaxical, self-concept, dialogue-thinking ego states, various personae

We were saying that during the late ego period, not only does an individual normally master his various personae, he starts to transcend them, to dis-identify with them. He thus tends to integrate all his possible personae into a "mature and integrated ego," and then he *starts* to dis-identify with the ego altogether. This, as we will see, marks the beginning of the Inward Arc, and all the stages from that point on are strictly trans-egoic (see Fig. 2 in Chapter 1).

The Egoic Realms: Summary

We see at this stage the same form of development that we mentioned in the two previous chapters—the triadic form of differentiation, transcendence, and operation. But if we look at that developmental triad in slightly more detail, here is what we find—at each major stage of development, there is: the *emergence* of a higher-order structure; the *identification* with that higher structure; the *differentiation* or *dis-identification* with the lower structure; which amounts to a *transcendence* of the lower structure; such that the higher structure can both *operate* upon and *integrate* the lower structures.

Thus, a fairly coherent mental-ego eventually emerges (usually between ages 4 and 7), differentiates itself from the body, transcends the simple biological world, and *therefore* can to a certain degree operate upon the biological world (and the earlier physical world) using the tools of simple representational thinking. This whole trend is consolidated with the emergence (usually around age 7) of what Piaget calls "concrete operational thinking"—thinking that can *operate* on the concrete world and the body using concepts. This cognitive mode dominates the middle ego/persona stage.

By the time of adolescence—the late ego/persona stage—another extraordinary differentiation begins to occur. In essence, the self simply starts to differentiate *from* the concrete thought process. And because the self starts to differentiate itself from the concrete thought process, it can to a certain degree *transcend* that thought process and therefore *operate* upon it. It is not surprising then, that Piaget calls this—his highest stage—"formal operational," because one can *operate* upon one's own concrete thought (i.e., work with formal or linguistic objects as well as physical or concrete ones), a detailed operation which, among other things, results in the sixteen binary propositions of formal logic. But the only point I want to emphasize here is that this can occur because consciousness differentiates itself from syntaxical-thought, thus transcends it, and hence can operate upon it (something that it could not do when it *was* it). Actually, this process is just beginning at this stage—it intensifies at higher stages—but the overall point seems fairly clear: consciousness, or the self, is *starting* to transcend the verbal ego-mind. It is starting to go trans-verbal, trans-egoic.

Finally, let us note that the verbal ego-mind is known in Mahayana Buddhism as the manovijnana,[162] in Hinduism as the manomayakosa,[94] in Hinayana Buddhism as the fourth and fifth skand-has.[107] It is also the fifth chakra, the visuddha-chakra or lower verbal-mind, and the lower aspects of the sixth or ajna chakra, or conceptual mind.[330] In the Kabbalah, it is Tiphareth (egoic self), Hod (intellect), and Netzach (desire).[338] And, I should not forget, it is Maslow's self-esteem needs.[363]

This brings us to the end of the Outward Arc, but not to the end of our story.

Symbols of Transformation

The Ascent of Consciousness

From what we have said thus far, it might be obvious that at each stage or level of evolution, both the mode of self and the correlative sense of reality are in the main generated by intricate transformations of the previous level. Each emergent level is thus not so much a total negation of the previous level, nor does it *come from* the previous level, but rather is a transformation (and transcendence) of it.

We will be examining the transpersonal dynamic of this transformation-upward in the next section and find at its core the Atman-project, or the attempt to attain ultimate Unity in ways that prevent it and force symbolic substitutes—each successive one being closer to the Source, as it were, but still merely substitutive. At this point, however, it would be worthwhile to look into the nature of the *transformers* themselves, and we will find that by-and-large each transformation is accomplished—or at least accompanied by—some type of *symbolic structure* (using "symbol" in its widest possible sense).

"The path of evolution," says Jungian psychologist Neumann, "leading mankind from unconsciousness to consciousness, is the path traced by the transformations and ascent of libido [which in Jungian psychology is not sexual energy but neutral psychic energy in general]."[279] And, as Jung so straightforwardly demonstrated, the *"mechanism that tranforms energy is the symbol."* Hence the (later) title of Jung's first pioneering book: *Symbols of Transformation.*[205]

Now we have already outlined in a half-dozen different major types of symbolic structures: the uroboric forms, the axial image, the concrete image, the word-and-name, and the membership-concept (and these, of course, cover only the Outward Arc). Each of these symbolic structures is capable of generating a different type of representation, and thus each of them is intimately connected with a particular type of transformation-upward or ascent of consciousness.

Let me now give a few examples of this symbolic transformation in order to make the idea as evident as possible. We have already noted the particular mode of time which is characteristic of each major Outward Arc stage: the timelessness of the pleromatic and uroboric stages; the immediate present tense of the axial-body; the extended present of the image-body; the rudimentary temporal sequences of the membership stage; and the extended linear time of the egoic stage. But how is it possible for the individual, in the course of his early evolution, to pass from one of these temporal forms to the next? How, or by what means, does one form of time give way to the next?

A large part of the general answer is: through and from the various symbolic structures which emerge at each stage in the growth of consciousness. Let us see:

The temporal mode of the pleromatic-uroboric stage (if I may take them together), is properly defined as timeless in the sense of pretemporal, beginningless and endless, prior to and ignorant of sequence and seriality. Although the infant is definitely aware of certain events, he cannot grasp them in temporal relation, nor, in fact, even separate himself from them. That, of course, was the pleromatic state—embeddedness in the material universe.

However, with the emergence or coming-into-play of the axial-images, this primitive, pre-temporal awareness is transformed into an apprehension of the passing present—vague and nebulous at first, but *present* nonetheless. Pretemporality thus gives way to the first form of time: the simple passing present, the *nunc fluens*, the durée réele, and this transformation, this growth of awareness, is made possible through the activity of the axial-image, for it confers on the infant the ability to lift his previously undifferentiated and pleromatic awareness onto specific, *present objects*.

Going further, with the rise of the concrete image, the simple present is transformed into an *extended present*, for the image can represent *absent* objects or persons, and thus recognize present moments other than the one immediately at hand. The infant's temporal world, at this image-body level, thus consists of an extended present or series of juxtaposed (parataxic) present moments. The growing world of time is thus slowly and painstakingly being constructed, and the concrete image plays a decisive role at this stage.

The image itself, however, cannot represent or constitute in awareness an extended serial duration or *sequence of events* in time. But the development of language—the symbolic structures of word-and-name—brings with it the ability to recognize series of events and sequences of actions, and thus to perceive the salient non-present world. In other words, the symbolic structures of language *transform* the present moment into a *tensed* moment, a moment surrounded by the past and the future. Thus does word-and-name transform the passing present of the axial-body level into the tensed duration of the verbal-membership level. It allows consciousness to *transcend* the present moment, which is a decisive and far-reaching ascent.

And—to cap this brief discussion—the next major symbolic structure, the syntaxical thought, creates a clear and enduring mental structure of times past and times future. So it is that at each stage of evolution an appropriate symbolic structure—itself emerging at that stage—transforms each particular mode of time into its successor, and thus marks the pace of the ascent of consciousness.

Similar transformations occur in the affective and motivational and conative life of the individual, ranging from the primal and archaic oceanic tones of the pleromatic-uroboric stages to the individual and specific goals, choices, and desires of the ego and persona. To simply outline one example of these transformative events, we can see that:

The original oceanic tone of the uroboric level is transformed by the axial-image into the individual bodily pleasure principle. For with the help of the axial-image, the infant begins to construct and represent the external world—he moves out of the infantile material and uroboric embeddedness and learns to focus his awareness from the material cosmos to the surface of his organism (his "body-ego"), while at the same time tentatively differentiating his body from the immediate environment. As we have seen, his sense of self is at this point gradually transformed from the pleromatic-uroboric mode to the axial-body mode, and the amorphous oceanic-tone is likewise transformed to the bodily pleasure principle, polymorphously perverse and free-floating at first, but bodily and not oceanic nonetheless. The axial-image transforms oceanic feelings and moods and euphoria into manifest bodily pleasure, which is decisive in helping to set and mold the bodily-base of the self-system—should this transformation fail to any large degree, the individual is left with a fixation to uroboric-euphoria (that is, he derives pleasure from losing consciousness in pre-personal pursuits).

The transformations continue: By most accounts, the infant early on associates bodily pleasure with the presence of certain significant objects—usually the "mothering one" and the "good breast." However, with the emergence of the next major symbolic structure, the image proper, the infant can simply *imagine* the pleasure-releasing event, so that the image itself can evoke and sustain a pleasurable response. The infant thereby can not only experience immediate pleasure, he can imagine a pleasure not yet present. In other words, he can *wish*. Thus, the image transforms the bodily pleasure principle into a measure of mental wishing.

And in similar fashion, the emergence of language—of word and name, of extended time, of membership-reality—transforms global wish-fulfillments into extended, specific, tensed desires; into temporal aims and goals. The further development of conceptual thinking and the consolidation of syntaxical cognition simply crystallizes and vastly extends, throughout the linear world of time, the specific goals and temporal desires now characteristic of the egoic self sense. Thus, from the amorphous and non-directed oceanic euphoria to "I want to study physics": the many transformations of desire.

Although we have only examined the Outward Arc and have said nothing of the Inward Arc of evolution, I think we can nevertheless begin to see that the evolution of consciousness—the ascent of consciousness—is marked by a series of significant transformations-upward, mediated or assisted by various types of symbolic structures. At each stage of ascent an appropriate symbolic structure—itself emerging at that stage—transforms each particular mode of consciousness into its higher successor. And, as we have consistently seen, once the higher successor emerges in consciousness, the self *identifies* with that structure, *differentiates* itself from the lower structure, hence *transcends* those lower structures and thus can both *operate* upon them and *integrate* them. Such is the ascent of consciousness, and it continues ultimately to Atman itself (which, alone of all the stages, is totally beyond all symbols and all forms—they are here no longer needed, and finally, are only an impediment to the Formless).

Transformation and Translation

There is a difference between transformation and translation, and it can be explained as follows:

Modifying the terms of linguistics, we can say that each level of consciousness consists of a *deep structure* and a *surface structure*. The deep structure consists of all the basic limiting principles embedded *as* that level. The deep structure is the defining form of a level, which embodies all of the potentials and limitations of that level. Surface structure is simply a *particular* manifestation of the deep structure. The surface structure is constrained by the form of the deep structure, but within that form it is free to select various contents (e.g., within the form of the physical body, one may select to walk, run, play baseball, etc. What all of those forms have in common is the deep structure of the human body).

A deep structure is like a paradigm, and contains within it all the basic limiting principles in terms of which all surface structures are realized. To use a simple example, take a ten-storey building: each of the floors is a deep structure, whereas the various rooms and objects on each floor are surface structures. The pleroma is on the first floor, the uroboros is on the second, the typhon is on the third, verbal on fourth and ego on fifth (we will later suggest that parapsychology is on the seventh floor, transcendence is on the ninth, God is on top and the building itself is Consciousness as Such). The point is that, for example, although all egos are quite different, they are all on the fifth floor: they all share the same deep structure.

The movement of surface structures we call *translation*; the movement of deep structures we call *transformation*. Thus, if we move the furniture around on the fourth floor, that is translation; but if we move up to the seventh floor, that is transformation. To give but a simple example, we can apply this to Jung's work on archetype elaboration (and it is not necessary that one believe in the existence of Jung's archetypes for this example to be effective. Keep in mind, too, that I am confining this whole discussion to examples from the Outward Arc—we have yet to examine the structures of the Inward Arc). The archetype of the magna mater—the prima materia of pleromatic-chaos—may be transformed at the body level into a concrete image of the Great Mother, which may in turn be transformed at the egoic-conceptual level into the *idea* of a loving wife. These are genuine transformations. But at each of these stages, and for a variety of reasons, a specific *translation* may occur. Thus, if the uroboric archetype of the magna mater is transformed into an image of a cave (on the body level), that image may undergo translation or displacement to the image of a cup, basket, house, womb, or box—as we saw with the magical primary process of this level. This translative process is not a gross change in levels, but merely a change in the "language" or form of the given level. The uroboric magna mater is *transformed* into a cave; the cave is *translated* into a cup—the former process is vertical, the latter horizontal.

Thus, translation results in a different "language" or form, but transformation results in a different type of language or form. The primitive uroboric-euphoria transforms to the bodily pleasure principle, which may then undergo various *translations* (Ferenczi's "amphixis of eroticisms") to different areas of the body, or may itself be *transformed* to egoic, temporal, and syntaxical desires or goals—the later, in turn, may then undergo translations or displacements, and so on. Transformations are movements from one level to another, while translations represent a movement of the elements of any given level.

Once a particular level of self sense comes into being, it maintains itself by a series of more-or-less constant translations. The particular mode of self translates both its internal milieu and its external environment according to the major symbolic deep structures and paradigms characteristic of that level. Thus, for instance, as the individual reaches the egoic-syntaxical level, he is committed to an almost perpetual "talking to himself," a constant sub-vocal chatter which unceasingly translates and edits his reality according to the symbolic structures of his language-and-thought as well as the major syntaxical rules and premises of his membership reality (and secondarily, his own philosophic bands).

In other words, his mode of self, now *transformed* to the egoic level, is maintained by an almost endless stream of specific *translations*. A given transformation, then, always helps create the possibility of new types of translations, and these translations help support and maintain that transformation. And thus, as we will see in the next sections, any time a series of translations fails its purpose and breaks down—either in the Outward or Inward Arc—the individual is precipitated into a major transformation. *Wherever translation fails, transformation ensues*—and it can be regressive transformation or progressive transformation, depending on factors we will later discuss.

We make one more important distinction: we define a *sign* as that form which points to, or represents, or is involved with any element *within* a given level; whereas a *symbol* points to, or represents, or is involved with an element of a different level (either higher or lower). This is in line with the traditional view of symbolism, explained by Huston Smith: "Symbolism is the science of the relationship between different levels of reality and cannot be precisely understood without reference thereto."[352] Anything I can point to on my present level of consciousness is only a sign; anything higher can only be discussed or thought about using symbols, and these symbols can only be finally understood upon transformation to that higher level itself. Therefore, we also say that *translation operates with signs, whereas transformation operates with symbols*. And we have just traced out several transformations, from pleroma to ego, which were mediated by *symbols*.

With all of that in mind, we can say that each transformation-upward marks the emergence in consciousness of a new and higher level, with a new deep structure (symbol-matrix), within which new translations or surface structures can unfold and operate (sign-matrix). And we can say that development or evolution is a series of such transformations, or changes in deep structure, mediated by symbols, or vertical forms in consciousness.

And most importantly, we say that all deep structures are *remembered*, in the precise Platonic sense of *anamnesis*, whereas all surface structures are *learned*, in the sense studied by Western psychologists. It is generally agreed that one does not learn to become a Buddha, one simply discovers or remembers that one is already Buddha. That is an incontrovertible fact of the perennial philosophy. Just so, no one learns any deep structure, but simply discovers or remembers it prior to (or concomitant with) the course of learning its surface structure. You don't learn to have a body, but you do learn to play baseball with it—you discover deep structures and learn surface structures. Among other things, this fundamental theorem (which we will explore later) relieves us of the tedium of trying to derive the existence of higher structures out of lower ones (e.g., trying to get the ego out of the id).

Translation, Transformation, and Psychopathology

To end this brief discussion of translation and transformation, we might point out that these two basic processes also play significant roles in psychopathology, for a particular type of transformation sets the stage for a particular type of dis-ease, while translation itself governs the nature of the specific symptoms which eventually surface.

Let me give a small example. But to begin with, note that repression is *not* transformation. We might say that repression is one type of *failure* to cleanly transform (there are also arrest, fixation, dissociation, and regression). Should the self, in the process of transforming from, say, the typhonic realm to the egoic, encounter severe repression of, for example, aggression, then the ascent of consciousness is halted with regard to that facet of self. Or rather, from that stage on, the anger-impulse will be *mis*-translated with regard to any deep structure which subsequently refuses the impulse. Thus transformation-upward is distorted because, *at every stage* past the repression, the impulse is mis-translated. And this mis-translation means that the individual cannot represent these impulses to himself with appropriate *signs*, but only with *symbols*, and these symbols represent the hidden aspects of self which now remain lodged in the lower levels of his own being. We might say that these symbols represent those aspects of the self which originate at a different level of consciousness (in this case, the typhonic) and *cannot* make it up to the present level. Without the repression, the anger would simply *transform* easily to the ego level, enter awareness as a *sign*, and the individual would correctly *translate* his situation as, "I'm madder 'n hell!" With repression, however, an aspect of the self *remains* at a lower level, cannot properly transform, and *therefore* enters awareness only as a *symbol* (since symbols, not signs, represent different levels)—and hence the individual *mis-translates* the true form of his present reality. And this mis-translation circles compulsively around a *symbol* lodged uncomfortably in his translative process, generating mystery in his awareness.

The anger is thus *transformed* into a *symbol*...and a symptom. A symptom is basically a symbol of some aspect of the self which has become dissociated from consciousness,[417] remains or regresses to a lower level of self, therefore cannot enter translation as a sign and thus shows up only as a symbol/symptom. (I am not now speaking of certain symptoms which are generated on *one* level alone, and involve only crossed signs, such as cognitive dissonance.[124] Nor am I speaking of what are, in fact, some of the most important symptoms of all: those which are symbols of *higher levels* trying to emerge in consciousness, symptoms which point not to the id but to God. We will deal with some of these later.)

Without repression, the angry impulse would be simply and easily discharged, or at least would be easily recognized and correctly translated. With the defenses, however, that impulse may be transformed and translated into any number of distorted languages or forms. It can be directly mis-translated or displaced onto other individuals or objects. The original anger can also be retroflected, or translated back onto the self, so that the person no longer feels angry but depressed (the classic psychoanalytic theory of depression). Or the anger may be projected entirely, or translated-in-origin onto another person, leaving the projector with feelings of fearful anxiety, since not he but the other person now seems hostile and angry at him. (Incidentally, the *type* of mis-translation is generally determined by the deep structure of the stage at which the original repression or defense occurred.)

Thus, at this level, the symptom of depression is but a *symbol* (or metaphor in Lacan's sense)[236] of the now unconscious or shadow-impulse of anger. To the individual himself, his symptom seems a foreign language altogether, and one which he cannot understand because he has, among other things, forgotten how to translate his symptom. The symptom of depression completely baffles him—he doesn't know why he is depressed, what causes it, how to control it. It's all Greek, all foreign language, to him.

Yet moment to moment his shadow anger is being transformed and translated into the symptom/symbol of depression. He is doing the translating and the transforming, but he has forgotten, first, *how* he's doing it, and second, *that* he's doing it.[418] He thus lives not as an "accurate" ego-concept, but as a persona dissociated from his shadow-anger. And the persona actually maintains its existence through the mis-translation (conversely, once the mis-translation is cleared up, the exclusive identification with this persona dissolves).

Therapy, on this level, thus proceeds in two basic steps: 1) The therapist helps the individual re-translate the symptom/symbol back to its original form. This is called "the interpretation," and a good therapist is a good interpreter.[165] The therapist might say, for example, "Your feelings of depression are masked feelings of anger and rage"—he translates the foreign language of the symptom back to the original form. He "tells" the individual the "meaning" of his depression (or helps him to discover it for himself), and thus helps him re-translate it in terms more consonant with the deep structure from which the symbols and symptoms originate. 2) The therapeutic translation continues in that fashion ("the working through") until a genuine and more-or-less complete *transformation* of consciousness from the lower to the upper level occurs, so that the symbol becomes sign, and the anger can enter awareness in its original form—which, as it were, dissolves the symptom.

* * * *

Thus far we have examined some of the prominent characteristics of the major stages in the Outward Arc of the life cycle, as well as the major symbolic structures which help mediate the transformations upward from stage to stage. At each major stage we have seen a broad but very strong agreement among Eastern and Western psychologists, and we have also seen a general form of development start to become apparent: each stage of development is marked by differentiation, transcendence, operation and integration. It is time now to turn to the Inward Arc—the *nivritti marga*, the path of understanding, the ascent to Source, the psychology of eternity. We have witnessed the growth from subconsciousness to self-consciousness; we witness now the growth from self-consciousness to superconsciousness.

7

Centauric Realms

At the late ego stage (ages 12-21), not only does an individual normally master his various personae, he tends to differentiate from them,
dis-identify with them, transcend them. He thus tends to *integrate* all
his possible personae into the *mature ego*—and then he starts to differentiate or dis-identify with the ego altogether, so as to discover, via
transformation, an even higher-order unity than the altogether egoic-
self. And that brings us, right off, to the centaur.

A Higher-Order Unity

As consciousness begins to transcend the verbal ego-mind, it can—
more-or-less for the first time—integrate the ego-mind with all the
lower levels. That is, because consciousness is no longer identified
with any of these elements to the exclusion of any others, all of them
can be integrated: the body, the persona, the shadow, the ego—all
can be brought into a higher-order integration.

This stage is variously referred to as the "integration of all lower
levels" (Sullivan, Grant, and Grant),[358] "integrated" (Loevinger),[243]
"self-actualized" (Maslow),[262] "autonomous" (Fromm,[146] Riesman[318]).
According to Loevinger this stage represents an "integration of physiological and psychological,"[243] and Broughton's studies[53] point to
this stage as one wherein "mind and body are both experiences of an
integrated self."[243] This integrated self, wherein mind and body are
harmoniously one, we call the "centaur."[410] The centaur: the great
mythological being with animal body and human-mind existing in a
perfect state of at-one-ment.

On the whole, we can say that as one contacts and stabilizes on the
centaur level, the elements of the gross personality—the body, the
ego, the persona, the shadow, the lower chakras—tend to fall into
harmony of themselves. For the individual is beginning to *transcend*

them, and thus he ceases to compulsively manipulate and exploit them. All in all, this is the stage variously described as one of autonomy, of integration, of authenticity, or of self-actualization—the ideal of Humanistic/Existential therapies, the "highest" stage to which orthodox Western psychology aspires. Instead of summarizing all the research data on this centauric stage of "self-actualization" or "integration", I will simply present one cogent and representative study:

James Broughton recently completed an extensive phenomenological study of what individuals at different stages of development see as the relationship between mind, body, and self.[53] He divides his results into six stages of increasing development (influenced by Kohlberg, Piaget, and Baldwin). At level 0, his lowest, the mind and body are not differentiated; self is "inside" and reality is "outside"—this is our bodyego realm. At levels 1 and 2, mind and body are differentiated, and self tends to reside in the mind which controls the body; both mind and body seem to be real and "substantial"—this is our early and middle egoic stages. At levels 3 and 4, the individual differentiates the social role or false appearance (our persona) from the "true" self-concept or "inner self"—which is our mature ego level. Going further, however, at level 5 (to use Loevinger's summary) not only has the individual dis-identified with the persona, he begins to dis-identify with the known ego, for "the self as observer is distinguished from the self-concept [our ego] as known.... The physiological body is recognized as a conceptual construction just as mind is."[243] Both ego-mind and body are no longer viewed as *substantial* but simply *constructural*. It appears to me that at level 5 the self is starting to shift to a center that is prior to both body and mind as separate entities, since both are recognized as mere *constructs*. And at level 6, Broughton's highest level, this shift seems complete, because at that highest level *"mind and body are both experiences of an integrated self."*[243] That, in my opinion, is the centaur, the integrated and total self, above and prior to body, mind, persona, and shadow, but embracing, as it were, all of them as *experiences* ("experiences of an integrated self," as Broughton's study showed).

Now in my opinion the existential psychologists have done much to explain, explore, and generally "resurrect" the centaur—which is one of the reasons I also call this level the "existential level". Beginning with Kierkegaard[223] and Nietzsche, through Husserl[192] and Heidegger[182] and Sartre,[331] to Binswanger,[36] Frankl,[131] Boss,[50] May,[266] Bugental,[64] and Maddi,[228] the potentials and crises of the total being were eloquently set forth in existential terms. Notions of authenticity, of concrete-being-in-the-world, of pure experiencing and true seeing, of Dasein, of intentionality, autonomy, meaning and the centered self—I am sorry to just toss out these terms, but the existential literature is so vast and so profound, that I can only hint at its essence by throwing out phrases and urging the reader to consult the original works. The point is that all these notions were brought forth as potentials for and of *being*, and all of them were underscored by the utterly central notion of the *total* bodymind.

Now of course I am not implying that all these authors—and the many others belonging generally to the "humanistic/existential" school—are in perfect agreement, or that they are all absolutely talking about the same "self," let alone what I am calling the centaur. But it does seem to me that they share a substantial and impressive number of common assumptions and conclusions (many of these writers acknowledge this fact by accepting in a general fashion the label "humanistic-existential"—see *Current Personality Theories*,[88] for instance, where the sections on Rogers, Adler, Existentialism, Holism, Organismic Theories, and Personalism *all* acknowledge their general similarities to each other). It is my opinion, however, that the existential-centaur is a real and higher level of consciousness, a higher-order unity of differentiation and transcendence, and that the broad similarities of these writers result from the fact that they all either intuit, or are personally alive to, this higher level of being and awareness.

Autonomy, Self-Actualization, and Intentionality

Now many of these existential-humanistic writers have gone to great lengths to explain, explore, and describe the *potentials* of the total bodymind or centaur. A prime concept in this regard is "self-actualization," a concept introduced by Goldstein and Karen Horney, and made popular by Maslow and Rogers and Perls and the whole human potentials movement. Roger's whole theory, for instance, "focuses renewed attention on the importance of *actualizing the full potential* of each individual and on the meaning of concepts such as experiencing, organismic valuing, and organismic sensing which the theory holds to be of crucial importance in fulfilling that unique potential (my ital.)."[187] The implication is that one's full potential springs from what Rogers calls the "total, ongoing psychophysiological flow" or "total organismic experiencing," and not from any aspect or fragment of that flow—ego, body, superego, self-concept, and so on. In our terms, self-actualization is intimately related to the centaur level, and is not directly available to the ego or persona levels.

Rollo May, for instance, states that "neither the ego nor the body nor the unconscious can be 'autonomous,' but can only exist as parts of a totality. And it is in this totality [the centaur] that will and freedom must have their base."[266] Presumably, then, actual autonomy (and self-actualization), would result, and could only result by definition, with the *conscious emergence of this totality*—a type of shift of identity from any of the fragments (ego, persona, body) to their prior and higher integration. According to general existential thought, when an individual's self is felt or prehended as the prior, total being, he assumes—*can* assume—responsibility for his entire being-in-the-world. He can, as Sartre put it, choose himself. From that higher, existential centaur, there is no reluctance to the present—no hidden corner of a self that balks at this existence. As such, the individual can start to move on the whole, as a whole—and that is what Leslie Farber has called the "spontaneous will."[118]

I particularly like the notion of the "spontaneous will," because—aside from its own intrinsic merits—it tends to point up the types of potentials available only to the centaur or total being, and not just the body or ego or persona. Rollo May explains Farber's conclusions: "Dr. Farber demarcates two realms of 'will,' the first consisting of an *experience of the self in its totality*, a relatively *spontaneous* movement in a certain direction. In this kind of willing, the body moves as a whole, and the experience is characterized by a relaxation and by an imaginative open quality. This is an experience of freedom which is anterior to all talk about political or psychological freedom."[265] We especially note here the imaginative and open mental set, the emphasis on the total self, and the notion of its being the movement of a whole.

"In contrast, the will of the second realm, as Dr. Farber sees it, is that in which some obtrusive element enters, some necessity for a decision with an element of an *against* something along with a *for* something. If one uses the Freudian terminology, the 'will of the super-ego' would be included in this realm."[265] The spontaneous will is of the total bodymind, whereas the second will is of the effortful and purposive ego (and super-ego).

Now I would like to point out that May equates in general terms the spontaneous will of the total self with what is called *intentionality* by the existentialists, which is why he says that intentionality "is the missing link between mind and body."[265] As I see it, the connection is fairly simple, and is pointed out by May himself: the body tends to be "involuntary" or "spontaneous", in the sense that—aside from voluntary muscles—we do not normally and consciously control its processes of circulation, growth, digestion, feeling, and all the millions of spontaneous variables that add up to the "natural wisdom of the body." The ego, on the other hand, we generally assume to be the home of many voluntary, controlled, and purposive activities. The total self, then, as the higher ego-and-body union, is a type of conjunction of both of these experiential realms—the voluntary and the involuntary. Thus, the "spontaneous will"—the "missing link between mind and body"—intentionality.

In this and subsequent chapters I am going to emphasize the notion of *intentionality*, and so by way of introduction (we will return to it later), let us note that according to May intentionality "is not to be identified with intentions but is the dimension which underlies them…, a dimension which cuts across and includes both conscious and unconscious, both cognition and conation."[265] Intentionality, that is, includes both a willing (conative) and a knowing (cognitive). For my own part, I will call the cognitive aspect of intentionality the *vision-image* or *higher-phantasy* process. "Imagination," says May, "is the home of intentionality." Or better: "Intentionality is an imaginative attention which underlies our intentions and informs our actions."[265] We might say that the cognitive aspect of intentionality is vision-image, and the conative aspect of vision-image is intentionality, both, I believe, springing from the higher-order unity of mind and body called centaur.

Intentionality is the spontaneous will of the bodymind centaur, and vision-image or high-phantasy is its language. Rollo May himself says as much: "Imagination is the home of intentionality and fantasy one of its languages. I use fantasy here not meaning something unreal to which we escape, but in its original meaning of *phantasitikous*, 'able to represent,' 'to make visible.' *Fantasy is the language of the total self.*" (my ital.).[265] Likewise, Perls *et al* note that phantasy in its purest form is simply an expression of the self-in-unity: "a unity of perceptual, motor, and feelingful functions,"[292] which they say is a type of "spontaneous contacting" (very like Farber's "spontaneous will").

Jung, too, was quick to spot the unifying role of the high-phantasy process. "The inner image," he says, "is a complex factor, compounded of the most varied material from the most varied sources. It is no conglomerate, however, but an integral product, with its own autonomous purpose. The image is a concentrated *expression of the total psychic situation*, not merely, nor even pre-eminently, of unconscious contents pure and simple (his ital.)."[214] For Jung, then, the complex-image—what I am calling the high-phantasy or vision-image—is an expression of the total being, including *both conscious and unconscious aspects* (remember that Rollo May said that intentionality is the "dimension which cuts across and includes both conscious and unconscious"). In Jung's own words, "the image is equally an expression of the unconscious as of the conscious situation of the moment. The interpretation of its meaning, therefore, can proceed exclusively neither from the unconscious nor from the conscious, but only from their reciprocal relation."[214]

Notice that in speaking of a "high" phantasy process, I am implying that there is also a "low" phantasy process. There is—and we have already seen it: it is the infantile primary process of whole-part equivalency and subject-predicate identity, the cognitive mode of the magical typhon. And these two modes, however similar they might appear to the untutored eye, simply cannot be equated.

But right here we are starting to see a principle emerge which is destined to be of the very utmost importance in grasping the nature of the higher realms of being and consciousness. Again and again we will see it emerge in reference to the more highly evolved and developed structures of the psyche, and it is just this: many structures on the Outward Arc that are "pre-" appear on the Inward Arc as "trans-". That is, pre-verbal deep structures give way to verbal structures which give way to trans-verbal structures; pre-personal gives way to personal which gives way to trans-personal; pre-egoic moves to egoic which moves to trans-egoic; pre-mental goes to mental which goes to trans-mental—and so on. I have sketched just a few of these major differences in Fig. 3.

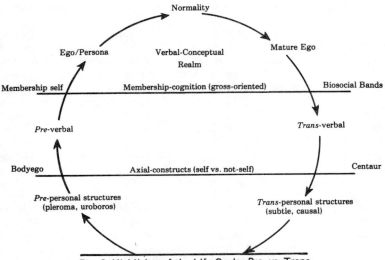

Fig. 3. Highlights of the Life-Cycle: Pre- vs. Trans-

Although there are naturally superficial similarities between pre- and trans-structures, the two simply cannot be equated. Since the trend in modern psychology and psychiatry is to try to reduce all trans-structures to pre-structures, I will try—as we move into the higher and trans-structures of consciousness—to explain the differences between these higher trans-states and their lower pre-state counterparts. For instance:

The Primary Process: Pre-Verbal

We can begin with the high-phantasy or vision-image of the centaur level—the cognitive aspect of intentionality (and for simplicity's sake one may think of vision-image and intentionality as being the same thing). For the mature phantasy of the centaur is definitely prior to language, but it is *not* pre-verbal. It is trans-verbal.

To understand this distinction, let us start with the *pre*-verbal primary process: On the infantile bodyego or typhon, which is incapable of real language structure and membership cognition, the phantasy process (or "phantasmic world" as Arieti calls it) is indeed *pre*-verbal and *pre*-conceptual, as psychiatrists have pointed out for over half a century. The pre-verbal primary process is a primitive wish which flourishes without any checks, without consensual validation, without any secondary channeling and binding by logic, will, and language—

because *none* of these yet exist. This is the pre-verbal primary process, rife with wish-fulfillment, adualism, and magical-distorted cognitions.

Furthermore, the primary process of the pre-verbal and infantile stages is heavily involved with and bound to simple instinctual, emotional, and vital-pranic needs and drives—with "anal" and "phallic" and "breast" phantasies, with self-assertive impulses, with power wishes and maternal incest/castration motifs, with lower chakra concerns—with all the bodyego categories that we discussed. There is, then, a close association of the pre-verbal phantasy process with instinctual urges—sexual and aggressive, ritually repetitive, vital and vegetal. This is why, I think, Freud always linked and usually equated the realms of the primary process and the instinctual urges.[135]

The primary process, then, is first and foremost body-bound—it not only dominates the bodyself level(s), it remains forever embedded in that structure of consciousness. "All schools [of psychoanalysis] agree that conscious mental activity is accompanied, supported, maintained, enlivened, and affected by unconscious phantasy, which begins in childhood, is primarily (originally) concerned with biological processes and relations, and undergoes symbolic elaboration."[327] More to the point is Susan Isaacs' summary of Klein's important analytic discoveries: "(a) Phantasies are the primary content of unconscious mental processes. (b) Unconscious phantasies are primarily about bodies, and represent instinctual aims towards objects."[327]

There is the lower phantasy, the primary process—it is "primarily about bodies" and "biological relations," and it can undergo "symbolic elaborations." If I may borrow Schafer's summary of the infantile bodyego categories, the primary process is tied to and "based on organs (mouth, anus, genitalia), substances (feces, urine, milk, blood), movements (sucking, fingering, straining, falling), and contacts (kissing, clinging, hitting)."[336] The primary process and the infantile bodyego go hand in hand, molded by the very categories Schafer lists.

Now I have frequently commented that the primary process and the infantile bodyself must eventually be surrendured and transformed; that consciousness has to detach itself from the vegetal body and open itself to the mental-egoic realm; that one's self sense must leave the hedonistic bodyego and transform to the ego-mind. A failure of this transformation at any point leaves the individual *fixated* at particularly *bodily zones*, bound by unconscious phantasies of achieving final satisfaction through those bodily areas (oral: achieve ultimate satisfaction by sucking, swallowing, or incorporating the world; anal, by possessing and manipulating the world; phallic, by "making" the world or sexually uniting with it).

If these fixations occur—and they do to some degree or another in all people; I am here especially concerned with the more severe cases— then "symbolic elaborations" tend to play off of these fixated modes. For example, a person fixated at the anal mode might—through the primary process—unconsciously equate mud with feces and then develop a phobia for dirt and an obsessive-compulsive cleanliness which drives him to wash his hands 20 or 30 times a day.[120] "Mud," in this case, is symbolic of "feces," so that a "symbolic elaboration" has spread out from a body-zone to encompass other, non-bodily areas. I personally believe that those "symbolic elaborations" do indeed occur much as psychoanalysis describes them.

The problem, however, is that psychoanalysis then tends to reduce *all* symbolism and even all higher modes of thought and being to the body mode of the infantile primary process. A derisive remark was once made against psychoanalysis that, "according to this doctrine, the unconscious sees a penis in every convex object and a vagina or anus in every concave one." Upon hearing that, the great analyst Ferenczi replied with straight face: "I find that this sentence well characterises the facts."[121]

With that type of approach, no wonder psychoanalysis has such awful difficulties with higher and transcendent modes of being—God Himself is just that great big Breast in the Sky. Actually, Ferenczi had a good point—it just wasn't the whole point. As he explains, "The child's mind (and the tendency of the unconscious in adults that survives from it) is at first concerned exclusively with his own body, and later on chiefly with the satisfying of his instincts, with the pleasurable satisfactions that sucking, eating, contact with the genital regions, and the functions of excretion procure for him; what wonder, then, if also his attention is arrested above all by those objects and processes of the outer world that on the ground of ever so distant a resemblance remind him of his dearest experiences."[121]

And here is Ferenczi's point: "Thus arise those intimate connections, which remain throughout life, between the human body and the objective world that we call *symbolic*. On the one hand the child in this stage sees in the world nothing but images of his corporeality, on the other he learns to represent by means of his body the whole multifariousness of the outer world."[121] The point is that, according to psychoanalysis, *all* symbolic activity is body-based, and refers ultimately to the body alone; whereas for us, that is true *only* when there occurs severe fixation on the body level which then necessitates a symbolic elaboration off of that fixation (as explained in Chapter 6). But for psychoanalysis, *all* symbolism is *only* bodily based. As Rycroft explains: "Psychoanalytical theory asserts that the object or activity symbolized is always one of basic, instinctual, or biological interest, the substitution or displacement always being from the body, i.e. and e.g. knives, aeroplanes, guns can be interpreted as *phallic symbols*, but the penis could never be a knife symbol."[327]

Aside from not seeing that that occurs only in cases of fixation, psychoanalysis fell into that reductionistic error by assuming, very simply, that what appears *first* in development is always the most basic, most fundamental, and most "real" of all structures. Note that Rycroft, in the first of the above quotes, equated *primary* with *original*: that which is most real and "most dear" (as Ferenczi himself put it) is that which was *first* in development—and as far as "mental" activity goes, that means the primary process and its association with the pleasure-principled body: those were the first truly substantial structures of the self sense to emerge in development, as we saw. In short, psychoanalysis assumes: first = most real; and thus *all* subsequent developments *must* be *symbolic* of those first and "most real" experiences.

For the perennial philosophy, however—and this is the view I am trying to represent—the highest and truest modes of being appear *last* in temporal development. Since the higher modes, by definition, must recapitulate the lower modes, they could only appear *after* the lower ones. In precisely the same way, humans appeared *last* in the evolutionary climb (to date), simply because they represent the highest mode of being yet to emerge.

Just because the primary process—with its bodily categories— appears first in development, psychoanalysis tries to make all subsequent developments into mere off-shoots and symbols of the primary process. For example, the primary process image of the breast most definitely enters consciousness long before the mature and extremely sophisticated concept of the mandala (which is a complex circular figure used in higher meditation practices), just as amoebas emerged on this earth long before human beings did. But to say—as psychoanalysis does—that the mandala is just a symbol of the breast is to say that a human being is just a symbol of an amoeba. That is precisely what the psychoanalytic theory of symbolism amounts to. Might as well say plants are symbols of dirt, just because dirt came first. With that simple fallacy, psychoanalysis solemnly promised humanity that it, psychoanalysis, would never be able to understand higher modes of being. Reducing the higher to the lower, it saw everywhere the beast. This type of approach would see an out-house and the Sistine Chapel as being pretty much the same, since both are made out of just a bunch of bricks—and after all, the bricks came first....

Vision-Image: Trans-Verbal

Almost from the very beginning of the scientific approach to psychology/therapy, there has been a continuous but subtle argument over the status of imaginative activity and phantasy: is it all just neurotic daydreaming? or is it a super-intuitive mode of knowing that reveals higher levels of reality? Is it archaic? or highly evolved? Is it valuable? or simply escapist and maladjusted?[93], [145], [265]

For my own part, I think both—hence the terms "higher" and "lower" phantasy. Lower phantasy, as epitomized by the primary process, is probably not much more than a rather sophisticated mode of imagery shared by numerous other primates—apes can form "paleo-symbols."[7] Being more-or-less body-bound, even as it images other objects, it tends to hold consciousness in a short-circuited pattern around the bodyself, and tends, in fact, to actually drag consciousness back into the narcissistic body-being. All of that has been very extensively covered, explained, and documented by psychoanalysis, and I mean for all of that to be evoked when we speak of the lower phantasy, the id-phantasy, the typhonic cognition.[120, 123, 134, 142]

But I am saying that that is true only of the infantile pre-verbal phantasy, and that the mature and high-phantasy process does not point backwards to instincts but upwards to higher modes of being and awareness which transcend the gross-body orientation. As Robert Masters puts it:

> The distinction between noetic imagination [vision-image] and fantasy [primary process] has been stated in various ways by philosophers and mystics through the ages. Paracelsus doubtless meant the same thing when he cautioned against confusing the *imagination vera* of the alchemists with fantasy, "that cornerstone of fools." The imaginal world is the visionary world, the world of theophanic as of other visions, and it becomes perceptible to us only through a special cognitive imagination.[271]

None of the problems of the pre-verbal phantasy process that we just listed inhere at the mature centaur. The individual has completed the formation of language and conceptual thought; he has *transformed* the infantile wishes of the typhon to more social and consensual forms; he has moved out of the infantile embeddedness structures (pleromatic and uroboric)—all of that is now more-or-less behind him (excluding, of course, fixations). The phantasy process is not now a way to regress to pre-verbal phantasies, but a way to contact trans-verbal realities. It serves as a *transition* (and a symbol of transformation) from the existential realm into the transpersonal. It is an extremely important cognitive mode, not just for the centaur level but for higher levels as well, which is why deep imagery and visualization, but never abstract conceptualization, are used in many forms of transpersonal meditation.[173] For this is the *trans*-verbal phantasy, and not only can it be pressed to entirely different ends than the pre-verbal primary process, it is of an entirely different realm.[106]

"Symbolic thinking," writes Mircea Eliade (in response to the psychoanalytic position), "is not the exclusive privilege of the child, of the poet or of the unbalanced mind: it is consubstantial with human existence, and it comes before language and discursive reason. The symbol reveals certain aspects of reality—the deepest aspects—which defy any other means of knowledge. Images, symbols, and myths are not irresponsible creations of the psyche; they respond to a need and fulfill a function, that of bringing to light the most hidden modalities of being."[106]

Now of course there can be fixation at and regression to the pre-verbal primary process, with pathological phantasies of infantile uroboric or maternal incest/castration and a heavy accent on instinctual urges and biological relations, sexual and aggressive and cannibalistic. And there *can* be progressive evolution to the trans-verbal phantasy process of the mature centaur level. This is not a return to infancy but a re-discovery of that portion of one's being that begins to go trans-personal and trans-historical, *not pre-historical.*

> When a historically conditioned being—for instance, an Occidental of our own days—allows himself to be invaded by the non-historical part of himself (which happens to him much oftener and more completely than he imagines), this is not necessarily [note Eliade says "not necessarily", as if he acknowledged that this could be regressive as well as progressive] a retrogression towards the animal stage of humanity [the bodyself stages] or a redescent towards the deepest sources of organic life [uroboric-repetilian]. Often he is re-entering, by means of the images and symbols that then come into play, a paradisiac stage of primordial humanity..., a lost paradise.[106]

And that lost paradise is not prior in time, but prior in depth. In the chapters on the subtle realms, we will explore just this non-historical portion of awareness.

What we have seen in the last few sections is that the entire existential/humanistic force—along with the Jungians, the Eastern tradition, Mircea Eliade, etc.—sees vision-image and high-phantasy and intentionality as being not a lower but a higher mode of cognition, reaching beyond *both* the infantile primary process and the secondary process of verbal reasoning. And now, even the most respected of orthodox psychiatrists are starting to say precisely the same thing. S. Arieti, for instance, recently wrote a highly influential book called *Creativity: the Magic Synthesis,* wherein he cogently argues that creativity—one of the highest and most valued cognitive processes in humans—is a *synthesis* of the primary process and the secondary process, and therefore reaches *beyond* the limitations of both.[8] And that, it seems to me, is precisely what we have been talking about with intentionality and vision-image: the magic synthesis, the higher-order synthesis and integration of the centaur itself. Thus, all in all I think it will soon be commonplace knowledge that there is *pre-verbal* (primary process), and there is *verbal* (secondary process)—and above and beyond both, as a magic synthesis, there is *trans-verbal*: intentionality, high-phantasy, and the vision-image.

Pre-Consensus and Trans-Consensus

The infantile bodyego was, recall, a stage wherein body and self or body and ego were undifferentiated. The mature centaur or total bodymind is the point where body and ego begin to go into trans-differentiation and high-order integration—that is to say, body and ego-mind, once having been differentiated, are now integrated. There are superficial similarities between the pre-differentiated bodyego and the trans-differentiated bodymind (or centaur), but the two are entirely different in structure. We have just examined briefly the cognitive processes of each level—but that, in a sense, is just the beginning.

In particular, I would like to point out that the infantile bodyego is pre-consensus, pre-membership, pre-social, pre-adjustment. The mature bodymind or centaur begins to go trans-consensus, trans-membership, trans-social, trans-adjustment. It seems to me that psychoanalysis, on the whole, is totally suspicious of, if not terrified by, trans-social and trans-conventional modes of being (because it confuses them with pre-social modes, which are indeed "scary"). Existential-humanistic therapy, on the other hand, announces—and rightly, I believe—that true authenticity occurs *only* as one goes trans-social in one's being.[228] This, for me, is easily explainable: psychoanalysis deals only with the ego/shadow/body realms, whereas existential-humanistic therapies continue through those realms (without denying their importance), and into the higher realm of the centaur—and the dividing line, as can be seen in Fig. 3, is membership-cognition.

Now this dividing line—the general dividing line between the mature and socially-adapted ego and the *authentic* centaur (using that italicized term as existentialists do)—is what I call the "Biosocial Bands."[410] "Bio-" denotes "body" (typhon) and "social" denotes "membership" and "membership concepts"—thus the biosocial band represents the upper *limit* of membership-cognition and gross bodily orientations, beyond which lie those realms of being which transcend conventional, egoic, institutional, and social forms—as indicated schematically in Fig. 3. By the same token, those realms of self and being which lie beyond the biosocial bands also tend to be trans-verbal, trans-conceptual, and trans-social. The interested reader will find the "Biosocial Bands" listed in all the appropriate Tables and Figures in this volume; for simplicity's sake, however, I will not dwell on this transitional plane, except to point it out—the only item I want to emphasize in this section is that there is a total world of difference between the *pre*-social being and the *trans*-social being, between those who have *not yet* arrived at the membership-stages and those who now start to transcend them and move beyond the biosocial realms. Because both pre-social and trans-social are *a*-social, the two have been horrendously confused by orthodox psychology, especially psychoanalysis, with a reductionistic fury.

I know of no better general introduction to this whole topic of pre-social and trans-social than Schachtel's work *Metamorphosis* (and notice: "metamorphosis" *means* "transformation").[334] Schachtel's primary interest is in the development of perception and attention, and he distinguishes two basic modes of perception (the terminology here is not that important—his point will soon become obvious): 1) autocentric, where emphasis is on the subject, on sensory qualities, on feelings in relation to perception, and 2) allocentric, where emphasis is on the object, what it is like, what it is. The gist of Schachtel's demonstration, to use Loevinger's excellent summary, is that the "child's allocentric openness to the world is lost in most adults. Schachtel uses the term sociocentric [membership-oriented] perception for shared autocentric perception. As secondary autocentricity [seeing the world through society's labels and categories and fixed concepts] and socio-centric [membership] perception become predominant, they interfere both with allocentric perception [seeing things as they are] and also with appropriate autocentric perception at the adult level [i.e., in its matured forms]. In everyday language, thinking and perceiving in terms of stereotypes and labels interferes both with realistic percep-tion of the objective world and with full enjoyment of the sensuous encounter with the world."²⁴³

Now here is the major point: the child's "allocentric openness" and an appropriate autocentric or sensory awareness can be "regained," as it were, but now in an entirely different context—so much so, in fact, that we must actually speak of different "kinds" or different "struc-tures." Thus, in the mature "*allocentric attitude*, there is an interest in and turning toward the object; it involves the whole object and *the whole being of the observer* (my ital.). Allocentric interest in the object leads to global perception of it, but it is a *different kind of glob-ality from that of infancy* (my ital.), which fuses subject and object [pleromatic-uroboric], or of early childhood, in which the distinct features of the object are not perceived [primary process]."²⁴³ Deik-man puts a similar point thus: "Rather than speaking of a return to childhood [pre-membership perception], it is more accurate to say that the undoing of automatic perceptual and cognitive structures permits a gain in sensory intensity and richness at the expense of abstract categorization [or membership-cognition in general]. It is... occurring in an adult mind, and the experience gains its richness from adult memories and functions now subject to a different mode of con-sciousness [that is, one which is now trans-membership]."³⁷²

Membership-cognition, once created (which is a necessary and desirable step), must now be transcended—that is how I read Schach-tel *et al.* On the whole, this higher "allocentric openness" and "rich sensory experience" (Roger's "organismic experiencing") involves learning to see and feel again, above and prior to schematization (Schachtel), and abstract categorization (Deikman), and ego-concep-tual translations (May)—and please note: this is now a trans-verbal perception, not a pre-verbal one. As Schachtel himself puts it, "It is in those experiences which transcend the cultural schemata [the biosocial bands of membership-perception]...that every new insight and every true work of art has its origin, and that the hope of progress, of a wid-ening of the scope of human endeavor and human life, is founded."³³⁴

The Immediate Present

To continue the general discussion: we saw that the infant bodyego was *only* aware of—and was literally confined to—the immediate here and now. Temporal sequences completely escape him, events just "seem to happen" (Sullivan—the parataxic mode). Most humanistic therapies place extreme stress on the "immediate here and now,"[292] and this has lead almost all orthodox psychologists and psychiatrists to the conclusion that these humanistic therapies are really throwbacks to the infantile typhon, that they are regressive and represent nothing more than "acting out." No doubt some of the more "pop therapies" are just that; but the psychiatric conclusion in general misses the entire point. At the mature centaur level, the immediate and vivid present is indeed the dominant mode of time, but the individual now has *complete access* to the entire conventional world of extended temporal realities as well. He is not confined to the present (like the child bodyego), he is simply grounded in it; and he is not ignorant of historical time, he is just no longer bound to it (like the ego). The typhon is pre-sequential time; the centaur is trans-sequential time. The former is ignorant of the world of linear time; the latter is beginning to transcend it. Naturally, then, they *appear* similar— but how different in fact they are, and how disastrous it is to equate them. Once linear time has been created (again, a necessary and utterly desirable step), then it *can* be transcended, and this is not regression but evolution.

Since the mode of time of the existential level is the immediate, vivid, and living present, many centaur therapists use this as one of the new *translations* given to the client.[291] That is (in addition to some of the other centaur translations we have discussed, such as vision-image and intentionality), the translation of "seeing all reality as *present*" is commonly used (as in Gestalt Therapy—"only the *now* is real"). The individual learns to see thoughts of yesterday as *present* occurrences, and anticipations of tomorrow as *present* activities (incidentally, this was St. Augustine's theory of time; that the past was *only* memory and the future *only* anticipation, *both* being *present* facts). To the extent that the individual succeeds globally in this translation, he then *transforms* to existential time; the whole abstract and ghostly world of linear time—now that it has served its purpose— collapses into the intensity of the present. The individual simply continues this translation (the "working through"), until the transformation is more-or-less complete and he is generally grounded in, but not confined to, the living present.[221, 292]

The ability to live fully in the present is a prime characteristic of the centaur as I have described it, and so it is not surprising that almost every developmental psychologist who has studied "highly developed" personalities—and the centaur is a highly developed being—has reported that "toleration for ambiguity and *ability to live intensely in the present* are aspects of the highest stages [of growth]."[243]

Is this then regression? I don't see how that conclusion can be soberly maintained. Rather, whereas the bodyego's present was a pre-sequence present, the centaur's present is a trans-sequence one: from above and beyond the temporal sequence, the self surveys the flow of linear events. It can see the past and the future *as* present thoughts *from* the present. It can *still see* the past and future, still remember yesterday and plan for tomorrow, but it can see them as movements *of* the present, a perception fantastically beyond the capacities of the typhon. The infantile bodyego can *only* see the present; the centaur can see *all time* from the present. Whatever else might be said, these are two entirely different modes of present-centered awareness.

Spontaneity

We also saw that the bodyego is dominated by its "impulsiveness" or its "uncontrolled spontaneity" or its "immediate discharge." In the mature centaur, this "immediate discharge" appears as spontaneity and impulse expression—precisely what we have seen as the "spontaneous will" or intentionality. And again, studies of impulse expression and spontaneity show that the child and the *most developed* adults share these traits, whereas the individuals in the intermediate stages (the average ego/persona realms) do not. Everyone agrees that the child (as bodyego) is spontaneous and impulsive, but "the increase in spontaneity, in being a home with one's impulses, is [also] a mark of the highest stages of...development, as many expositions agree."[243] Now this means one of two things; either the most highly developed adults are *regressing* to infancy and the pre-egoic-control stages, or the most developed adults are *progressing beyond* the rigid controls of the ego to the trans-egoic-control stages. Naturally, my own opinion is that the infant bodyego has a pre-verbal, pre-control, pre-inhibition spontaneity, whereas the mature centaur evidences a trans-verbal, trans-control, trans-inhibition freedom. But let us finish this discussion by noting, with Loevinger, that this fact "does not justify the conclusion that intermediate stages of [membership and egoic] rigid controls can be bypassed."[243]

Summary: the Centaur

There are a few final things that I would like to say about the peculiar role and nature of the existential or centauric level in the over-all context of the spectrum of consciousness. As we have seen, although this level has *access* to language, membership-cognition, egoic logic and will, it can and does reach beyond them, to a pristine sensory awareness and ongoing psychophysiological flow, as well as to the high-phantasy process of intuition and intentionality. This level is above language, logic, and culture—yet it is not pre-verbal and pre-cultural but trans-verbal and trans-cultural.

And here is the point I want to emphasize: while this level is trans-verbal, it is *not* trans-personal. That is, while it transcends language, gross concepts, and the gross ego, it does not transcend existence, personal orientation, or waking psychophysiological awareness (see Fig. 3). It is the last stage dominated by normal forms of space and time—but those forms are still there.

But sensory awareness itself, cleansed of the overlay of egoic and cultural schematization, begins taking in the waking realm with a clarity and richness that is striking. And at this point, sensory awareness is no longer just "vegetal" or "animal" or merely "organic"—it is rather a type of super-sensory (and almost, but not quite, suprasensory) awareness, an influx of higher subtle and even transpersonal energies. As Aurobindo explains, "By an utilization of the inner senses,—that is to say, of the sense-powers, in themselves, in their purely...subtle activity...—we are able to take cognition of sense-experiences, of appearances and images of things other than those which belong to the organization of our material environment."[306] This "super-sensory" awareness is reported by many centaur therapists (Rogers,[322] Perls,[291] etc.); it is discussed by Deikman[92] and is also reported as one of the *beginning* stages of mystical insight (as one ascends to, and then transcends, the centaur).[329]

I also believe—and would even like to emphasize—that the trans-verbal, trans-conceptual centaur is the home of Bergson's "intuition" and Husserl's "pure seeing." I do not mean to deny that either Bergson or Husserl saw beyond the centaur and into higher realms; I only feel that by and large their philosophies reflect most brilliantly the reality of centauric intentionality, vision-image, and immediate perceptual apprehension. Husserl is also one of the few who clearly understood the vast difference between body sensory awareness (typhonic), which is incapable of mental reflection, and true experiential awareness (centauric), which *includes* acts of mental reflection. Immediate experiential awareness was, for Husserl, a trans-verbal consciousness and intentionality (which was his term), not a pre-verbal sensory awareness—a point, it seems to me, which is by-and-large lost on most modern "experiential therapists," who glorify typhonic excesses. For an expanded discussion of these themes, the reader is referred to Bergson's *Introduction to Metaphysics* and Husserl's *Ideas*.

A higher-order unity, a higher-order integration: trans-verbal, trans-membership, but *not* trans-personal—this mature centaur is the point, I believe, that higher energies begin to rush into the organism, even transfiguring it physiologically. This whole level—which is a dis-identification with the ego and a higher-order identification with the total bodymind—marks the highest potential that can be reached in the existential or "gross" realm. It is very much what John Lilly (following Gurdjieff) called "state +12," which is "blissful state; cosmic love, reception of grace [higher energies], heightened bodily awareness [super-sensory]; highest function of bodily consciousness."[242] And it is important to note that Lilly places this bodymind level above or higher than the conceptual level or the level of "absorption and trans-mission of new data and programs; teaching and learning."[242] Above, that is, the egoic secondary process and syntaxical cognition. This state is also similar to the initial stages of the path of Bubba Free John, where, relaxing thought and desire through attentive inquiry, one intuits an "unqualified sense of relationship. This unqualified sense of relationship, enjoyed while, paradoxically, still aware of the perception of the world and *one's bodily presence within it*, is intuition of the all-pervading Divine Presence."[59]

THE CENTAURIC SELF	
• cognitive style—	transverbal vision-image, high-phantasy, synthesis of primary and secondary processes; trans-consensual
• affective elements—	prehension, spontaneity, impulse expression, supersensory, heart-felt
• conative/motivational factors—	intentionality, creative wish, meaning, spontaneous will, self-actualization, autonomy
• temporal mode—	grounded in the present moment, aware of linear time as exfoliating from the present
• mode of self—	integrated, autonomous, trans-biosocial, total body-mind being

This is one of the reasons, I think, that even existentialists tend to start intuiting *transpersonal* realities—*to use their own words*. Both Husserl and Heidegger tended eventually toward strongly transcendent philosophies (not to mention the theistic existentialists, Marcel, Jaspers, Tillich). Dr. May himself speaks of the movement "from an impersonal through a personal to a transpersonal dimension of consciousness."[265] And George Brown, one of the great heirs to Fritz Perls in Gestalt Therapy—which, by Perls' own account, is a purely existential therapy—describes what happens as individuals are given the centauric-translation of centering on the here and now, but eventually reach an impasse:

> The impasse experience could be described in a lot of ways. There are transpersonal energies involved. People talk about floating sensations, tranquility and peace. And we don't push them. We say, "That's fine, keep reporting what's happening to you." And sometimes we ask them if they can touch anything where they are; if they can't, that's fine. If they do, what usually happens is that they begin to see some light [true subtle realm]. This might very well be a movement towards the transpersonal. They frequently see light and go towards it, and they come out and there is sun and beautiful things: green trees and blue sky and white clouds. Then, when they are finished with that experience and open their eyes, they see colors more clearly, their vision is more

acute, their perception heightened, [super-sensory
centaur awareness], they've cut out the filters [egoic and
membership filters] which their fantasies and patholo-
gies have placed over them at that moment of time.[55]

The existential-centaur, then, is not only the higher-order integration of ego, body, persona, and shadow, it is also the major transition
towards the higher subtle and transpersonal realms of being. (Notice
that Stan Grof's research seems to support this thesis very strongly).[166] This is so in both the centaur's "super-sensory" modality, and
in its cognitive process of intuition, intentionality, and vision-image.
They are all *intimations* of the higher realms of transcendence and
integration.

And it is now time to look to those higher realms themselves.

8

Subtle Realms

The Nirmanakaya: the Gross Realms

So far, we have seen these major levels of increasing differentiation, integration, and transcendence: the simple and primitive fusion-unity of the pleroma and uroboros; the next higher-order unity of the biological bodyself; then the mental-persona, which, if integrated with the shadow, yields the higher-order unity of the total ego; and finally the centaur, which is a higher-order integration of the total ego with all preceding and lower levels—uroboros, body, persona, and shadow.

But *all* of that belongs to what traditional psychologies would call the "gross realm," beyond which lie the subtle and causal realms (see Table A). In Hinduism, the gross realm is called the *sthula-sarira;*[94] in Kabbalah it is everything below the *Tiphareth;*[338] in Buddhism, it is the *Nirmanakaya* (which is the term I use most often, next to "gross" itself).[332] The gross realm, the Nirmanakaya—the realm of ordinary waking consciousness—is simply composed of all those levels which are based on, or centered around, or take as their final referent the gross physical body and its constructs of ordinary space and time. The physical or axial body itself is called the "gross level," and all *aspects of the psyche that reflect this level* are called the "gross-reflecting mind" (or just the "gross mind" for short). Taken together, they constitute the overall gross realm—the gross bodymind of ego, body, persona, shadow, and centaur.

This "gross-reflecting mind" is what Aurobindo means when he speaks of the average individual as possessed of a "twilit or obscure *physical mentality*," or of "the ordinary *material intellect* which takes its present organization of consciousness for the limit of its possibilities."[306] For in the ordinary egoic state "the mind, habituated only to the evidence of the senses and associating reality with corporeal fact, is either unaccustomed to use other means of knowledge or unable to

TABLE A.

Major Realms	General Levels	Cognition
NIRMANAKAYA Five vijnanas plus Manovijnana	Bodyself (axial, pranic, image) Membership-self Ego/persona (gross-adapted) Centaur/existential	Sensorimotor Low-phantasy Membership-cognition Intellection High-phantasy (vision-image)
SAMBHOGAKAYA Manas	Low subtle High subtle	Clairvoyant-cognition Higher-mind High-intuition Literal-inspiration Illumination
DHARMAKAYA Alayavijnana	Low causal High causal	Final-illumination Radical Insight Jnana/formless
SVABHAVIKAKAYA Dharmadhatu/Tathata	Ultimate	Supreme enlightenment Sahaja

extend the notion of reality to a supraphysical experience."[306] And, in a phrase I particularly like, he speaks of the true subtle mind (as opposed to the gross mind) as "a mind and sense not shut up in the walls of the *physical ego* (ital. mine)."[306]

All of this—the gross body and the gross ego as constituting the overall gross realm—is in close agreement with standard Buddhist psychology. For the Nirmanakaya is said to consist of the five senses *plus* the *manovijnana*, and the manovijnana is the "mind involved with the senses."[332] D.T. Suzuki unequivocally equates the manovijnana with both the ego of Western psychology and the logical-empirical intellect.[365] He also speaks of this overall realm as the one of "sense and thought," and places all the data of Western psychology precisely in that realm—and that realm only.[362] Thus, besides the gross or physical body, we see that the gross realm in humans consists of, or is inextricably intermeshed with, the lower or gross-reflecting mind, so that the entire realm itself is best referred to as the *realm of the gross bodymind*.

It follows, then, that almost all of the data generated by orthodox Western psychology pertains only to the gross realm. Huston Smith is quite clear on that point.[352] So is René Guénon: Western psychologists "recognize...scarcely anything except the corporeal modality [the gross bodymind]." That is, Western psychology aims at what Guénon calls the "corporeal individuality," very like Aurobindo's "physical ego." As Guénon so bluntly but correctly puts it: "As for modern Western psychology, it deals only with quite a restricted portion of the human individuality, where the mental faculty is in direct relationship with the corporeal modality, and given the methods it employs, it is incapable of going any further."[168]

But *is* there "any further"? According to the mystics—whom we agreed at the very beginning of this book to adopt as models of higher evolution—indeed there is. "The ordinary man," says Aurobindo, "lives in his mind and senses [the gross bodymind] as they are touched by a world which is outside him, outside his consciousness. When the consciousness subtilises, it begins to come into contact with things in a much more direct way, not only with their forms and outer impacts but with what is inside them, but still the range may be small. But the consciousness can also widen and begin to be first in direct contact with a universe of range of things in the world, then to contain them as it were—as it is said to see the world in oneself—and to be in a way identified with it. To see all things in the self and the self in all things... that is universalization."[306] That is, there are higher and higher orders of unity and identity and integration, leading finally to universal unity itself and the Supreme Identity.

To put it all very plainly, *evolution can continue*. It has already brought forth humans from amoebas—why on earth should we think that after that prodigious feat lasting billions of years, evolution just petered out and wound down? And if the ratio "amoeba to human" is repeated, the result could only be God. The mystics simply show us the stages of higher evolution leading to that Summit. "Certainly, if that body, life and consciousness were limited to the possibilities of the gross body which are all that our physical senses and physical mentality [gross ego] accept, there would be a very narrow term for this evolution," says Aurobindo. However, according to many sages, "there are behind our waking mentality vaster ranges of consciousness...superconscient to it of which we become sometimes abnormally aware, [and] there are behind our gross physical being other and subtler grades of substance with a finer law and a greater power...; by our entering into the ranges of consciousness belonging to them [we can] substitute their purer, higher, intenser conditions of being for the grossness and limitation of our present physical life and impulses and habits."[306] Thus, our present gross "mind, life and body are an inferior consciousness and a partial expression which strives to arrive in the mould of a various evolution at that superior expression of itself already existent to the beyond-mind [the "beyond-mind" is simply the realms beyond body, mind, and centaur]. That which is in the beyond-mind is the ideal which in its own conditions it is labouring to realise..."[306]

And the first stage of the beyond-mind, the realms beyond the gross, is simply the world of the subtle sphere.

The Sambhogakaya: the Subtle Realm

For indications as the nature of any higher levels of consciousness, beyond the ego and centaur, we have to turn to the great mystic-sages, Eastern and Western, Hindu and Buddhist, Christian and Islamic. It is somewhat surprising, but absolutely significant, that all of these otherwise divergent schools of thought agree rather unanimously as to the nature of the "farther reaches of human nature." There are indeed, these traditions tell us, higher levels of consciousness—as far above the ego-mind as the ego-mind is above the typhon. And they look like this:

Beginning with (to use the terms of yogic chakra psychology), the sixth chakra, the Ajna chakra, consciousness *starts* to go trans-personal. Consciousness is now going trans-verbal *and* trans-personal. It begins to enter the true "subtle sphere," known in Hinduism as the *suksma-sarira*,[94] in Buddhism as the *Sambhogakaya* (the technical term I have adopted).[161] This process quickens and intensifies as it reaches the highest chakra—called the sahasrara—and then goes supra-mental as it enters the seven higher stages of consciousness beyond the sahasrara.[350] The ajna, the sahasrara, and the seven higher levels are, on the whole, referred to as the subtle realm.

For convenience sake, however, we speak of the "low-subtle" and the "high-subtle." The low-subtle is epitomized by the ajna chakra—the "third eye," which is said to include and dominate both astral and psychic events. That is, the low-subtle is "composed" of the astral and psychic planes of consciousness. Whether one believes in these levels or not, this is where they are said to exist (or rather, where they are said to reach maturity).

The astral level includes, basically, out-of-body experiences, certain occult knowledge, the auras, true magic, "astral travel," and so on. The psychic plane includes what we would call "psi" phenomenon: ESP, precognition, clairvoyance, psychokinesis, and so on. Many individuals can occasionally "plug in" to this plane, and evidence random or higher-than-random psychic abilities. But to actually *enter* this plane is to more-or-less master psychic phenomena, or at least certain of them. Patanjali has an entire chapter of his Yoga Sutras devoted to this plane and its structures (which are *siddhis,* or paranormal powers).[370,398] I should also mention that most researchers in the field of parapsychology feel that the astral and psychic realms are really the same body, and so in general we speak of this realm as the astral-psychic.[399]

The whole point of the low-subtle—the astral-psychic—is that consciousness, by further differentiating itself from the mind and body, is able in some ways to *transcend* the normal capacities of the gross bodymind and therefore *operate* upon the world and the organism in ways that appear, to the ordinary mind, to be quite fantastic and far-fetched. For my own part, I find them a natural extension of the transcendent function of consciousness.

THE LOW-SUBTLE SELF	
• cognitive style—	clairvoyant perception and cognition; extra-egoic and extra-sensory
• affective elements—	transpersonally sensitive, suprasensory (the stage beyond the supersensory centaur)
• motivational/conative factors—	siddhi; paranormal and parapsychological drives
• temporal mode—	trans-axial or trans-physical; "point-source" time; able to read world lines with precognition or postcognition
• mode of self—	astral-psychic

The High-Subtle

The high-subtle begins at the sahasrara and extends into seven more levels of extraordinarily high-order transcendence, differentiation, and integration. I am not going to present an exhaustive break-

down of this realm—the reader is instead referred to the works of
Kirpal Singh,[349], [350] who deals with this entire realm—of nada and
shabd yoga—in a brilliant fashion. I will simply say that this realm
is universally and consistently said to be the realm of high religious
intuition and literal inspiration; of bijamantra; of symbolic visions; of
blue, gold, and white light; of audible illuminations and brightness
upon brightness; it is the realm of higher presences, guides, angelic
beings, ishtadevas, and dhyani-buddhas; all of which—as we will soon
explain—are simply high archetypal forms of one's own being (although they initially and necessarily appear "other"). It is the realm
of Sar Shabd, of Brahma the Controller, of God's archetypes, and of
Sat Shabd—and beyond these four realms to three higher and totally
indescribable levels of being. Dante sang of it thus:

> Fixing my gaze upon the Eternal Light
> I saw within its depths,
> Bound up with love together in one volume,
> The scattered leaves of all the universe....
> Within the luminous profound subsistence
> Of that Exalted Light saw I three circles
> Of three colors yet of one dimension
> And by the second seemed the first reflected
> As rainbow is by rainbow, and the third
> Seemed fire that equally from both is breathed.

Keep in mind that this is what Dante *saw*, literally, with his eye of
contemplation. He is not simply waxing poetic, but using poetry and
vision-image to sing of what he *directly saw*.

The psychiatrist Dean, a pioneer in the new field of "metapsychia-
try," reports this:

> An intellectual illumination occurs that is quite impos-
> sible to describe. In an intuitive flash, one has an aware-
> ness of the meaning and drift of the universe, an identi-
> fication and merging with creation, infinity and immor-
> ality, a depth beyond depth of revealed meaning— in
> short, a conception of an over-self, so omnipotent....[91]

In Hinduism, this realm is called the *vijnanamayakosa*;[94] in Mahayana Buddhism, this is the *manas*;[362] in Kabbalah, it is *Geburah* and
Chesed.[338] Aspects of this subtle realm have been called the "over-
self" or "over-mind"—as in Aurobindo and Emerson (Aurobindo uses
the term to cover aspects of the causal as well).[12] The point is simply
that consciousness, in a rapid ascent, is differentiating itself entirely
from the ordinary mind and self, and thus can be called an "over-self"
or "over-mind"—almost like calling the ego an "over-body" or "over-
instincts," since the mental-ego transcends and reaches over the
simple feelings and perceptions of the typhon. The over-mind simply
embodies a transcendence of all mental forms, and discloses, at its
summit, the intuition of That which is above and prior to mind, self,
world, and body—something which, as Aquinas would have said, all
men and women would call God.

But this is not God as an ontological other, set apart from the cosmos, from humans, and from creation at large. Rather, it is God as an Archetypal summit of one's own Consciousness. John Blofeld quotes Edward Conze on the Vajrayana viewpoint: "'It is the emptiness of everything which allows the identification to take place—the emptiness which is in us coming together with the emptiness which is the deity.' By visualizing that identification 'we actually do become the deity. The subject is identified with the object of faith. [As is said,] The worship, the worshipper and the worshipped, those three are not separate.'"[43] At its peak, the soul becomes one, literally one, with the deity-form, with the dhyani-Buddha, with God. One dissolves into Deity, *as* Deity—that Deity which, from the beginning, has been one's own Self or highest Archetype. In this way only could St. Clement say that he who knows himself knows God. We could now say, he who knows his over-self knows God. They are one and the same.

THE HIGH-SUBTLE SELF

• cognitive style—	actual-intuition and literal-inspiration, archetypal Form, audible illuminations, revelations of light and sound
• affective elements—	rapture, bliss, ecstatic release into superconsciousness
• motivational/conative factors—	karuna, compassion, overwhelming love and gratefulness
• temporal mode—	trans-temporal, moving into eternity
• mode of self—	archetypal-divine, over-self, over-mind

The Subtle Realms: Summary

I have deliberately kept this chapter short so as not to introduce an excessive amount of information on what is, after all, a rather unknown and unfamiliar realm for most individuals. I will do the same thing in the next chapter. But I would like you to simply consider the implications of the possible *existence* of the subtle realm. What *if* the mystic-sages are right?

The whole point would be that in the subtle realm—and especially in the high-subtle—a very high-order differentiation and transcendence is occurring. Mediated through high-archetypal symbolic forms—the Deity-forms, illuminative or audible—consciousness is following a path of transformation-upward which leads quite beyond the gross bodymind. This transformation-upward, like *all* the others we have

studied, involves the *emergence* (via remembrance), of a higher-order
deep structure, followed by the shifting of *identity* to that higher-
order structure and the differentiation or *dis-identification* with the
lower structures (in this case, the ego-mind). This amounts to a *transcendence* of the lower-order structures (the gross mind and body),
which thus enables consciousness to *operate* on and *integrate* all of
the lower-order structures.

Lex Hixon has described one form of the subtle deep-structure
called an "ishtadeva."[185] The ishtadeva is simply a high-archetypal
deity-form which is *evoked* (and thus *emerges*), in certain meditations
and is *literally* visualized with the mind's eye using the high-phantasy
or vision-image process. I realize some people would say that the
ishtadeva is "just a mental image" and doesn't *really* exist—but that
is to simultaneously reduce *all* mental productions: might as well say
that mathematics is just a mental production and therefore doesn't
really exist. No, the ishtadeva is real—more than real—in its emergence from the ground unconscious.

Hixon describes it thus: "The Form or Presence of the ishtadeva
[which is evoked by vision-image as he clearly explains] appears as
vibrantly alive, composed from the radiance of Consciousness. We are
not projecting the ishtadeva. The primal radiance which assumes the
form of the ishtadeva is actually projecting us and all the phenomena
that we call the universe." This high archetypal symbol eventually
mediates the ascension of consciousness to an *identity* with that Form:
"Gradually we realise that the Divine Form or Presence is our own
archetype, an image of our own essential nature."[185]

This, however, is not a *loss* of consciousness but an *intensification*
of consciousness through a higher-order development, evolution,
transcendence and *identification*: "The ishtadeva does not disappear
into us; we as individuals disappear into the ishtadeva, which now
remains alone. Yet there is no loss of our individual being as we blend
into the object of our contemplation, for it has been our own archetype from the beginning, the source of this fragmentary reflection we
call our individual personality."

The whole point is that the gross ego has not simply swallowed
the high Archetypal Form, but that the prior *nature* of the ego is
revealed to *be* that Form, so that consciousness reverts to—or remembers—its own prior and higher identity: "We remain now as a transcendental center of consciousness expressed through the Form or
formless Presence of the ishtadeva. We are now experiencing the life of
the ishtadeva from within. We are consciously meeting and becoming
[via higher identification] ourselves in our archetypal and eternal
nature."[185] Such, then, is one form of true transformation or development into the subtle realm, the discovery or remembrance of a higher-
order unity that is now approaching Unity—that enters the transpersonal sphere of superconciousness and discloses only Archetypal
Essence.

9

Causal and Ultimate Realms

The Dharmakaya: the Causal Realms

As the process of transcendence and integration continues, it discloses even higher-order unities, leading, consumately, to Unity itself.

Beyond the high-subtle lies the causal region, known variously as the *alaya-vijnana* (Yogacara Buddhism),[362] the *ananda-mayakosa* (Hinduism),[94] pneuma (Christian mysticism),[352] *karana-sarira* (Vedanta),[94] *Binah* and *Chokmah* (Kabbalah).[338] In general Mahayana Buddhist terms, this is the Dharmakaya realm (the term I will use). Again, for convenience, we divide it into the low-causal and the high-causal. As in the last chapter, I will be deliberately succinct:

The low-causal, which classically is revealed in a state of consciousness known as savikalpa samadhi,[309] represents the pinnacle of God-consciousness, the final and highest abode of Ishvara, the Creatrix of all realms.[94] This represents the *culmination* of events which began in the high-subtle. In the high-subtle, recall, the self was dissolved or re-absorbed into the archetypal deity, *as* that deity—a deity which from the beginning has always been one's own Self and highest Archetype.

Now at the low-causal, that deity-Archetype itself condenses and dissolves into final-God, which is here seen as an extraordinarily subtle audible-light or bija-mantra from which the individual ishtadeva, yidam, or Archetype emerged in the first place. Final-God is simply the ground or essence of all the archetypal and lesser-god manifestations which were evoked—and then identified with—in the subtle realms. In the low-causal, all of these archetypal Forms simply reduce to their Source in final-God, and thus, by the very same token and in the very same step, one's own Self is here shown to *be* that final-God, and consciousness itself thus transforms upwards into a higher-order identity with that Radiance. Such, in brief, is the low-causal, the ultimate revelation of final-God in Perfect Radiance and Release.

THE LOW-CAUSAL SELF

• cognitive style—	final-illumination, essence of audible revelation, root of bija-mantra, savikalpa samadhi
• affective elements—	radiant bliss/ananda
• motivational/conative factors—	only karuna, or transcendent love-in-oneness
• temporal mode—	utterly trans-temporal, eternal
• mode of self—	final-God, point Source of all Archetypal Forms

---

The High-Causal

Beyond the low-causal, into the high-causal, all manifest forms are so radically transcended that they no longer need even appear or arise in Consciousness. This is total and utter transcendence and release into Formless Consciousness, Boundless Radiance. There is here no self, no God, no final-God, no subjects, and no thingness, apart from or other than Consciousness as Such.

Note the overall progression of the higher unity structures: In the subtle realm, the self dissolves into archetypal Deity (as ishtadeva, yidam, dhyani-buddha, etc.). In the low-causal, that Deity-Self in turn disappears into final-God, which is its Source and Essence. Here, in the high-causal, the final-God Self is reduced likewise to its own prior Ground: it dissolves into Formlessness. Each step is an increase in consciousness and an intensification of Awareness until all forms return to perfect and radical release in Formlessness.

John Blofeld describes beautifully this progression from the Vajrayana Buddhist view: "As the rite progresses, this deity [ishtadeva] enters the adept's body and sits upon a solar-disc supported by a lunar-disc above a lotus in his heart; presently the adept shrinks in size until he and the deity are coextensive [the beginning of the subtle realm]; then, merging indistinguishably [becoming *one* with deity in the high-subtle realm], they are absorbed by the seed-syllable from which the deity originally sprang [the low-causal]; this syllable contracts to a single point [final-God]; the point vanishes and deity and adept in perfect union remain sunk in the samadhi of voidness [the high-causal]...".[43]

We already heard Lex Hixon, representing the Hindu view, describe the progression into the subtle realm. But he naturally continues the account into the causal: After the ishtadeva-archetype has emerged and one has identified with it (in the high-subtle realm), then "that Archetype dissolves into its own essence, or ground [the causal realm].... There is now perfect release into the radiance of formless Consciousness. There is no ishtadeva, no meditator, and no meditation, nor is there any awareness of an absence of these. There is only radiance."[185]

Precisely the same sequence is described by Zen texts on koan study.[220, 258, 364] After the initial stages of concentrating on the koan (this is equivalent to visualizing the ishtadeva or dhyani-buddha), a point is reached where the individual dissolves into the koan—he becomes *one* with the koan in a super-abundance of consciousness: not a loss of awareness but an extraordinary intensification of it. This is called "the man forgotten"—that is, the separate subject is forgotten in union with the koan, which now *alone* is. This is the subtle state. As this process intensifies, the koan itself is forgotten—that is, it dissolves itself into its own prior ground of Formlessness. This is called "the dharma (the koan) forgotten" or "both man and dharma forgotten"—and this is the high-causal of formless samadhi. This overall process is so consistently and similarly described by all the traditions which reach this high realm that we can now be quite certain of its general features . They are unmistakable.

Let us note that this state itself—the high-causal of "both man and dharma forgotten" or "both subject and object forgotten"—is known as nirvikalpa samadhi (Hinduism),[94] nirodh (Hinayana Buddhism),[160] jnana samadhi (Vedanta)[309]—and it is the eighth of the ten Zen ox-herding pictures which depict the stages to supreme Enlightenment.[220]

THE HIGH-CAUSAL SELF	
• cognitive self—	unknowing or perfectly divine ignorance in cessation, nirvikalpa samadhi, boundless Consciousness
• affective elements—	primal or formless Radiance, perfect Ecstatic
• motivational/conative factors—	only karuna, or transcendent love-in-oneness; final spontaneity, or *lila* and *tzu jan*
• temporal mode—	trans-temporal, eternal
• mode of self—	Formless Self-Realization, transcendent Witness

Svabhavikakaya: the Final Transformation

Passing through nirvikalpa samadhi, Consciousness totally awakens as its Original Condition and Suchness (tathata), which is, at the same time, the condition and suchness of all that is, gross, subtle, or causal. That which witnesses, and that which is witnessed, are only one and the same. The entire World Process then arises, moment to moment, as one's own Being, outside of which, and prior to which, nothing exists. That Being is totally beyond and prior to anything that arises, and yet no part of that Being is other than what arises.

And so: as the center of the self was shown to be Archetype; and as the center of Archetype was shown to be final-God; and as the center of final-God was shown to be Formlessness—so the center of Formlessness is shown to be not other than the entire world of Form. "Form is not other than Void, Void is not other than Form," says the most famous Buddhist Sutra (called the "Heart Sutra").[81] At that point, the extraordinary and the ordinary, the supernatural and mundane, are precisely one and the same. This is the tenth Zen ox-herding picture, which reads: "The gate of his cottage is closed and even the wisest cannot find him. He goes his own way, making no attempt to follow the steps of earlier sages. Carrying a gourd, he strolls into the market; leaning on his staff, he returns home."[220]

This is also sahaja samadhi, the Turiya state, the Svabhavikakaya—the ultimate Unity, wherein all things and events, while remaining perfectly separate and discrete, are only One. Therefore, this is not itself a state apart from other states; it is not an altered state; it is not a special state—it is rather the suchness of all states, the water that forms itself in each and every wave of experience, as all experience.[408] It cannot be seen, because it is everything which is seen; it cannot be heard, because it is hearing itself; it cannot be remembered because it only is. By the same token, this is the radically perfect integration of all prior levels—gross, subtle, and causal, which, now of themselves so, continue to arise moment to moment in an irridescent play of mutual interpenetration. This is the final differentiation of Consciousness from all forms in Consciousness, whereupon Consciousness as Such is released in Perfect Transcendence, which is not a transcendence from the world but a final transcendence as the World. Consciousness henceforth operates, not on the world, but only as the entire World Process, integrating and interpenetrating all levels, realms, and planes, high or low, sacred or profane.

"Followers of the Way," said Zen Master Rinzai, "once and for all sit down and cut off the heads of both the Sambhogakaya Buddha and of the Nirmanakaya Buddha. Those satisfied with merely completing the ten stages of the Bodhisattva are like serfs. Those content with universal and profound awakening are but fellows carrying cangue and chains. Awakening and Nirvana are like tethering posts for donkeys. And why is this so? Because, followers of the Way, you fail to see the emptiness of the three great world ages [that is, the whole universe, past, present, and future]; this is the obstacle that blocks you."[148] But when this is understood, where are the three realms of being or the three bodies of Buddha (gross, subtle, and causal)? Rinzai answers:

> The pure light of your heart at this moment is the Dharmakaya Buddha in your own house. The non-differen-

tiating light of your heart at this moment is the Sambhogakaya Buddha in your own house. The non-discriminating light of your own heart at this instant is the Nirmanakaya Buddha in your own house.[148]

For, adds Rinzai, "This trinity of the Buddha's Body [gross, subtle, and causal] is none other than he here before your eyes, listening to my expounding of the Dharma. Who is he then who understands all this? This is the One who is right in front of you, in all awareness, with no divisible shape, and in solitary brightness. This One understands how to talk about the Dharma and how to listen to it.... The scholars of the Sutras and Treatises take the Three Bodies as absolute. As I see it, this is not so. These Three Bodies are merely names, or props, they are only mental shadows [to one who has transcended them all in Perfect Liberation]. Venerable Ones, get to know the One who plays with these shadows. He is the original source of all the Buddhas. Knowing him, wherever you are is home."[148]

Every conscious being, then, precisely as he or she is, is a perfect embodiment and expression of the Ultimate. What every individual *is*, before he is anything else, is the Dharmakaya—the Body of very Truth. What he feels, before he feels anything else, is the Sambhogakaya—the Body of Playful Bliss. What he sees, before he sees anything else, is the Nirmanakaya—the Body of manifest-life-as-samadhi. These three Bodies of Buddha are one as the only Heart, and these three realms play in irridescent Unity through all eternal gestures.

And this, finally is the ultimate Unity towards which all evolution, human and cosmic, drives. And, it might be said, cosmic evolution— that holistic pattern—is completed in and as human evolution, which itself reaches ultimate unity consciousness and so completes that absolute Gestalt towards which all manifestation moves.

Eternity: God or Id?

I have said that I would try in the sections on the higher realms to briefly discuss the differences between *pre* and *trans* so as to help avoid confusing the two. We discussed the differences pre and trans with regard to the centaur, and now—in the subtle and causal realms— I would like to center the discussion on the notion of timelessness: pre and trans.

From the high-subtle on, time itself begins to evaporate, as it were, until in the causal realms there is only Timeless Eternity, a timelessness that is not a lack, not a privation, not an absence, but a superabundance of Radiance that cannot be contained in spatial or temporal categories. It is not exactly that time itself disappears—it is not that consciousness goes blank into darkness. Rather, in the state of Transcendence (subtle and causal), time both collapses into the Eternal Now *and* continues to flow through it and from it. Just as your eye can take in or see all four corners of this page in a single glance, so the eye of Eternity sees all time in one Moment. All of eternity is in every point of time, so that all time is Present in Eternity. Each point of time remains perfectly itself, by itself, and unfolds of itself quite naturally—*and* each point of time is only in Eternity, moment to moment. This is called the *nunc stans*—the Eternal Moment which embraces all time without obliterating any of it, because "Eternity is in love with the productions of time."

And here we run into the problem of pre and trans. Long ago Freud had stated that *the id is timeless*. "Unconscious mental processes are in themselves timeless," he said. "In the id there is nothing corresponding to the idea of time."[57] Because of Freud's immensely influential thoughts on the "timeless id," two things have happened:

(1) Whenever psychoanalysts encountered a "timeless state of awareness", they immediately assumed that this *must* be a resurgence of timeless id material. Eternal consciousness was thus interpreted as being merely a throwback to instinctual, oceanic, and primitive modes of awareness. God, in this system, is just an infantile symptom which needs desparately to be cured. Freud himself took this view in *Civilization and Its Discontents*.

(2) Many psychoanalysts, especially recently, have realized that Freud's thoughts on the matter were too naive; that psychoanalysis must make room for transcendent states of timeless being. Thus, they tried to legitimize unity consciousness and timeless consciousness by *redefining the id*, or the unconscious itself. Norman O. Brown said the id was actually Noumenal Reality itself;[57] Matte Blanco said the id was really an infinite set;[39] Loewald said the id was something like a primary being or ground.[246]

This second type of formulation—however preferable to the first—results nonetheless in some very awkward compromises. Matte Blanco, for instance, makes it very clear that the unconscious—the Freudian unconscious—is just like Freud said: the home of the primary process, instinctual, emotional, that seething cauldron of primal green goo. It is the source of totally over-powering and disrupting emotions, and thus the job of psychoanalysis is to *defuse* this unconscious set by translating it into secondary process thinking. Yet, because Blanco also identifies the *same* unconscious with the ultimate ground of being—Parmenides' One, he says—even God, he hints—then he unwittingly arrives at the conclusion that the job of psychoanalysis, since it must defuse the unconscious, is to defuse God and relieve the soul of Infinity.

This confusion exists because the difference between pre and trans is not clearly understood. Let me quickly review the temporal modes of each of the major levels of consciousness, and I think the whole problem will open up (I'll condense the levels into five for this summary):

On the first floor of the building of consciousness is the pleromatic and uroboric state. The mode of time is totally pre-temporal and a-temporal: no past, no present, no future—only pleromatic ignorance.

This is *not* a trans-temporal state; the infant does not transcend time, he is totally ignorant of it.

On the second floor is the typhonic self—the primary process, the prana-id, the emotional-sexual being. Here there is no *linear* time (no past and no future), but only a simple *present*. The mode of time is embedded in this simple present, ignorant of linear time.

On the third floor is egoic time—linear, historical, syntaxical, with a past, a present, and a future.

On the fourth floor is the centaur. The mode of time is again the immediate present, but it is a trans-linear present, whereas the typhon was a pre-linear present. The centaur is grounded in the present while *still aware* of linear time.

On the fifth floor are all the truly trans-temporal realms. This is utter Eternity, which is aware of linear time and aware of the immediate present, but is anchored in neither. This is *not* the immediate passing present, which lasts only a second or two, but the eternal present, which—lasting not at all—underlies and embraces all duration.

Now levels one and two—the pleroma-uroboros and the typhon—are approximately what psychoanalysis means by the "id." And those levels are, more or less, timeless in the sense of pre-temporal. They are either totally timeless (like the pleroma), or confined to the present without access to linear time (like the typhon). Psychoanalysis is thus right on that account: the id is indeed timeless. But it is timeless by way of *ignorance*, not transcendence. There is no time in it because it is too primitive—too dumb—to grasp such notions.

Freud said "In the id there is nothing corresponding to the idea of time," and from that point on, whenever analysts heard of timeless states of awareness, they thought they were dealing with the id. But Freud's statement hardly covers the matter: it is true that all id states are timeless, but it does not follow that all timeless states are id. The id is simply part of the *pre-temporal* universe. In rocks there is nothing corresponding with the notion of time—nor in plants nor in lower animals. All of the developmental stages of evolution prior to language are basically timeless (either completely a-temporal, like rocks and the pleroma, or pre-linear time, like plants, animals, and the typhonic realms). But there is nothing special—and certainly nothing Noumenal or Ultimate—about those states or about the id. To put it crudely, the id is pre-temporally dumb.

That pre-temporal id cannot in any way be equated with trans-temporal states—the difference is as vast as between, say, rocks and humans or humans and gods; and the trans-temporal realm most certainly cannot be reduced to the pre-temporal. The first school of psychoanalysis (listed above), makes the error of refusing to admit at all the existence of trans-temporal states, and thus merely tries to reduce trans to pre. Since they are well acquainted with the first two floors of consciousness, whenever a level-5 or transcendent state emerges, they simply claim it to be a throwback to level-1. Since they know nothing of trans-temporality, they simply subsume it under pre-temporality. Level-5 is reduced to level-1 and the Mystery dispersed. The second school of psychoanalysis, on the other hand, tries to admit the existence of trans-temporal states, but since they are not quite sure what to make of them, they simply redefine the pre-temporal id so as to include all timeless phenomena in it. They thus arrive at the problematic conclusion that the same id which is so primitive and so seething in its instinctual blindness is also the home of God Himself, that primal Ground of Being which rises beyond all distinctions.

The id *is* timeless—but it is pre-temporal. God *is* timeless—but it is trans-temporal. My own opinion is that psychoanalysis (and orthodox psychiatry and psychology), must recognize this incredible difference, and thus cease identifying God and id simply because both are outside the stream of linear time. Might as well equate rocks and rockets since both lack propellers.

The same holds true for every other central characteristic of the mystic union versus the infantile oceanic state. The infant-pleromatic fusion is pre-subject/object differentiation, which means the infant cannot distinguish subject from object. But the mystic union (*sahaj samadhi*) is trans-subject/object, which means that it transcends subject and object, while remaining perfectly aware of that conventional duality, much as language transcends sensory awareness without obliterating it. To say that trans-dual *samadhi* is really regression to pre-dual narcissism is precisely to say that a forest is really regression to an acorn.

In short, the infantile fusion state—the pleroma, uroboros, typhon, the whole id region—is pretemporal, prespatial, preverbal and prepersonal. The true mystic union, on the other hand, is transtemporal, transspatial, transverbal and transpersonal. Because both pre-x and trans-x are (in their own ways) non-x, they appear similar at first glance, which is fine. But two glances ought to be enough to convince any sane person of the actual and profound differences involved. Pre and trans can be seriously equated only by those whose intellectual inquiry goes no further than superficial impressions. But until that type of mentality loses its appeal, orthodox psychiatry will continue to see saints as insane and sages as psychotic, thereby proving itself a proudly tenacious impediment to the growth and evolution of humanity on the whole.

10

The Form of Development

This chapter—the most important in the book—will be short and succinct, because I would like its major points—simple in themselves—to stand alone. For what has so amazed me, as I surveyed the overall stages of development, is that although the content of each developmental growth is quite different, the *form* is essentially similar. The form of development, the form of transformation—this is constant, as far as I can tell, from the womb to God.

What we have seen—at every major stage of growth—is that the process of psychological development proceeds in a most articulate fashion. At each stage, a higher-order structure—more complex and *therefore* more unified—*emerges* through a differentiation of the preceding, lower-order level. This higher-order emergence is mediated or assisted by various types of symbolic structures (some of the major ones we saw: uroboric form, axial-form, image, word-and-name, concept, vision-image, ishtadeva-archetype, final-God, and then the Formless itself). That is, at each stage of ascent an appropriate symbolic form—itself emerging at that stage—transforms each particular mode of consciousness into its higher-order successor.

This higher-order structure is introduced to consciousness, and eventually (it can occur almost instantaneously or it can take a fairly prolonged time), the self *identifies* with that emergent structure. For example, when the body emerged from its pleromatic fusion with the material world, consciousness became, for the first time, a bodyself: which means, *identified with the body*. The self was then no longer *bound* to the pleromatic fusion, but it *was* bound to the body. As language emerged in consciousness, the self began to shift from a solely biological bodyself to a syntaxical ego—the self eventually identified itself with language, and operated *as* a syntaxical self. It was then no longer bound exclusively to the body, but it *was* bound to the mental-ego. Likewise, in advanced evolution, the deity-Archetype emerges, is introduced to consciousness (in the subtle realm), the self then identifies with and as that Deity, and operates from that identification. The self is then no longer exclusively bound to the ego, but it *is* bound to its own Archetype. The point is that as each higher-order structure emerges, the self eventually identifies with that structure—which is normal, natural, appropriate.

As evolution proceeds, however, each level in turn is differentiated *from* the self, or "peeled off" so to speak. The self, that is, eventually *dis-identifies* with its present structure so as to *identify* with the next higher-order emergent structure. More precisely (and this is a very important technical point), we say that the self detaches itself from its *exclusive* identification with that lower structure. It doesn't throw that structure away, it simply no longer exclusively identifies with it. The point is that because the self is differentiated from the lower structure, it *transcends* that structure (without obliterating it in any way), and can thus *operate* on that lower structure using the tools of the newly emergent structure.

Thus, when the bodyego was differentiated from the material environment, it could operate on the environment using the tools of the body itself (such as the muscles). As the ego-mind was then differentiated from the body, it could operate on the body and world with *its* tools (concepts, syntax, etc.). As the subtle self was differentiated from the ego-mind, it could operate on the mind, body and world using its structures (psi, siddhi), and so on.

Thus, at each point in psychological growth, we find: 1) a higher-order structure emerges in consciousness (with the help of symbolic forms); 2) the self identifies its being with that higher structure; 3) the next-higher-order structure eventually emerges; 4) the self dis-identifies with the lower structure and shifts its essential identity to the higher structure; 5) consciousness thereby transcends the lower structure; 6) and becomes capable of operating on that lower structure from the higher-order level; 7) such that all preceding levels can then be integrated in consciousness, and ultimately as Consciousness. We noted that each successively higher-order structure is more complex, more organized, and more unified—and evolution continues until there is only Unity, ultimate in all directions, whereupon the force of evolution is exhausted, and there is perfect release in Radiance as the entire World Flux.

Every time one remembers a higher-order deep structure, the lower-order structure is subsumed under it. That is, at each point in evolution, what is the *whole* of one level becomes merely a *part* of the higher-order whole of the next level. We saw, for example, that the body is, during the earlier stages of growth, the *whole* of the self sense—that is the bodyego. As the mind emerges and develops, however, the sense of identity shifts to the mind, and the body becomes merely one aspect, one part, of the total self. Similarly, as the subtle level emerges, the mind and body—which together *had* constituted the whole of the self-system—become merely aspects or parts of the new and more encompassing self.

In precisely the same way, we can say that at each point in evolution or remembrance, a *mode* of self becomes merely a *component* of a higher-order self (e.g., the body was *the* mode of the self before the mind emerged, whereupon it becomes merely a component of self). This can be put in several different ways, each of which tells us something important about development, evolution, and transcendence: 1) what is *whole* becomes *part*; 2) what is *identification* becomes *detachment*; 3) what is *context* becomes *content* [that is, the context of cognition/experience of one level becomes simply a content of experience of the next]; 4) what is *ground* becomes *figure* [which releases higher-order ground]; 5) what is *subjective* becomes *objective* [until both of these terms become meaningless]; 6) what is *condition* becomes *element* [e.g., the mind, which is the *a priori* condition of egoic experience, becomes merely an element of experience in the higher-order realms; as it was put in *The Spectrum of Consciousness*, one is then looking at these structures, and therefore is not using them as something with which to look at, and thus distort, the world].[410]

Each of those points is, in effect, a definition of *transcendence*. Yet each is also a definition of a stage of *development*. It follows that the two are essentially identical, and evolution, as has been said, is actually "self-realization through self-transcendence."

The point is that development and transcendence are two different words for the very same process. "Transcendence" has often been thought of as something odd, strange, occult, or even psychotic—whereas in fact there is nothing special about it at all. The infant learning to differentiate his body from the environment is simply *transcending* the pleromatic world; the child learning mental language is simply *transcending* the world AND the simple body; the person in subtle-body meditation is simply transcending the world AND the body AND the mind. The soul in causal-body meditation is transcending the world AND the body AND the mind AND the subtle-realm.... The form of each growth is essentially the same, and it is the form of transcendence, the form of development: it traces a gentle curve from subconsciousness through self-consciousness to superconsciousness, remembering more and more, transcending more and more, integrating more and more, unifying more and more, until there is only that Unity which was always already the case from the start, and which remained both the alpha and omega of the soul's journey through time.

11

Types of the Unconscious

The preceding chapters have been devoted to outlining some of the major stages and levels in the growth of consciousness; the following chapters will draw out some of the implications of that model. We will look at the dynamics of evolution—which is nothing other than the incredible Atman-project. We will look at meditation, at the unconscious, at involution (the opposite of evolution), at schizophrenia and mysticism. And we start with the "types" of the unconscious:

Many accounts of "the unconscious" simply assume that it is there, either as process or as content, from the start, and then proceed to describe its layers, levels, grounds, modes or contents. But I believe that approach must be supplemented by developmental or evolutionary concerns on the one hand, and dynamic factors on the others.

Let me give a few examples of the problem itself: Transactional Analysis speaks of unconscious (or preconscious) script programming, containing *verbal* injunctions such as "feel guilty" or "collect anxiety."[33] The job of the script analyst is to discover these injunctions, make them explicit and conscious, and thus release the client from their compulsive power. For simplicity's sake, let's call this the "verbal-script unconscious."

Let us now note a rather simple point: a pre-verbal child cannot have a verbal-script unconscious. Rather, language itself will have to *emerge* developmentally, then be loaded with script injunctions which will then have to sink back below the ordinary threshold of consciousness—at which point, and not before, we may speak of the unconscious script. In the same way, a child in the pre-phallic stage cannot have a phallic fixation, the pre-egoic infant doesn't possess unconscious ego-character structure, and so on.

Clearly, what exists in "the" unconscious depends in large measure on developmental concerns—*all* of the unconscious, in all its forms, is not just given at the start. Yet, to continue the story, many modern writers seem to assume that there is a "transpersonal unconscious" that is present but repressed from the beginning, whereas—if it is like verbal forms, character structure, mental capacity, abstract thinking, and higher structures in general—it is *not yet repressed* because it has not yet developmentally had the chance to emerge. It is not yet repressed from awareness because it has not yet even tentatively emerged in awareness in the first place.

With this developmental and dynamic, as opposed to static and given, viewpoint in mind, I will now outline five basic types of unconscious processes. These are *types* of unconscious processes, not *levels* of the unconscious (although we will mention these as well). This outline is meant to be neither exhaustive nor definitive, but only indicative of concerns that I feel transpersonal psychology must address.

Ground-Unconscious

By "ground" I intend an essentially neutral meaning; it is not to be confused with "Ground of Being" or "Open Ground" or "Primal Ground." Although in a certain sense it is "all-encompassing," it is basically a developmental concept. The fetus "possesses" the ground-unconscious; in essence, it is *all the deep structures existing as potentials ready to emerge, via remembrance, at some future point.* All the deep structures given to a collective humanity—pertaining to every level of consciousness from the body to mind to soul to spirit, gross, subtle, and causal—are enfolded or enwrapped in the ground unconscious. All of these structures are unconscious, but they are *not* repressed because they have not yet entered consciousness (in this lifetime; we can speak of repression of these higher states in involutional or pre-birth psychology, for which see the last chapter). Development—or evolution—consists of a series of hierarchical transformations or *unfoldings* of the deep structures out of the ground-unconscious, starting with the lowest (pleroma and body), and ending with the highest (God and Void). When—and if—*all* of the ground-unconscious has emerged, then there is *only* consciousness: all is conscious *as* the All. As Aristotle put it, when all potential has been actualized, the result is God.

Notice that the ground-unconscious is largely (but I don't think we can say totally) devoid of surface structures, for these are basically *learned* during the unfolding (remembrance) of deep structures. This is similar—but only similar—to Jung's idea of the archetypes as "forms devoid of content." As Jung put it, an archetype (deep structure), "is determined as to its content [surface structure] only when it becomes conscious and is therefore filled out with the material of conscious experience."[213] Everyone "inherits" the same basic deep structures; but everyone learns individual surface structures, which can be quite similar or quite dissimilar from those of other individuals (within, of course, the constraints of the deep structures themselves).

Finally, let us note that the closer a deep structure is to emergence, the more profoundly it affects the already-emerged consciousness. This fact turns out to be of the utmost significance.

Now, all of the following four types of the unconscious can be defined *in relation* to the ground-unconscious. This gives us a concept of unconscious processes that is at once structural and dynamic, layered and developmental.

Archaic-Unconscious

Freud's initial pioneering efforts in psychoanalysis led him to postulate two basically distinct psychic systems: the system-unconscious, as he called it, and the system-conscious. The unconscious was, he felt, *generated* by repression: certain impulses, because they were dynamically resisted by the system-conscious, were forcefully expelled from awareness. "The unconscious" and "the repressed" were basically one and the same.[39]

Eventually, however, Freud came to speak, not so much of the system-conscious and the system-unconscious, but rather of the ego and the id, and these two formulations did not overlap very clearly.[140] That is, the ego was *not* the same as the system-conscious, and the id was *not* the same as the system-unconscious. First of all, parts of the ego (the super-ego, the defenses, and the character-structure), were *unconscious*; and parts of the id were unconscious *but not repressed*. In his words, "We recognize that the *Ucs.* does not coincide with the repressed; it is still true that all that is repressed is *Ucs.*, but not all that is *Ucs.* is repressed."[140]

Not all that is unconscious is repressed because, as Freud came to see, some of the unconscious simply finds itself unconscious from the start—it is not first a personal experience which is then repressed, but something that, as it were, *begins* in the unconscious. Freud had once thought that the symbols in dreams and phantasies could be traced back to real life personal experiences, but he came to see that many of the symbols found in dreams and phantasies could not possibly have been generated by personal experience. "Whence comes the necessity for these phantasies, and the material for them?" we hear him ask. "There can be no doubt about the instinctual sources; but how is it to be explained that the same phantasies are always formed with the same content? I have an answer to this which I know will seem to you very daring. I believe that these *primal phantasies*...are a phylogenetic possession. In them the individual...stretches out...to the experiences of past ages."[144] This phylogenetic or "archaic heritage" included, besides instincts, "abbreviated repetitions of the evolution undergone by the whole human race through long-drawn-out periods and from prehistoric ages." Although Freud differed profoundly from Jung on the nature of this archaic heritage, he nevertheless stated that "I fully agree with Jung in recognizing the existence of this phylogenetic heritage."[145]

For Jung, of course, the "phylogenetic heritage" consisted of the instincts and the mental-forms or images associated with the instincts, which he eventually termed the "archetypes." For Jung, instinct and archetype were intimately related—almost one. As Frey-Rohn explains it, "The connection between instinct and archetypal image appeared to [Jung] so close that he drew the conclusion that the two were coupled.... He saw the primordial image [the archetype] as the *self-portrait of the instinct*—in other words, *the instinct's perception of itself.*"[145] As for the archaic-images themselves:

> Man inherits these images from his ancestral past, a part that includes all of his human ancestors as well as his prehuman or animal ancestors. These racial images are not inherited in the sense that a person consciously remembers or has images that his ancestors had. Rather they are predispositions or potentialities for experiencing and responding to the world in the same ways that his ancestors did [they are, that is, archaic deep structures].[175]

Such is the archaic-unconscious, which is simply the most primitive and least developed structures of the ground-unconscious—the pleroma, the uroboros, and the typhon. They are initially unconscious but unrepressed, and some tend to remain unconscious, never clearly unfolded in awareness except as rudimentary deep structures with little or no surface content. Self-reflexive awareness is out of the question with these structures, so they always retain a heavy mood of unconsciousness, *with or without* repression (which is a significant point). The "prevailing quality of the id," said Freud, "is that of being unconscious,"[143] and that is the *nature* of the id, not something *created* by repression.

Incidentally, I do not share Jung's enthusiasm over the archaic images; and I do not equate the archetypes, which are highly advanced structures lying in the high-subtle and low-causal, with the archaic-images, which are (as Jung himself said) instinctual or typhonic counterparts. I agree with most everything Jung says about the archaic-images *as* archaic images, but I do not equate them with the archetypes per se. The archetypes are exemplary patterns of manifestation, not old images.

At any rate, following both Freud and Jung, we can say in general that the somatic side of the archaic-unconscious is the id (instinctual, limbic, typhonic, pranic); the psychic side is the phylogenetic phantasy heritage. On the whole, the archaic-unconscious is not the product of personal experience; it is initially unconscious but not repressed; it contains the earliest and most primitive structures to unfold from the ground-unconscious, and, even when unfolded, they tend towards unconsciousness. They are pre-verbal, and most are sub-human.

Freud himself came to realize the significance of differentiating the personal unconscious (which we will examine in the next section), from the archaic-unconscious. In analyzing a client's symptoms, dreams, and phantasies, it is important to distinguish those which are the products of actual past experience or personal phantasy, and those which were never personally experienced in this life, but which enter consciousness through the impersonal archaic heritage. My own feeling is that the former are best treated analytically, the latter, mythologically.

Submergent-Unconscious

Once a deep structure has emerged from the ground-unconscious and taken on some sort of surface structure, it can for various reasons be returned to a state of unconsciousness. That is, once a structure has emerged, it can be submerged, and the total of such structures we call the submergent-unconscious. The submergent-unconscious is that which was once conscious, in the lifetime of the individual, but is now screened out of awareness.

Now the submergent-unconscious can include, in principle, every structure that has emerged, whether collective, personal, archaic, subtle, etc. It can contain collective elements that have clearly and unequivocally emerged and then been suppressed, or it can contain personal elements molded in this lifetime and then suppressed, or it can contain a mixture of both. Jung has written extensively on just that subject, and we needn't repeat him here.[214] But we should notice that even Freud was aware of the difference between the archaic-unconscious id and the submergent-unconscious id, even if it was occasionally hard to perfectly differentiate them. "In the course of this slow development certain contents of the id were...taken into the ego; others of its contents remained in the id unchanged, as its scarcely accessible nucleus. During this development, however, the young and feeble ego put back into the unconscious state some of the material it had already taken in, dropped it, and behaved in the same way to some fresh impressions it might have taken in, so that these, having been rejected, could leave a trace only in the id. In consideration of its origin we speak of this latter portion of the id as *the repressed* [in contradistinction to the first part which is simply unconscious from the start: the archaic-unconscious]."[143] There is the difference, or rather one of them, between the original archaic-unconscious and the repressed or submergent-unconscious. But, as Freud says, "It is of little importance that we are not always able to draw a sharp line between these two categories of contents in the id. They coincide approximately with the distinction between what was innately present originally [the archaic-unconscious] and what was acquired in the course of the ego's development [the submergent-unconscious]."[143] Notice that Freud arrives at these conclusions on the basis of developmental thinking, "in consideration of its *origin*...".

The submergent-unconscious *becomes* unconscious for various reasons, and these reasons lie along a *continuum of inattention*. This continuum ranges from simple forgetting through selective forgetting to forceful/dynamic forgetting (the latter alone being repression proper). Of the *personal* submergent-unconscious, Jung states:

> The personal unconscious...includes all those psychic contents which have been forgotten during the course of the individual's life. Traces of them are still preserved in the unconscious, even if all conscious memory of them has been lost. In addition, it contains all subliminal impressions or perceptions which have too little energy to reach consciousness. To these we must add unconscious combinations of ideas that are still too feeble and too indistinct to cross over the threshold. Finally, the personal unconscious contains all psychic contents that are incompatible with the conscious attitude.[208]

Simple forgetting and lack of threshold response constitute the *subliminal submergent-unconscious*. Dynamic or forceful forgetting, however, is repression proper, Freud's great discovery. The *repressed submergent-unconscious* is that aspect of the ground-unconscious which, upon emerging and picking up surface structures, is then forcefully repressed or returned to unconsciousness due to an incompatibility with conscious structures (for which, see the next section).

The personal aspect of the repressed submergent-unconscious is the *shadow*. Once returned to unconsciousness, the shadow can be strongly influenced by the archaic-unconscious (following primary process laws and the pleasure principle, which dominate the typhonic realms), although this is definitely a relative affair. I agree with Jung, for instance, that the shadow *can* be verbal and highly structured (similar in structure and content to the ego/persona).[210] Actually, there seems to be a continuum of structure, ranging from the highly structured verbal components of the unconscious all the way down to the primal chaos of the unstructured *materia prima*, the pleromatic base of the archaic-unconscious (a point made also by Matte Blanco, and one of the points of his presentation with which I strongly agree).[39] Needless to say, one of the major reasons for repressing the shadow is that it becomes a vehicle for the archaic-unconscious: loaded with instinctual impulses which are felt to be incompatible with the ego.

Embedded-Unconscious

We come now to that aspect of the unconscious which most puzzled Freud, but which is nonetheless one of his greatest discoveries. Recall that Freud abandoned the conscious-unconscious model in favor of the ego-id model because "we recognize that the *Ucs.* does not coincide with the repressed; it is still true that all that is repressed is *Ucs.*, but not all that is *Ucs.* is repressed." Besides the archaic-unconscious, which was unconscious but unrepressed, Freud found that "it is certain that much of the ego is itself unconscious."[139] At the same time, he began to locate the *origin* of repression in the ego, because "we can say that the patient's resistance arises from his ego...".[139]

The point was this: repression *originates* in some part of the ego; it is some aspect of the ego that represses the shadow-id. But Freud then discovered that part of the ego was itself unconscious, *yet it was not repressed*. He simply put two and two together and concluded that the *unrepressed* part of the ego was the *repressing* part. This part he called the super-ego: it was unconscious, unrepressed, but repressing. "We may say that repression is the work of this super-ego and that it is carried out either by itself or by the ego in obedience to its orders... portions of the both of them, the ego and the super-ego themselves, are unconscious."[142] But *not* repressed.

Before we try to make sense of this unrepressed but repressing structure, I must briefly recap my general theory of repression, a theory based on the works of Piaget,[297] Freud,[120] Sullivan,[359] Jung,[214] and Loevinger.[243] In essence, we have this: the process of *translation*, by its very nature, tends to screen out all perceptions and experiences which do not conform to the basic limiting principles of the translation itself. This is normal, necessary, and healthy, and forms the basis of "necessary and normal defense mechanisms"—it prevents the self-system from being overwhelmed by its surroundings, internal or external. This is normal "inattention," and—in contrast to a plethora of theories which maintain that "filtering" is reality-corrupting—it is absolutely essential for normal equilibration.

Should, however, binds arise in the translation process of any level, then the individual mis-translates his self and his world (which means that he distorts or deletes, displaces or condenses, aspects of the deep structure that could just as well exist correctly as surface structures). This can occur in any number of ways, and for any number of reasons—and it can be expressed in terms of "energy thresholds" or "informational distortion." The essential point is that the individual is now selectively inattentive or forcefully restrictive of his awareness. He no longer simply translates his self and world (via "normal inattention"), he translates *out*, or edits, any aspects of his self and world which are threatening (via *selective* inattention). This mis-translation results in both a *symptom* and a *symbol*, and the job of the therapist (as we saw), is to help the individual re-translate ("the interpretation") his symbolic symptoms back into their original forms by suggesting "meanings" for the symbol-symptoms ("Your feelings of anxiety are *really* feelings of masked rage.") Repression is simply a form of mis-translation, but a mis-translation that is not just a mistake but an *intentional* (even if unconscious) editing, a dynamic repression with vested interests. The individual does not just forget: he doesn't want to remember.

We saw that at each level of development, the self sense *identifies* with the newly-emergent structures of that level. When the body emerged from the pleroma, the self identified with it; when the verbal-mind emerged, the self identified with it; and so on. Further, it is the nature of an exclusive identification that one does not and cannot realize that identification without *breaking* that identification. In

other words, all exclusive identification is unconscious identification—
by definition and fact. At the moment the child realizes that he *has* a
body, he no longer is *just* the body: he is aware of it; he transcends it;
he is looking at it with his mind and therefore he cannot be *just* a body
any longer. Likewise, at the point the adult realizes he has a mind, he
is no longer just a mind—he is actually starting to perceive it from the
subtle regions beyond mind. Prior to those points, the self was more or
less exclusively identified with those structures and therefore *could
not realize it*. The self could not see those structures because the self
was those structures.

In other words, at each level of development, one cannot totally
see the seer. No observing structure can observe itself observing. One
uses the structures of that level as something with which to perceive
and translate the world—but one cannot perceive and translate those
structures *themselves*, not totally. That can occur only from a higher
level. The point is that each translation process sees but is not seen; it
translates, but is not itself translated; *and it can repress, but is not
itself repressed*.

The Freudian super-ego, with the defenses and the character-
structure, are those aspects of the ego level with which the self is
unconsciously *identified*, so much so that they cannot be *objectively*
perceived (as can the rest of the ego). They translate without being
translated—they are repressing but unrepressed. This fits very well
with Freud's own thoughts on the matter, because he himself felt that
1) the super-ego is created by an *identification* ("identifications replace
object-choices"), and 2) one of the aims of therapy is to make the
super-ego conscious—to see it as an object and thus cease using it as
something through which to see and (mis)translate the world.[46] This is
simply an instance of the overall evolution process we earlier described,
where—once one has identified with a newly-emergent structure,
which is necessary and desirable—one *then* becomes free of that structure by dis-identifying with it, later to integrate it in a higher-order
unity. I should quickly mention that, according to Freud, the super-
ego is frequently severe and "masochistic" because contaminated by
the archaic-unconscious.[141]

Anyway, the super-ego is simply one instance of what we call the
embedded-unconscious: because it is embedded *as* the self, the self
cannot totally or accurately see it. It is unconscious, but *not* repressed.
It is that aspect of the ground-unconscious which, upon emergence,
emerges *as* the self-system and so remains essentially unconscious,
possessing the power to send other elements to the repressed-uncon-
scious. Again, it is unrepressed but repressing. This can occur at any
level of consciousness, although the specifics naturally vary consider-
ably, because the tools of resistance are simply the structures of the
given level, and each level has quite different structures (for example,
when the bodyego *was* the embedded-unconscious, it used not repression but introjection and projection as the modes of mis-translation,
because introjection and projection are part of the primary process

which dominates the typhonic-body realms).[225] However, this whole
process assumes its most violent, pathological, and characteristic
forms with the ego-mental level and the low-subtle realms. Levels
lower than these are not really strong enough to sustain fierce repression (the archaic-id is originally unrepressed and unrepressing); levels
higher than this become so transcendent and integrated that repression—as we ordinarily think of it—tends to fade out. The higher realms
do possess their own forms of resistances, but this is a matter for a
separate study.

Emergent-Unconscious

Let us now examine someone who has evolved from the pleroma to
the bodyself to the ego-mind. There still remain in the ground-unconscious the deep structures of the subtle and causal realms. These
structures have not yet emerged; they cannot, as a rule, emerge in
consciousness until the lower structures have emerged. Since the higher structures encompass the lower ones, the higher have to unfold last.
At any rate, it is certainly ridiculous to speak of realizing the transpersonal until the personal has been formed. The transpersonal (the
subtle and causal) realms are not yet repressed—they are not screened
out of awareness, they are not filtered out—they have simply not yet
had the opportunity to emerge. We do not say of a two-year-old child
that he or she is resisting the learning of geometry, because the child's
mind has not yet developed and unfolded to the degree that he or she
could even begin to learn mathematics. Just as we do not accuse the
child of repressing mathematics, we do not accuse him of repressing
the transpersonal...not yet, that is.

At any point on the developmental cycle, those deep structures
which have not yet emerged from the ground-unconscious are referred
to as the emergent-unconscious. For someone at the ego (or centaur)
level, the low-subtle, the high-subtle, the low-causal, and the high-
causal are emergent-unconscious. They are unconscious, *but not repressed* (in this lifetime—again, I am excluding involutional and pre-
birth psychology, for which see the last chapter of this book).

Notice that the subtle/causal emergent-unconscious shares several
characteristics with the archaic-unconscious, namely: they have never
(or never yet) been conscious within the lifetime of the individual, and
thus are not repressed, and yet find themselves in the unconscious
from the start. The difference, other than the important fact that one
is low and primitive and the other is high and transcendent, is that the
archaic-unconscious is humanity's past; the emergent-unconscious is
humanity's future. But the unconscious-future is determined only as
regards deep structures: the surface structures are not yet fixed. The
unconscious-past, on the other hand, contains deep structures as well
as surface structures (such as the shadow), because both of these have
already emerged and been determined by awareness.

Now supposing that development is not arrested at the ego-centaur realm—which is usually the case at this point in history—the subtle will of itself begin to emerge from the ground-unconscious. It is not really possible to set timetables for these higher realms and stages, because a collective humanity has only evolved to the ego level, and thus only levels leading up to that have been determined as to emergence. In general, however, the subtle *can* begin to emerge after adolescence, but rarely before. And for all sorts of reasons, the emergence of the subtle can be resisted and even, in a sense, repressed. For the ego is strong enough to repress not only the lower realms but also the higher realms—it can seal off the superconscious as well as the subconscious.

That part of the ground-unconscious whose emergence is resisted or repressed, we call, naturally enough, the emergent-repressed unconscious. It is that part of the ground-unconscious which—*excluding developmental arrest*—remains unconscious *past* the point at which it could just as well become conscious. We are then justified in looking for reasons for this lack of emergence, and we find them in a whole set of defenses, actual defenses, against transcendence. They include rationalization ("Transcendence is impossible or pathological"); isolation or avoidance of relationship ("My consciousness is supposed to be skin-bounded!"); death-terror ("I'm afraid to die to my ego, what would be left?"); desacralizing (Maslow's term for refusing to see transcendent values anywhere); substitution (a lower structure is substituted for the intuited higher structure, with the pretense that the lower *is* the higher); contraction (into forms of lower knowledge or experience). Any or all of these simply become part of the ego's translation processes, such that the ego merely continues to translate whereas it should in fact begin transformation.

Because psychoanalysis and orthodox psychology have never truly understood the nature of the emergent-unconscious in its higher forms, then as soon as the subtle or causal begins to emerge in awareness—perhaps as a peak experience or as subtle lights and bliss—they are all in tithers to explain it as a breakthrough of some archaic material or some past repressed impulses. Since they know not of the emergent-unconscious, they try to explain it in terms of the *submergent*-unconscious. They think the subtle, for example, is not a higher structure emerging but a lower one remerging; not the trans-temporal coming down but the pre-temporal coming back up. And so they trace samadhi back to infantile breast-union; they reduce transpersonal unity to prepersonal fusion in the pleroma; God is reduced to a teething nipple and all congratulate themselves on explaining the Mystery. This whole enterprise is starting to fall apart, of its own weight, because of the ridiculous number of things psychoanalysis is forced to attribute to the infant's first four months of life in order to account for *everything* that subsequently emerges.

At any rate, with an understanding of these six types of the unconscious (the ground-unconscious, archaic-unconscious, submergent-unconscious, embedded-unconscious, emergent-unconscious, and emergent-repressed unconscious), as well as of translation/transformation and the stages of development presented in the first part of this book, we can now turn to a quick study of meditation and the unconscious.

12

Meditation and the Unconscious

Most of the accounts of meditation and the unconscious suffer from a lack of concern with developmental or evolutionary factors. They tend simply to assume that the unconscious is *only* the submergent-unconscious (subliminal, filtered, screened, repressed, or automated), and thus they see meditation as a way to *reverse* a nasty state of affairs created in this lifetime: they see it as a way to force entry into the unconscious. Meditation is pictured as a way to lift the repression, halt the filtering, de-automate the automating or de-focalize the focalizing. It is my own opinion that those issues, however significant, are the most secondary aspects of all types of meditation.

Meditation is, if anything, a sustained instrumental path of transcendence. And since—as we saw—transcendence and development are synonymous, it follows that meditation is simply *sustained development* or growth. It is not primarily a way to reverse things but a way to carry them on. It is the natural and orderly unfolding of successively higher-order unities, until there is only Unity, until all potential is actual, until all the ground-unconscious is unfolded as Consciousness. It is what an individual, at this present stage of human evolution, has to do in order to develop beyond this present stage of human evolution, and advance towards that only God which is the goal of all creation.

Meditation thus occurs in the same way all the other growth/emergences did: one translation winds down and fails to exclusively dominate consciousness, and transformation to a higher-order translation occurs (a higher-order deep structure is remembered, which then underlies and creates new surface structures). There is differentiation, dis-identification, transcendence and integration. Meditation *is* evolution; it *is* transformation—there is nothing really special about it. It seems quite mysterious and convoluted to the ego because it is a development beyond the ego. Meditation is to the ego as the ego is to the typhon: developmentally more advanced. But the same process of *growth* and emergence runs through the whole sequence—the way we got *from* the typhon to the ego is the same way we go from the ego to God. We grow, we don't dig back.

My first point is that most accounts of meditation assume that the transpersonal realms—the subtle and causal—are parts of the submergent-unconscious or repressed-submergent-unconscious, and that meditation means lifting the repression. And I am suggesting that the transpersonal realms are really part of the emergent-unconscious and meditation is just speeding up the emergence.

However, when a person—say a young adult—begins meditation, all sorts of different things begin to happen, some of which are only incidentally and remotely related to the actual growth and transcendence process, and this greatly complicates the overall picture of meditation. With that problem in mind, I would first like to discuss the nature of the meditative stance itself, and then its general and complete course.

To begin with, we note that every transformation in development necessitates the surrendering of the particular present translation (or rather, the exclusiveness of that translation). For the average person, who has already evolved from the pleroma to the typhon to the ego, transformation into the subtle or causal realms demands that egoic-translation wind down and be surrendered (not destroyed). These egoic-translations are usually composed of verbal-thoughts and concepts (and emotional reactions to those thoughts).[378] Therefore meditation consists, *in the beginning*, of a way to *break conceptual translating* in order to open the way to subtle-level transformation.[59, 333, 345, 374]

In essence, this means *frustrate* the present translation and encourage the new transformation. As explained in *No Boundary*,[426] this frustration/encouragement is brought about by *special conditions*—such as the moral precepts, diet regulation, vows, and the more internal conditions of prayer, chanting, and meditation.

The heart of the special conditions is an activity which embodies any of the major characteristics of the sought-after higher sphere. That is, the individual is taught to begin translating his reality according to one of the major characteristics of the desired higher realm. He is therefore using *symbols*, not signs, and thus is open to *transformation* instead of mere translation. For example, the yidan (or ishtadeva): the individual is shown a symbol of the yidam-deity, a symbol which, precisely because it is a symbol, corresponds to nothing in his present reality. He constructs or translates this symbol into his own consciousness, to the point that the subtle-yidam actually *emerges* from the ground-unconscious into full awareness. The individual *identifies* (as we explained with *all* development) with this higher structure, which breaks his lower translation as ego and raises him to a higher structure. He then *sees* (translates) reality from the higher viewpoint of Deity: the high-subtle has emerged in his case, because he has evoked it as a process of growth and transcendence from his own ground-unconscious.

The Master (guru, roshi, etc.) simply continues to frustrate the old translations, to undermine the old resistances, and to encourage the new transformation by enforcing the special conditions. This is true in *all* forms of meditation—concentrative or receptive, mantric or silent. In concentrative meditation, the special condition has a defined form; in receptive meditation, it is "formless"—both are enforced special conditions, however, and the individual who drops his formless or defocal awareness is chastised just as severely as the one who drops his koan.

In principle, this is no different than asking a child to put into words something he would rather act-out typhonically. We are asking the ego to go one step further and put into subtle forms that which he would rather think about conceptually. Growth occurs by adopting higher translations until one can actually transform to that higher realm itself. Since some of the major characteristics of the higher realms include trans-temporal timelessness,[111] love,[215] no avoidances or attachments,[59] total acceptance,[71] and subject-object unity,[365] these are most often the special conditions of meditation ("Stay in the Now always;[345] recognize your avoidances;[60] be only love in all conditions;[268] become one with your meditation and your world;[220] accept everything since everything is Buddha,[43]" etc.). Our parents helped us move from the first floor to the fifth floor by imposing the special conditions of language and egoic self-control. Just so, the Master helps us from the fifth to the tenth floor by imposing the special conditions of the tenth upon us as practice.

It does not, in essence, matter whether the special conditions use a concentrative-absorptive or a receptive-defocal mode of meditation. The former breaks the lower and egoic translation by halting it, the latter by watching it. What they both have in common is what is essential and effective about both: jamming a translation by concentration or watching a translation by defocalizing can only be done from the next highest level. They both accomplish the same goal, the breaking of a lower-order translation. Both are also intensely *active* processes. Even "passive receptivity" is, as Benoit said, activity on a higher plane.[27] (This is not to say, however, that the receptive-defocal mode and the concentrative-absorptive mode are identical, or that they produce the same secondary results. This will become obvious when we outline the course of a typical meditation).

Before discussing what transpires in meditation, however, it is important to realize that not all schools of meditation aim for the same general realm of consciousness. Rather, as we have already suggested in the previous chapters, the transpersonal and superconscious realms really break down into several different levels (low and high subtle, low and high causal, etc.). Very few religions are aware of all of these distinctions, and thus many have more-or-less "specialized" in one level or another. Hence, meditative practices themselves break down generally into three major classes (cf. Bubba Free John).[59]

The first is the Nirmanakaya class, which deals with bodily or typhonic energies and their transmutation into the lower-subtle region, culminating at the sahasrara. This includes hatha yoga, kundalini yoga, kriya yoga, pranayama, and particularly all forms of tantric yoga. The goal of the Nirmanakaya class, as I mentioned, is the sahasrara, the crown chakra, and it is exemplified by Patanjali.[270, 329, 370]

The second is the Sambhogakaya class, which deals with the high-subtle regions, and aims for the seven (or ten) inner spheres of bliss and audible realization secreted within and beyond the sahasrara. This includes Nada yoga and Shabd yoga, and is exemplified by Kirpal Singh.[348, 349, 350]

The third is the Dharmakaya class, which deals with the causal regions. It operates through neither tantric energy manipulation nor subtle light and sound absorption, but rather through inquiry into the causal field of consciousness itself, inquiry into I-ness or the separate-self sense, even in and through the Transcendent Witness of the causal region, until all forms of subject-object dualism are uprooted. This class is exemplified by Sri Ramana Maharshi,[308] Bubba Free John,[60] Zen Buddhism[364] and Vedanta Hinduism.[94] At the terminal point of each path, one *can* fall into the prior Suchness of all realms, the Svabhavikakaya, although this is both easier and more likely the higher the path one initially adopts.

Let us now assume that a young adult takes up the practice of Zen, in either its concentrative-koan or receptive-shikan-taza form. Both of these are Dharmakaya practices, if employed correctly, and so we will expect to see all sorts of lower-level manifestations in the intermediate stages.

To start with, the meditation practice begins to break the present egoic-translation by either halting it (koan), or watching it (shikan). Washburn has given a nice account of some of the specifics of this process (his "reduction of intensity threshold" and "immobilization of psychic operations" are two ways of describing the winding down of a level's translations, which is pre-requisite for both lower level de-repression and upward-transformation).[388] As the present egoic-translation begins to loosen, then the individual is first exposed to the subliminal-submergent unconscious (the non-repressed submergent-unconscious in general), which includes, among other things, the "innumerable unnoticed aspects of experiences, aspects tuned out due to habit, conditioning, or the exigencies of the situation."[388] All sorts of odd memories float up, screen memories, insignificant memories, memories that are not repressed, merely forgotten or preconscious. Months can be spent "at the movies" watching the subliminal-submergent re-emerge in awareness and dance before the inward eye.

As meditation progresses, however, the more resistant aspects of the egoic-translation are slowly undermined and dismantled in their exclusiveness. That is, the embedded-unconscious is jarred loose from its unconscious identification with the self and thus tends either to emerge as an actual object of awareness or to at least lose its hold on awareness. Washburn states that psychic immobilization (the halting of egoic-translation) "brings unconscious psychic operations into awareness by interfering with their normal functioning," so that "one can begin to look *at* it, rather than, as hitherto had been the case, merely looking *through* it."[388] I think that is a good point, but I would add that it applies basically to the embedded-unconscious; we don't, for example, bring the causal-emergent unconscious into awareness by "interfering with it" but rather by allowing it to emerge in the first place, just as we don't bring mathematics into awareness by interfering with it but by first learning it.

At any rate, the embedded-unconscious, by being "interfered with," starts to shake loose its habitual hold. Now recall that the embedded-unconscious translations were the unrepressed but repressing aspects of the self-system of a given level. Naturally, then, as the repressor is relaxed, the repressed tends to emerge. That is to say, the repressed-submergent unconscious now tends to float—or sometimes erupt—into awareness. The individual confronts his shadow (and, on occasion, primal or archaic phantasies from the archaic-unconscious). An individual can spend months or even years wrestling with his shadow, and this is where orthodox therapy can certainly complement meditation. (Incidentally, notice that what is released here is the repressed-submergent unconscious, and not *necessarily* the subtle or causal emergent-unconscious, unless they are part of the emergent-repressed unconscious screened out by the *same* defenses wielded against the shadow. This is indeed possible and even probable to a certain degree, but on the whole the defenses against the repressed shadow and those against an emergent God are of a different order.)

What has happened, up to this stage in meditation, is that the individual—through the loosening of the egoic-translation and embedded-unconscious—has "relived" his life up to that point. He has opened himself to all the traumas, the fixations, the complexes, the images, and the shadows of all of the prior levels of consciousness which have so far emerged in his life—the pleromatic, the uroboric, the typhonic, the verbal, and the mental-egoic. All of that is up for review, in a sense, and especially up for review are the "sore spots"—the fixations and repressions that occurred on the first five floors of his being. Up to this point in meditation, he has seen his past, and perhaps humanity's past. From this point on he sees his future—and humanity's future as well.

Incidentally, Washburn has suggested that only receptive meditation leads directly and immediately to the unconscious, whereas absorptive meditation "is so immersed in its object that all else, including messages from the unconscious, is unavailable to awareness; and for this reason confrontation with the unconscious can occur only after the object has been discarded, or after the practice has been concluded."[388] Again, I think that is quite true, but it applies to only some aspects of the developmental unconscious, particularly the archaic, submergent, and embedded unconscious. While the concentrative practice is fully active, none of those aspects of the unconscious can "squeeze in." However, it does not apply to, for example, the subtle emergent-unconscious, because in the state of subtle absorption in the yidam, mantra, or nada, one *is* directly in touch with that previously unconscious state. Even if one doesn't cognize it as an object, which one doesn't, one is still intuitively alive to the subtle, as the subtle. The concentrative path *disclosed* this subtle-realm aspect of the emergent-unconscious in a perfectly direct and immediate way, *during* the practice itself.

But while in the subtle, concentratively absorbed, it is true that no *other* objects tend to arise in awareness, and that would include, for example, the shadow. The subtle meditation does help to break the egoic-translation, however, so that when one ceases subtle absorption, one is indeed open to shadow-influx, just as Washburn describes. With receptive meditation, of course, one is open to whatever arises whenever it arises, and so one "sees" the shadow on the spot as it de-represses. Thus Washburn's point, in my opinion, applies significantly to the shadow, but not to the emergent-unconscious.

As the subtle emerges from the ground-unconscious into awareness, various high-archetypal visions, sounds, and illuminations occur. I described the subtle realm earlier, and so needn't repeat it here. The point is that subtler and subtler translations emerge, are eventually undermined, and transformation to new and subtler translations occurs. This is nothing more than *development* in the subtle realm. One version of this runs as follows:

> It is the strongest impulses that are affected first, and as they dim, the meditator begins to discern more subtle ones—just as the setting of the sun brings the stars into view. But these more subtle impulses themselves wane, which allows even more subtle ones to be discriminated. Interestingly, this is not an absolutely continuous process, for during sitting meditation there occur interludes of virtual silence during which, it seems, one passes through some kind of psychic "membrane" that divides the present level from the next, subtler level. Once this divide has been passed, psychomental activity resumes...; but its character is now much finer and more rarefied.[388]

The "membranes" are simply the translation-processes of each level, which screen-out the other levels and divide the present level from the rest; the "passing of this divide" is simply transformation to a higher, subtler, and "more rarefied" translation. "The new threshold [the new translation] that is established in this way can itself be reduced [transformed] by continued meditation, and this one too, and so on. In each case a new spectrum of lower-intensity, subtler objects becomes accessible to the meditator's inner sight."[388]

Although these subtle sounds and illuminations are the goal of the Sambhogakayas, they are all viewed as makyo (or inferior productions) by the Dharmakayas. Thus, if meditation continues into the causal realm, all prior objects, subtle or gross, are reduced to gestures of Consciousness as Such, until even the transcendent Witness or I-ness of the causal realm is broken in the Great Death of Emptiness, and the unparalleled but only Obvious state of sahaj is resurrected. This is called *anuttara samyak sambodhi*. It is without recourse. At this final transformation, there are no longer any exclusive translations occurring anywhere, because the translator died. The mirror and its reflections are one and the same.

And so proceeds meditation, which is simply higher development, which is simply higher evolution—a transformation from unity to unity until there is simple Unity, whereupon Brahman, in an unnoticed shock of recognition and final remembrance, grins silently to itself, closes its eyes, breathes deeply, and throws itself outward for the millionth time, losing itself in its manifestations for the sport and play of it all. Evolution then proceeds again, transformation by transformation, remembering more and more, until each and every soul remembers Buddha, as Buddha, in Buddha—whereupon there is then no Buddha, and no soul. And that is the final transformation. When Zen Master Fa-ch'ang was dying, a squirrel screeched on the roof. "It's just this," he said, "and nothing more."

13

The Atman-Project

We have seen that psychological development in humans has the same goal as natural evolution: the production of ever-higher unities. And since the ultimate Unity is Buddha, God, or Atman (to use those terms in their broadest sense as "ultimate reality"), it follows that psychological growth aims at Atman. And that is part of what we call the Atman-project.

We saw that the individual being, from the very start, contains all the deep structures of consciousness enfolded and enwrapped in his own being. And in particular, he contains or participates in prior Atman-consciousness—*from the start*. The infant is not enlightened, obviously. But just as obviously, the infant is not without Atman. "All sentient beings," says the *Nirvana Sutra*, "possess the Buddha Nature."[364] "Wherever there is consciousness," proclaims the *Tibetan Book of the Dead*, "there is Dharmakaya."[110] *Anima Naturaliter Christiana*, said Tertullian, by which he meant that "the soul is endowed *from the outset* with the knowledge of God and that whatever God imparts in this manner can at most be obscured, but never entirely extinguished."[307] Likewise. "This is what the Jewish midrash means when it ascribes knowledge to the unborn babe in the womb, saying that over its head there burns a light in which it sees all the ends of the world."[279] From the outset, the soul intuits this Atman-nature, and seeks, from the start, to *actualize* it as a reality and not just an enfolded potential. That drive to actualize Atman is part of the Atman-project.

But it is only part, because—even though each stage of psychological growth is a step closer to God—each stage is *still* only a stage. That is, each stage towards God is still not itself God. Each stage is a search for God which occurs under conditions which fall short of God. The soul must seek Unity through the constraints of the present stage, which is not yet Unity. And *that* is the other side of the Atman-project: each individual wants only Atman, but wants it under conditions which prevent it. Only at the end of psychological growth is there final enlightenment and liberation in and as God, but that is the *only* thing that is desired from the beginning. But notice: since at every stage of growth the soul wants only Unity or Atman, but since each stage is less than Atman, then each stage tends to become, in effect, a compromise and a *substitute* for Atman—and this occurs consciously or unconsciously. It occurs at every level, from the lowest to the highest, as a simple reflex of manifestation.

The point is that each stage or level of growth seeks absolute Unity, but in ways or under constraints that necessarily prevent it and allow only compromises: substitute unities and substitute gratifications. The more primitive the level, the more primitive the substitute unity. Each successive stage achieves a higher-order unity, and this continues until there is *only* Unity. The Atman-project continues until there is only Atman. There is the dynamic, and there the goal, of evolution and development.

If we look carefully at that definition of the Atman-project, we can see that it has three different strands. "Each stage or level of growth seeks absolute Unity"—that we call the Atman-trend or Atman-telos. "But in ways or under conditions that necessarily prevent it"—that we call the Atman-constraint or Atman-denial or contraction. "And allow only substitute unities and substitute gratifications"—that is the Atman-project proper, a compromise formation between the Atman-trend and the Atman-constraint. Because I don't want to be over-technical about this, I will usually just refer to the whole complex as the Atman-project. The interested reader will be able to tell, from the context, which of these three strands I intend.

Variations on the Atman-Project

What I would like to do in this section, simply, is describe the nature of the Atman-project from several different angles, in the abstract, so that we may better grasp its general and overall structure. Then, in the succeeding chapters, we will examine the stage-specific forms of the Atman-project which appear throughout development.

According to the perennial philosophy, the ultimate nature of reality is *sunyata* or *nirguna*,[364] which is usually translated as "emptiness," "voidness," or "nothingness." But sunyata does *not* mean blankness or vacant absence. The "void," as R.H. Blyth remarked, does not mean featureless, but *seamless*—"the seamless coat of the universe," as Whitehead put it. Sunyata simply means that, just as the arms and legs and fingers are quite different entities but also are parts of *one* body, so all things and events in the universe are aspects of one fundamental Whole, the very source and suchness which is the Real itself.[426] This holds, obviously, for men and women as well. The ultimate psychology is a psychology of fundamental Wholeness, or the superconscious All. At any rate, let us simply note that this Wholeness, according to the perennial psychology, is *what is real and all* that is real. A radically separate, isolated and bounded entity does not exist anywhere.[389] There are no seams in the world, in things, in people or in God.

It follows, then, that to erect a self boundary or barrier, and hold a separate-identity feeling *against* the prior Wholeness, not only involves *illusion*, it requires a constant expenditure of energy, a perpetual *contracting* or restricting activity. This, of course, obscures the prior Wholeness itself, and this—as I have elsewhere suggested— is the primal repression.[410] It is the illusory repression of universal consciousness and its projection as an inside-self vs. an outside-world, a subject vs. an object.

Let us note, then, that a separate-subject or self-identity, such as most normal individuals possess, is based upon the superimposition of an illusory *boundary* upon prior Wholeness. That prior Wholeness then *appears* as a subject-in-here vs. a world-out-there. There is a boundary; and thus there is a subject vs. an object—and if this boundary is exclusively executed, it obscures (but does not destroy) the prior Wholeness of Atman.

According to the perennial philosophy, the re-discovery of this infinite and eternal Wholeness is men and women's single greatest need and want.[193] For not only is Atman the basic nature of all souls, each soul or each subject knows or intuits that this is so. Every individual—every sentient being—constantly intuits that his prior Nature *is* the infinite and eternal, All and Whole—he is possessed, that is, with a true Atman-intuition. *Anima Naturaliter Christiana.*

But, at the same time, the subject is terrified of real transcendence, because transcendence entails the "death" of his isolated and separate-self sense. The subject can find the prior Whole only by letting go of the *boundary* between subject and object—that is, by dying to the exclusive subject. And the subject, obviously, is terrified of this. And because he can't or won't let go of and die to his separate self, he cannot find true and real transcendence, he cannot find that larger fulfillment as the Whole. Holding on to himself, his subjectivity, he shuts out Atman; grasping only his own ego, he denies the rest of the All.

Yet, notice immediately that men and women are faced with a truly fundamental dilemma: above all else, each person wants true transcendence, Atman-consciousness, and the Whole; but, above all else, each person fears the loss of the separate self, the "death" of the isolated ego or subject. All a person wants is Wholeness, but all he does is fear and resist it (since that would entail the death of his separate self). Atman-telos vs. Atman-restraint. And there is the fundamental double-bind in the face of eternity, the ultimate knot in the heart of the separate self.

Because man wants real transcendence above all else, but because he cannot or will not accept the necessary death of his separate-self sense, he goes about seeking transcendence in ways, or through structures, that *actually prevent* it and *force symbolic substitutes*. And these substitutes come in all varieties: sex, food, money, fame, knowledge, power—all are ultimately substitute gratifications, simple substitutes for true release in Wholeness. As Gilson put it, "Even in the midst of the lowest pleasures, the most abandoned voluptuary is still seeking God." That can now be said with absolute assurance. And that is why human desire is insatiable, why all joys yearn for infinity—all a person wants is Atman; all he finds are symbolic substitutes for it. This attempt to regain Atman consciousness in ways or under conditions that prevent it and force symbolic substitutes—this is the Atman-project.

The Subjective Wing

Even an individual's feeling of being a separate, isolated, and bounded self is a mere substitute for one's own true Nature, a substitute for the transcendent Self of the ultimate Whole. Every individual *correctly* intuits that he is of one nature with Atman, but he *distorts* that intuition by applying it to his separate self. He feels his separate self is immortal, all-embracing, central to the cosmos, all-significant. That is, he *substitutes* his ego for Atman. Then, instead of finding actual and timeless wholeness, he merely substitutes the wish to live forever; instead of being one with the cosmos, he substitutes the desire to possess the cosmos; instead of being one with God, he tries himself to play God.

This is what we call the *subjective wing* of the Atman-project. Since the Atman-project is created by the split between subject and object, the Atman-project can be played out through a manipulation of both the subjective and objective sides of awareness (we will return to the objective wing shortly). The subjective wing of the Atman-project is the *impossible* desire that the individual self be immortal, cosmocentric, and all-important, but based on the *correct* intuition that one's real Nature is indeed infinite and eternal. Not that his deepest nature is *already* God, but that his ego *should* be God—immortal, cosmocentric, death-defying and all-powerful—there is his Atman-project. And there is either Atman, or there is the Atman-project.

Hubert Benoit has an exquisite quote on the nature of the subjective wing of the Atman-project. "One should ask oneself," he begins, "how this thing can be, how [any person] can come to believe that he accepts his temporal state, this limited and mortal state [of being only a separate self and not the Whole] which is in reality affectively inacceptable, how can he live this way?" That is, how can one live without Atman? The answer, of course, is to create substitutes for that Estate: to create an Atman-project by (consciously or unconsciously) making the separate self *appear* to be Atman-like—cosmocentric, immortal, deified, central to all that is and the prime mover of all that is. And so, says Benoit, how does this soul live with this inacceptable situation of not realizing Atman? "He arrives at it, essentially, through the play of his imagination, through the faculty which his mentality possesses of recreating a *subjective world* whose unique motor principle this time he is. The man would never resign himself to not being the unique motive-power of the real universe [i.e., to not being Atman] if he had not this consoling faculty of creating a universe for himself, a universe which he creates all alone."²⁷ And that is part, the subjective part, of the Atman-project.

Life and Death

Once this false, individual, and separate self sense is created out of prior Wholeness, then that self is faced with two major drives: the perpetuation of its own existence (Eros) and the avoidance of all that threatens its dissolution (Thanatos). This inward, isolated, pseudo-self is fiercely defended against death, dissolution, and transcendence (Thanatos), on the one hand, while aspiring and pretending to cosmocentricity, omnipotence, and immortality on the other (Eros). These are simply *the positive and negative sides* of the Atman-project: Life and Death, Eros and Thanatos, Vishnu and Shiva.

Thus, arising as a function of the subject vs. object boundary, are the two major dynamic factors: Eros and Thanatos, Life and Death. Eros ultimately is the desire to recapture that prior Wholeness which was obscured when the boundary between self and other was constructed. But to actually gain a true re-union of subject and object, self and other, requires the death and dissolution of the exclusively separate self—and this is precisely what is resisted. Thus Eros cannot find true union, real Wholeness, but is instead driven to find symbolic substitutes for the lost Whole, and these substitutes, in order to work, must *present as fulfilled* the wish for prior Unity. Eros, then, is the underlying power of seeking, grasping, wishing, desiring, perpetuating, loving, living, willing, and so on. And it is *never* satisfied because it finds only substitutes. Eros is ontological hunger.

We come, then, to Thanatos. Thanatos—death and the fear of death. What has been so very difficult for Western psychology to grasp is that there are at least two major but quite different forms of fear and anxiety. One form is pathological or neurotic terror: any type of anxiety that can legitimately be traced to "mental illness," pathological defense mechanisms, or neurotic guilt. But the other form of terror is not due to a mental aberration or neurotic illness but to a perception of the *truth*—it is a basic, unavoidable, inescapable terror *inherent* in the separate self sense. Man's prior Nature is the Whole, but once he splits that Nature into a separate self vs. an external other, then that separate self necessarily is faced with an awareness of death and the terror of death. It is existential, given, inherent (as long as the boundary exists between subject and object)—and the perception of this terror is a perception of the truth of the situation, not a perception of mental illness.

The Upanishads put this fact beautifully: "Wherever there is other, there is fear."[191] That has been perfectly obvious to the East for at least 3000 years. But fortunately, the existential psychologists in the West have finally—after decades of orthodox psychiatry's trying to reduce existential dread to neurotic guilt—exposed and explained this essential point with such clarity that it can only be overlooked by exposing one's ignorance. "The essential, basic arch-anxiety (primal anxiety)," wrote the great existential psychologist Boss, is *"innate to all isolated, individual forms of human existence.* In the basic anxiety human existence is afraid *of* as well as anxious *about* its 'being-in-the-world.'"[25] Most of us, of course, are not directly aware of this primal fear underlying our work-a-day egos, but Zilboorg explains why:

> If this fear were as constantly conscious, we should not
> be able to function normally. It must be properly re-
> pressed to keep us living with any modicum of comfort....
> We may take it for granted that the fear of death is
> always present in our mental functioning.... No one is
> free of the fear of death.[436]

This death terror is *inherent* in the separate-self sense, the separate subject, and it arises in one form or another wherever there is boundary. And once this death-imprint awakens there are two, and only two, things that can be done with it. Men and women, that is, have two choices in the face of death and Thanatos: they can deny and repress it, or they can transcend it in the superconscious All. As long as one holds on to the separate-self sense, one must repress death and its terror. In order to transcend the death-terror, one must transcend the self. That is, there is *nothing* the separate self can do to *actually* get rid of death terror, since the separate self *is* that death-terror—they come into existence together and they only disappear together. The only thing the separate self can do with death is deny it, repress it, dilute it, or otherwise hide it. Only in the superconscious All, in actual transcendence, is the death-terror uprooted, because the separate self is uprooted as well. But until that time—and to borrow Becker's phrase—*"consciousness of death* (his ital.) is the primary repression, not sexuality."[25]

The death-terror, the reflex against Thanatos. But what precisely is the nature of this Thanatos? What ultimately does it signify? Perhaps we can give a simple answer in this fashion:

We saw that there are *no* radically separate entities anywhere—that the boundary between subject and object is ultimately illusory. Thus that boundary between subject and object, self and other, has to be constantly and unceasingly recreated moment to moment—and for the simple reason that it isn't real in the first place. At the same time, the simple force of reality, the "pull" of the Whole, acts moment to moment to tear down that boundary. *And that force is Thanatos.* As the individual, moment to moment, recreates his illusory boundaries, so reality, moment to moment, conspires to tear them down.

Such is Thanatos, and its real meaning is transcendence. Thanatos is not a force trying to reduce life to inorganic matter (that, as we will see, is the force of "involution"), or a repetition compulsion, or a homeostatic principle, or a suicidal wish. Thanatos is the power of sunyata—the power and push to transcend illusory boundaries—but it *appears*, to a self that will not or cannot surrender its boundaries (at any level), as a threat of literal death and physical mortality.

The point is this: wherever there is boundary, the Thanatos of one's deeper Nature acts, moment to moment, to remove it or to sacrifice it. As long as there is boundary, there is Thanatos. And one will either submit to Thanatos, sacrifice, and transcendence *or one will have to find something else to do with that death wish*, that self-sacrificial drive. That is, one will have to find *substitute sacrifices*. And, as I tried to show in *Up From Eden*,[27] all that is wretched in human affairs, all that marks man as the most insidious of the beasts, all that brands him as a mass murderer and victimizer comes under the heading of *substitute sacrifices*. This was perfectly explained by Otto Rank's formula, which brilliantly summarizes everything we might say on the subject: "The death fear of the ego is lessened by the killing, the sacrifice, of the other; through the death of the other, one buys oneself free from the penalty of dying, of being killed."[25] Freud said, "the desire to kill replaces the desire to die," and Becker summarized it as "the offering of the other's body in order to buy off one's own death."[26]

Now please notice: the denial of death (and the finding of substitute sacrifices), is part of the Atman-project—we call it the *negative side*, the "negative" side of the attempt to regain Atman-consciousness. We saw that once the self is created out of prior Wholeness it is faced with two major drives: the perpetuation of its own illusory existence (Eros), and the avoidance of all that threatens its own dissolution (Thanatos). On the *positive side* (and that does *not* mean "on the good side," it simply means on the Eros side, like the positive pole of a magnet), it searches out all sorts of *substitute gratifications* that pretend to fulfill its desire to be infinite, cosmocentric, all powerful, heroic, godlike. On the *negative side* (the Thanatos side), it screens out or represses anything that threatens death, dissolution, transcendence, letting-go—it then creates *substitute sacrifices*. And we say both of these drives—substitute gratification and substitute sacrifice—are forms of the Atman-project because they are both driven ultimately by a correct intuition that one is indeed infinite and eternal. But it is an intuition that is distorted by its application to the separate self sense, which is absolutely finite and mortal.

Thus Eros—the desire to more life, the desire to have everything, to be cosmocentric—is driven by the correct intuition that in reality one *is* the All. But, when applied to the separate self, the intuition that one *is* the All is perverted into the desire to *possess* the All. In place of *being* everything, one merely desires to *have* everything. That is the basis of all substitute gratifications, and that is the insatiable thirst lying in the soul of all separate selves. That is the positive side of the Atman-project, and it is quenched only by Atman.

In the same way, the *denial of death* (the negative or Thanatos side of the Atman-project) is based upon the correct intuition that one's prior Nature *is* indeed timeless, eternal, immortal beyond all forms. But when that intuition of timelessness is applied to the separate self, it is perverted into the desire to simply live forever, to go on going on, to avoid death everlastingly. Instead of being timeless in transcendence, one merely substitutes the desire to live forever. In place of eternity one substitutes death-denial and immortality strivings and substitute sacrifices. And that, again, is the negative side of the Atman-project: the rancid immortality of death denial.

The separate self sense, then, is under sway of the Atman-project, the attempt to regain prior Wholeness in ways that prevent it and force symbolic substitutes. Instead of finding true Wholeness, it is thus driven by concerns over its mere existence: Eros drives it to continue its pseudo-separateness, and Thanatos involves it in death and the fear of death. And the battle of Life vs. Death, Eros vs. Thanatos, is the arch battle and the basic anxiety and dilemma *inherent* in all separate selves—a primal mood of fear removed only by true transcendence into Wholeness.

Objective Wing

This brings us to the last major aspect of the Atman-project: the separate self, although it pretends and aspires to immortality and cosmocentricity, necessarily fails its purpose to some degree or another. It cannot altogether pull off the charade that it is stable, permanent, enduring, and immortal. James put it that the fearful background of death is there to be thought of, and the skull will grin in at the banquet.[198] Once the separate self emerges, the foggy atmosphere of death becomes its constant consort. No amount of compensations or defenses or repressions is enough to finally and totally screen out this background dread. That is, nothing the inward self can do will finally choke out this horrifying vision, and so "external" or "objective" props are brought in to help support the Atman-project, to help alleviate the terror of death and present the self as immortal.

Now these external props can be positive or negative; they can service Eros or Thanatos. An individual will create, or latch on to, a whole host of external or objective wants, desires, properties, and possessions, goods and materials; he searches for wealth, fame, power, and knowledge, all of which he tends to imbue with either infinite worth or infinite desirability. But since it is *precisely* infinity that men and women truly want, all of these external, objective, and finite objects are, again, merely substitute gratifications. They are *substitute objects*, just as the separate self is a *substitute subject*.

Once again, Hubert Benoit has a brilliantly precise statement on the nature of the Atman-project in general, and substitute objects in particular: "Man only seeks to deify himself in the temporal sphere because he is ignorant of his real divine essence [Atman]. Man is born the son of God, participating totally in the nature of the Supreme Principle of the Universe; but he is forgetful of his origin, illusorily convinced that he is only this limited and mortal body which his senses perceive. Amnesic, he suffers from illusorily feeling himself abandoned by God (while he is in reality God himself), and he fusses about in the temporal sphere in search of affirmations to support his divinity which he cannot find there...".[27] Because man forgets and even denies God, while still intuiting Him, he "fusses about in the temporal sphere" in search of *substitute objects*, while, at the same time, trying inwardly to deify himself (the substitute subject). Both manipulations result inevitably from the loss of that radical Oneness which alone is Complete.

And so there are the two wings of the Atman-project—the subjective and objective—and there are the two sides of the Atman-project—positive and negative, Eros and Thanatos (and all four become totally intermixed: you can have Eros subject and Eros object, Thanatos subject and Thanatos object). But all are simply a product and function of boundary: wherever a boundary is placed upon prior Wholeness, that Wholeness appears as a subject vs. an object, a self vs. an other. This subjective self then wishes to recover the prior Wholeness (using Eros), but it fears its own dissolution (Thanatos). As a compromise, it arranges the Atman-project: it applies *to the subject* the intuited characteristics of the Whole, and thus tries to make the part appear Whole—cosmocentric, immortal, death-defying. The substitute subject chasing substitute objects—and all for the want of God.

The Form of Death and Remembrance

The Atman-project appears in all sorts of different forms—it appears wherever Atman *seems* lacking. That is, it appears throughout the manifest realm. It is really just another name for *maya*. The way I explained it above is simply a form it most often takes in human beings, and then only the most general form. It takes on all sorts of various structures and forms in human development, from the lowest to the highest, from the pleroma to the edge of the ultimate. It appears even in the womb, but of course in the most primitive and weakened form. We do not accuse the infant of denying God—actual Atman-realization has not yet had (in this lifetime) a chance to *emerge* (which occurs, as a rule, in the second half of life, on the Inward Arc). We say, however, that *all* individuals are touched by God, and all sentient entities intuit God; that is the only thing that holds the cosmos together. Sentient beings—at whatever age and in whatever condition—intuit their own essence as Atman, and strive for that essence within or under or through the conditions, restrictions, and potentials of their particular level of adaptation. And to the extent they intuit Atman, they apply Atman to their own level.

But notice that *part* of the Atman-project is indeed the *search* for Atman (that is "Atman-telos"). From the very beginning, all creatures intuit God. From the start, men and women intuit their prior Atman nature, and this acts like a huge unconscious magnet, so to speak, drawing them onward and upward toward that perfect release in the superconscious All. But it also forces them, as a temporary and remedial measure, to fashion all sorts of substitutes for Atman—substitute subjects, substitute objects, substitute gratifications, substitute sacrifices, immortality projects, and cosmocentric designs, and tokens of transcendence.

Under this pressure, successive structures of consciousness are created and then abandoned, fashioned and then transcended, constructed and then passed by. *They are created as a substitute for Atman, and abandoned when those substitutes fail.* And evolution proceeds by a series of such abortive attempts to reach Atman-consciousness—proceeds, that is, via the Atman-project, with each step, as it were, getting a bit closer.

It is true, then, that successively higher structures emerge in the course of evolution and development, but they emerge *as* substitute gratifications, and only as the lower substitutes are eventually relinquished, only as the lower forms of Eros-grasping wind down, can new and higher ones claim attention, subtler and subtler, until *all substitutes for Unity are tried and found wanting, and only Unity itself remains.*

Once a new level of evolution—a new but higher-order substitute self—is created by a vertical transformation of the deep structure of the previous level, the Eros of the new level proceeds by means of horizontal translations to integrate the surface structures of that stage into some sort of higher-order wholeness. Since it cannot have true and real Union, it at least attempts (as a substitute) to unify itself. These Eros-translations proceed to organize and develop the emergent characteristics and surface structures of the new level, to stabilize and preserve that level by *integrating* the new and higher symbolic substitutes. And this overall translative process continues until—for various reasons—this type of translation is found inadequate. And then? And then translation fundamentally fails and transformation ensues.

Now the reasons for the failing of translation are numerous, and they differ from level to level of the spectrum. In general, however, we may state that whenever Eros (of that level) exceeds Thanatos (of that level), translation proceeds and stabilization occurs. The seeking-and-grasping of that particular level is happy with its substitute gratifications, which present as fulfilled the desire for Unity. When Thanatos exceeds Eros, however, the particular translation involved winds down and is eventually surrendered, and transformation to a different mode of self and a different type of translation ensues: a new deep structure is remembered so that new surface structures can be learned.

Essentially, this means that consciousness abandons its exclusive identity with the lower structure—*it "dies" to it*; it accepts the Thanatos of that lower level, dies to that level, and thus *dis-identifies* with that lower structure. By *accepting the death* of the lower-level, it *transcends* that level.

As the higher-order level then emerges, the self, as we saw, *identifies* with that higher structure. It thus creates a *new* mode of self—with *new* forms of Eros-seeking. And this new mode of self faces a *new type* of death-terror or death-seizure. Namely, the new type of terror is that generated by the self's attempts to defend its new form of identity: new self, new other, and therefore new death-seizures *and* new death-denials. The new translation will now continue as long as the Eros of this level exceeds Thanatos—as long as the grasping exceeds the emptiness (sunyata), as long as the new structure serves as a substitute gratification and does not go tasteless in its desire. But once that occurs, once Thanatos outweighs Eros, then the self accepts the "death" of that level, dis-identifies with it—thus transcending that lower level—and thereby switches its identity to the next higher emergent structure, which *itself* then possesses new forms of Eros, and faces new seizures of Thanatos and death.

We will be going over all of that in the following chapters, but I will give a few quick examples now.

We saw that at the bodyego stage, the self was almost exclusively identified with the body's simple emotions and instincts. Its Eros-seeking is instinctual, biological, visceral-hunger, and if these instincts are traumatically *frustrated* (say, the hunger drive of the infant at the mother's breast), then that disruption is experienced as a death-seizure—to disrupt the instinct is to disrupt the self, because they are identical at that stage.

As the verbal mind emerges, however, the self differentiates or dis-identifies from its *exclusive* attachment to the instincts, and switches its essential identity to the verbal self (let's say the persona). It can now accept—within obvious limits—the frustration of the eating-instinct: it no longer "dies" when food is not immediately forthcoming—it simply gets hungry. But it now has a new self, and this new self has *new wants* and *faces new forms of death-seizure*. Humiliation, for instance, is a death-seizure of the persona. The self—which is now identified with the persona—suffers a literal death-seizure if the persona "loses face" or is fundamentally humiliated or shown to be ridiculous, and so on. The persona says, "I could have died of embarrassment!" This occurs, and will occur, *as long as the self remains identified with the persona* (as long as its Eros outweights Thanatos)—and it ceases only when and if the self dis-identifies with the persona, *accepts its death*, transcends it, and moves to a higher and more inclusive self structure. *This type of process is*, as we will see, *repeated at every stage of development*. And when all structures have been dis-identified with and transcended, there is only the Boundless; when all deaths have been died, there is only God.

All of this sounds, of course, a little abstract. What we will be doing in the next few chapters, therefore, is simply examining the forms of the Atman-project which appear on each of the levels of consciousness. We will see each level striving, consciously or unconsciously, for Unity (Atman-telos), but under or through conditions that necessarily prevent it (Atman-restraint), and force substitute unities (Atman-project). When these substitutes cease to satisfy, then that lower level is abandoned (through accepting its death), a new and higher-order level is created—which is still a substitute, although closer to the Real—until there is only the Real and the soul grounds itself in that superconscious All which was the first and last of its only desire.

14

Evolution Through the Lower Levels

Uroboric Incest and Castration

The simplest, earliest, and crudest form of the Atman-project is that of the pleromatic state. We saw that the self at this stage was autistic, adual, totally devoid of differentiation. Further, the pleromatic self was totally one with the environment. As Piaget put it, the self is *material*. The self is not yet bodily, not yet mental, not yet subtle—it is almost literally material: one with *materia prima* and *virgo mater*. The unity of this stage is purely physical; it is a unity of pre-differentiation, a unity by default. Primal in its paradise of ignorance, it is the most primitive of unities.

That primal and primitive paradise does not long obtain, however, because as soon as the uroboric forms begin to emerge out of the ground-unconscious, the material and pleromatic consciousness is transformed. The non-differentiated mass of the pleromatic stage gradually disperses into two vague prehensions, which we have earlier named and explained as the uroboric self vs. the uroboric other. The neonate begins to realize that the environment and his self are not one and the same. The infant starts to recognize that something exists apart from his self, and this "global something" we call the "uroboric other." I am being deliberately vague about these terms because, by all accounts, this is an extremely vague state of consciousness, and I don't want to over-interpret what the infant is actually experiencing. Nonetheless, there are some excellent accounts of these early stages by Margaret Mahler and Louise Kaplan,[218] Piaget,[295] Klein,[225] and (for the one I have selected to here discuss) Erich Neumann.[279]

Neumann, in his exhaustive *History and Origins of Consciousness*, has given a very detailed account of what he sees as the three major (with several minor) phases of self-evolution: the uroboric, the maternal, and the paternal (all of which we will eventually discuss). He examines this earliest of stages—the pleromatic and uroboric—

and concludes that the self at this level is driven by what he calls *uroboric incest/castration*.

I should point out that Neumann uses the terms "incest" and "castration" in a very general sense: as "desire" (incest) and "painful disruption" (castration). When he intends purely sexual connotations, he says so. With some reservations, I will follow his example, because "incest" and "castration" are quite similar to Eros and Thanatos, but they are much more graphic and carry a livelier impact. It should also be said that "castration" properly used is not sexist. *Webster's* gives it three definitions: 1) to remove the testicles, emasculate, geld; 2) to remove the ovaries, spay; 3) to deprive of essential vigor or significance by mutilating, expurgating, subjugating. Obviously, I mean that last, unless otherwise specifically stated.

What, then are we to make of uroboric incest/castration? According to Neumann, uroboric incest is the tendency to fall back into embryonic and pleromatic states—we would say, the desire to unite with the uroboric other and sink back into pre-differentiated oblivion. "So long as the infantile...consciousness is weak and feels the strain of its own existence as heavy and oppressive, while drowsiness and sleep are felt as delicious pleasure, it has not yet discovered its own reality and differentness. So long as this continues, the uroboros [and pleroma, if we may treat them together] reigns on as the great whirling wheel of life, where everything not yet individual [pre-personal] is submerged in the [pre-differentiated] union of opposites."[279] Thus, "in uroboric incest [Eros], the emphasis upon [sexual] pleasure and love is in no sense active, it is more a desire to be dissolved and absorbed; passively one lets oneself be taken, sinks into the pleroma, melts away...".

In other words, uroboric incest is simply the most primitive form of Eros, the most archaic and least developed form of the Atman-project. Uroboric incest is the tendency to seek out that *lowest-level unity* of all—simple material embeddedness, wherein all conscious forms melt back into the utter darkness of the prima materia. But please note: that *is* a drive towards unity; it is just the lowest imaginable form of that drive, the lowest form, we would say, of the Atman-project.

Now as long as the self-system is caught in or driven by uroboric incest, then it is open, for just that reason, to uroboric castration (death-seizure). As long as the self wants pleromatic fusion, then it opens itself to being innundated by that primal pleroma—it can be "castrated" or over-run by the uroboric other and the pleroma. This is why, I think, Neumann frequently speaks of "the deadly uroboric incest, where the embryonic [self] dissolves like salt in water."[279] And that "dissolution" is uroboric castration: the simple uroboric self is overthrown and dissolved by the pleroma. Neumann's point, however vague it might initially appear, is simply that as long as the self is involved with uroboric incest, then it is opened to uroboric castration. *As long as life* (Eros) *is geared to that level, then death* (Thanatos) *is geared to that level.* And just there is the uroboric Atman-project.

Notice, however, that Thanatos and castration are not precisely the same thing. Although I will occasionally use them interchangeably—since I don't want to introduce too many definitions here—castration is actually Thanatos *resisted*. As long as the self cannot die to uroboric incest-Eros, then it is open to uroboric castration. Because it cannot surrender uroboric incest-Eros, because it cannot die to that desire, because Eros outweighs Thanatos, *then* Thanatos appears as castration, as a threat. Instead of transcending the uroboric self by moving upwards to the typhonic realms, the self is simply castrated, dissolved, destroyed, and returned to pleromatic embeddedness. This whole point will, I think, become clearer as we advance in the discussion.

Uroboric translation continues as long as uroboric Eros outweighs Thanatos, as long as uroboric seeking and desire and incest is not surrendered. But as soon as the self is strong enough to accept the death of the uroboros, as soon as the self can surrender or die to the exclusively uroboric incest, then Thanatos outweighs Eros, uroboric translation ceases and transformation upward ensues.

Should this transformation-upward be less than "clean" or less than complete, then aspects of consciousness will remain "stuck" or fixated in uroboric incest; that is, the individual will take secret pleasure in self dissolution, in abandoning consciousness in pre-personal pursuits. But if all goes well, uroboric incest will be surrendered—it is only a substitute gratification anyway, and once it is tasted and found wanting, and relinquished, then higher substitutes can emerge from the ground-unconscious. And notice: once uroboric incest is relinquished, uroboric castration is transcended.

The entire point is that, to put it poetically, the self figures (and rightly so), that it has no future at this stage, that Unity is not here, and thus it carries its Atman-project to the next stage of evolution.

The Atman-Project in the Typhonic Realms

Throughout the alimentary uroboric stage, the infant's awareness floated in an oceanic state, differentiated only by the very vague line between the uroboric self and the uroboric other. But as the organism itself begins to mature physiologically, and especially in its capacity for imagery, the primitive uroboric self-feeling begins to shift to the individual bodyself, and the uroboric other begins to focus as the "mothering one." The infant thus begins to grow out of the purely pre-personal and uroboric realm into the typhonic plane of existence, where it will face the existential battle of being vs. nullity, a battle centered around the figure—now loving, now terrifying, now benevolent, now devouring—of the Great Mother.

The mothering one initially is not merely a caretaker, but the literal focus of the child's entire world. "The pre-Oedipal mother is the mother who, in consequence of the biological basis of the family, must become the whole world of the child."[57] As the infant begins to transcend and differentiate his pleromatic-uroboric narcissism into an inside-world on the one hand and an outside-world on the other, the mothering one is all of a piece with the outside-world. The infant's relationship with the mothering one, then, is not one of feeder to fed nor suckling to sow, but of being to non-being and self to existence. This is why all schools of psychiatry place so much emphasis on this early phase of development—it is a profoundly influential level. The infant's relationship with the mothering one is really a relationship with existence per se, existence as a whole. Therefore, the mothering one in this capacity is best thought of as the mythological Great Mother—the Great Surround, Great Environment, or Great Ground. The Great Mother is the first thing the self sees as it awakens from pleromatic-uroboric slumber—and imagine the impact!

Because the self sense is just starting to emerge at this stage, the self cannot initially differentiate itself from the Great Mother. That is to say, the infant is—*by all accounts—originally one with the Great Mother.*[46, 97, 214] But as the differentiation between the body and the environment begins to mature—a differentiation which in very vague form had begun in the uroboric state—as this differentiation matures, new and higher forms of self and other spring into existence. The body begins to tease itself apart from the material world around it; the inside-world of the organism starts to differentiate from the Great Mother. And thus, the minor skirmish begun between the uroboric self and the uroboric other now rages with full force as the drama between the bodyself and the Great Mother. The self-identity which was so fleeting in the uroboric state now begins to stabilize, and thus the life-death factors come into play with a violent action at this typhonic level.

In the pleromatic state, the infant's self was dispersed as simple material unity—the crudest form of the Atman-project; at the uroboric stage, he groped vaguely for unity with the uroboric other (uroboric incest). At the body stage, the infant again comes up with a new type of Atman-project, with a new type of substitute self. But remember the condition of a substitute self: it must pretend to fulfill the desire for Atman-unity, the desire to be cosmocentric, central to the universe. If you simply remember that the infant is struggling for UNITY, then even the most bizarre aspects of psychoanalytic theory become very obvious and very straightforward.

For instance, according to psychoanalysis, the infant at this stage translates his situation (*in images*) so as to present itself as the center of the cosmos by—as psychoanalysis puts it—"incorporating" or "swallowing" the world (the Great Mother, or just initially the "breast") in image form. The infant tries to take the whole world, in image form, into his separate self! He tries to take the world into himself and thus make his separate self the whole world. "Melanie Klein has shown [that] the ego 'is based on object libido reinvested in the body'; the self is a *substitute* for the lost other, a substitute which pretends to be the lost other; so that we may embrace ourselves thinking we embrace our mother [the whole world]. [The self structure] results from the desire to [attain] union with the mother, by the device of pretending to have swallowed her, i.e., to have incorporated her into oneself."⁵⁸ There is a cosmocentric substitute indeed! If he can't *be* the world, then he'll try to swallow it instead. Next to pleromatic-uroboric dispersal, probably the most primitive form of the Atman-project we will encounter.

That is one form of his simple Atman-project, driven by Eros struggling to find its true world and Real Self; there is his "incest," his desire to discover some sort of unity consciousness, but carried out under conditions that forestall it and force image substitutes of the real World and union with it.

And so the infant proceeds to translate his self and his world, attempting to gain some sort of prior Unity. In this manner, then, we can view the stock in trade phenomenon of psychoanalysis: infantile thumb-sucking. For by virtue of the magical primary process which, as we saw, dominates this body level, the infant can *translate* the Great Environment or Great Mother into the breast-image into the thumb-image, and thus by thumb-sucking he can pretend to unite himself with his world. That is, he can translate himself into his whole world and his whole world into himself. This is a very clever substi-tute union—but it obviously works only in images—that is, only in phantasy and in imagination. It is not real Union; it is a *substitute union*.

All of the above is simply part of typhonic Eros-incest—the desire to find some sort of unity through merging with the Great Mother by incorporating or swallowing the Great Mother. When psychoanalysis speaks of "oral eroticism," it simply means oral-Eros, oral-seeking—trying to find Unity through the mouth—trying to be one with the world by eating the world. We saw that at this stage (the oral-typhonic stage), the infant's major connection with the world is through the mouth; how natural, then, to seek real Unity with the world through the oral connection! The psychoanalytic stage of "oral eroticism" is just that simple—the Atman-project is centered on the mouth of the body. At this stage, says Fenichel, "The ideas of eating an object or of being eaten by an object [are] the ways in which any re-union with objects is thought of unconsciously."¹²⁰ To find Atman, to find Unity, the infant eats the world, the Great Mother. Personally, I believe that psychoanalysis is absolutely correct in its assessment of this stage (which does not, of course, exclude the contributions of other research-ers, such as Piaget; I am simply using psychoanalytic theory as one example of the Atman-project).

And yet, of course, where there is oral incest there is oral castra-tion. Says Fenichel, "Corresponding to the specific aims of oral eroti-cism...we find specific oral fears, especially the fear of being eaten."¹²⁰ These oral fears go back, as we saw, to the alimentary uroboros, but the overall point is very clear: typhonic life vs. death, typhonic Eros vs. Thanatos—as long as the self desires to swallow the world, eat the world, then it will be open to being swallowed and eaten—castrated—

by the same world. The Great Mother is the first food—and the first Destroyer....

Thus, because the infant is incestuously involved with the Great Mother—because the infant wants to merge with the Mother, swallow and incorporate the Mother—then the infant is open to terrible death-seizures and castrations at the hands of the Great Mother. "The human child, which at the mother's breast experiences a new and intense mode of union [Eros-incest]..., must also experience a new and intenser mode of separation...and death. It is because the child loves [or is attached to] the mother so much that it feels separation from the mother as death."[57]

And the child *does* feel separation from the Great Mother as a death—*because the Great Mother was once part of the child's self-system*. The self was once literally *identified* with the Great Mother, and thus separation or differentiation from the Great Mother is initially a death-seizure. And note: as long as the self desires this maternal fusion—as long as it retains its oral-incest—then separation from the Great Mother will be a death-seizure, a primal anxiety.

But the self must eventually accept the death of its oral-incest; it must sooner or later accept the death of the maternal fusion state so that it can *differentiate* itself from the Mother and thus *transcend* that primitive maternal embeddedness. This can occur only as oral-incest winds down, and the *death* of oral-incest is accepted.

Notice that if the death or Thanatos of this level is not eventually accepted, then the self will continue to experience oral-incest and *therefore* oral-castration. Because it cannot give up this level, because it continues to exclusively identify with this level, then it continues to suffer castration when anything happens to this level. The infant will not be able to break its oral-incest; it will not be able to break its fusion with the Great Mother (it remains a "momma's body"); and therefore, it will continue to experience separation from the Mother as a death-seizure. For this primal "separation anxiety" is, as Otto Rank clearly explained, nothing other than the terror of death.[25] And since it is an over-powering death-terror, the self caught in it will cease to differentiate and separate (because that is too painful, too death-demanding). It will cease, that is, to develop and transcend. *Because it cannot accept the death of this level, it cannot transcend this level.*

Psychoanalysis puts this in its own way: "The special concentration of libido [Eros-seeking] in the mouth in earliest infancy, the hypercathexis of the act of suckling, results from the inability to accept separation from the mother...and represents the residue of human incapacity to accept death.... And the effect is to burden the [Atman] project of loving union with the world the unreal project of becoming oneself one's whole world."[57] I do not see that our case could be put any more plainly. If the self cannot accept the death of that old incest or fusion with the Mother, if the self cannot accept the separation and differentiation from the Mother, then it remains stuck at this primitive unity state, at this primitive form of the Atman-project, wherein one tries to achieve real Unity by swallowing the world and becoming one's own world.

The point is that *separation anxiety* is really *differentiation anxiety*—which is really the anxiety of *transcendence*. Separation anxiety occurs at *every stage of development*, because differentiation and transcendence occurs at every stage of development—as we saw in chapter 10. And this separation anxiety continues until the *death* of that stage is accepted, whereupon the self can then differentiate itself from that stage and thus transcend that stage. Separation anxiety on any level is the inability to accept the death of that level, and if that inability persists, then development *stops* at just that stage.

But if development proceeds more or less normally, then eventually, to return to the typhonic level, this oral-incest will wind down; Thanatos will exceed Eros, and transformation-upward will ensue. Most of this low form of the Atman-project is surrendered (image-only cosmocentricity, Freud's "omnipotence of images," Ferenczi's "omnipotence by magic gestures," oral-incest and swallowing the world, etc.), a surrender that allows higher, but still substitutive, gratifications to emerge from the ground-unconscious into awareness. On the other hand, failure to surrender these early and archaic forms of the Atman-project results in fixation: part of consciousness itself is prevented from continuing its transformation-upward and its ascent towards Atman, but remains instead lodged in these lower realms. From this fixation point, *symbols* will irradiate into awareness, and probably symptoms as well. The soul has remained incestuously involved with these lower realms, and unconsciously receives its token Atman-feelings through an erotic (Eros) involvement with its lower past, its primitive roots.

The Anal/Membership Phase of the Atman-Project

In the above sections we saw, in effect, that the self had begun to emerge from the subconscious. The typhonic self developed a fairly stable differentiation between self and other, and thus managed to transcend the old pleromatic-uroboric fusion state. Because the self had tentatively emerged as a separate entity, it naturally developed certain forms of Eros-seeking (self-preservation, oral-incest, magical omnipotence), and was opened to certain forms of vulnerability-death (maternal castration, oral-castration, dissolution). Thus, there already existed some very crude forms of the Atman-project. On the Eros side, the self already wanted to expand itself, enrich itself, blow itself up as the center of the cosmos—even to the point of trying to swallow the whole world! On the negative side—the Thanatos side— the self already was attempting rudimentary forms of death-denial, trying to protect itself from the terror of dissolution and the terror of isolation and separation and emergence. "The great scientific simplification of psychoanalysis," wrote Becker, "is the concept that the whole of early experience is an attempt by the child to deny the anxiety of his emergence."[25] That is, the anxiety of emergence, separation, and death....And that starts as soon as there is *any* sort of emergence—all the way back to the uroboros.

Eventually, these lower-order incests are more-or-less surrendered, and thus the lower-order castrations and death-terrors are relaxed as well. But what is not relaxed and cannot be relaxed is the Atman-project: it is simply transformed to the next higher-order level. A new and higher mode of self emerges, is faced with new types of other, and therefore experiences new desires and new Eros-impulses, and likewise suffers new death-seizures and so creates new death-denials. Life vs. death is carried to a higher level, and the Atman-project swings into action on the new plane. There are new growths, new potentials... and new terrors.

At this point in our story, we are just reaching the verbal-membership stage (which usually occurs in conjunction with the psychosexual stage of anality—without confusing the two, I will still discuss them together). This overall stage, remember, marks the point where the verbal-mind is *starting* to emerge from the ground-unconscious and differentiate itself from the body. That is, the typhonic body-ego is *starting* to differentiate naturally into the mental-ego and the physical-body; the verbal-mind thus *begins* to transcend the simple body. At the previous stage, we witnessed the differentiation of the body from the environment (and the Great Mother). At this stage, we see the start of the next higher-order differentiation of the ego from the body itself.

In the previous stages, the developmental "action"—Eros and Thanatos, incest and castration—occurred *across* the boundary between the bodyself and the Great Environment (since that was the major boundary of differentiation). Here, the developmental action occurs predominantly across the boundary between the body and the emerging ego (since that is now the growing tip of differentiation). Thus, the separation drama—the drama of life and death, Eros and Thanatos, the whole Atman-project—shifts from that between the body and the environment to one between the ego and the body.

The verbal-self is the new and higher, but still substitutive, self. It is capable of higher-order unities because it is capable of ideation. With the verbal mind, consciousness begins to grow and, as it were, spill over the confines of the physical being. No longer is consciousness tied to the naive present. Through language, one can anticipate the future, plan for it, and thus gear one's present activities in accordance with tomorrow. Through language and its symbolic, tensed structures, one can postpone the immediate and impulsive discharges of simple biological drives. One is no longer totally dominated by instinctual demands but can, to a certain degree, transcend them. Through membership-cognition, the self can participate in the higher-order unity of sharing a verbal community (comm-*unity*), a community which far transcends the simple and immediate perceptions of the physical body. The child, then, proceeds to *translate* his world and his self in terms of the higher-order forms of verbal ideas and membership symbols; his reality is representational.

Yet precisely because the verbal-self is *starting* to differentiate from the body, the body starts to become a special, *objective* focus of interest—a special home of incest and a special concentration of death. And this, quite simply, is part and parcel of the whole psychoanalytic "problem of anality."

I realize that the concept of "anality" is not very popular nowadays—especially with humanistic and transpersonal psychologists. But it is my own feeling that the concept of anality—set in the context of the entire spectrum of consciousness—is a perfect and even brilliant expression of real humanistic and even transpersonal concerns. It is really a problem of life and death and transcendence—all focused on the body. That psychoanalysis frequently uses this concept in a reductionist fashion is no reason to discard the concept itself, only its reductionistic use. In my opinion, thinkers such as Becker[25] and Brown[57] and Rank[311] have recast this psychoanalytic concept in such a brilliant fashion that it not only becomes acceptable to humanistic and transpersonal psychology, it is now indispensable. In fact, "anality" is simply a code-word for the Atman-project of this level.

To begin with, allow me to briefly summarize the works of Ernest Becker on developmental psychology.[25] Becker has recast psychoanalytic concepts in *existential/humanistic* terms, thus preserving and synthesizing the best of psychoanalysis and existential psychology. Hence, to recast Becker in *transpersonal* terms is to salvage the best of all three of these important schools of thought—psychoanalytic, existential/humanistic, and transpersonal/mystic. My own opinion is that if each of these three schools can give just a little, we achieve a remarkably faithful account of what is actually occurring in development on the whole.

Becker begins with what has become an old and very honorable task of psychology: trying to figure out what men and women *really* want. Becker surveys the entire literature on the subject, and decides that it is *heroism*: "What I have tried to do," he concludes, "is to suggest that the problem of heroics is the central one of human life, that it goes deeper into human nature than anything else." If we carefully examine the nature of *heroics*, Becker says, "then we must admit that we are dealing with *the* universal human problem."[25]

And heroics? The drive to be heroic? What is that? According to Becker, it is simply the drive toward "what we might call 'cosmic significance.' The term is not meant to be taken lightly, because this is where our discussion is leading. [To take one example]We like to speak casually about 'sibling rivalry,' as though it were some kind of by-product of growing up, a bit of competitiveness and selfishness of children who have been spoiled, who haven't yet grown into a generous social nature. But it is too all-absorbing and relentless to be an aberration, it expresses the heart of the creature: the desire to stand out, to be *the* one in creation. When you combine natural narcissism with the basic need for self-esteem, you create a creature who has to feel himself an object of primary value: first in the universe, representing in himself all of life."[25] Heroism, Becker makes plain, simply means the drive to be central to the cosmos, to be God-like, to be first and last and ultimate in all the world. As we have put it, it is the drive to be *cosmocentric*.

At the same time, heroism also means avoiding anything that subtracts from one's own cosmocentricity. Since death is the ultimate substraction, death is the ultimate terror. As Becker puts it, "Heroism is first and foremost a reflex of the terror of death." *Likewise*, the "repression of death is the primary repression."[26] Heroism, therefore, is also a reflex against death and Thanatos—it embodies the urge to be immortal, death-less, blood-immune and everlastingly triumphant.

In short, heroism is the drive to be God-like, cosmocentric, immortal. Heroism, obviously, is the Atman-project: the drive to be Atman, timeless and All, spaceless and infinite, One and Whole. The positive or cosmocentric side and the negative or death-denial side of Becker's heroism are simply the Eros and Thanatos sides of the Atman-project.

Becker also addresses the subjective and objective wings of the heroic Atman-project. The subjective side is what he calls the "vital lie" of character—the fact that the separate self is basically a lie, a vital lie, about the possibilities of heroism. Character is the "inward" Atman-project, the inside story of heroism. The objective side of the heroic Atman-project is, for Becker, the whole world of culture, since all culture is basically "a codified hero system" which promises immortality and death-denial. All cultures, said Otto Rank, are based on "immortality symbols". Mankind erects monuments of stone, gold, and steel which do not themselves decay or die, thereby to assuage his fear of impermanence and insubstantiality.[26] Culture is what men and women do with death....

All-in-all, Becker's works cover the subjective and objective wings, and the Eros and Thanatos sides, of the heroic Atman-project—the attempt of the creature to be Infinite, to be All, to be Atman. And, up to this point, Becker and I are in perfect agreement. But Becker thinks that men and women want to be God because they are spineless liars, whereas I maintain they want to be God because their ultimate potential *is* God. For Becker—and to use my terms—the Atman-project is a fundamental lie about Atman. The individual heroically wants eternity and infinity, but since (according to Becker) there *is no* eternity and infinity, the heroic urge—the Atman-project—is just a lie, plain and simple. And the self is a lie, and culture is a lie, and religion is a lie (to which Huston Smith responded: I have made many generalizations, but "none, we trust, as irresponsible as this.").[26a]

For myself, the Atman-project is not a lie about Atman, but a *substitute* for Atman. The Atman-project is only partly a lie—and partly the *truth* as well. Men and women *are* ultimately Atman, and they are driven to heroics as a substitute for that Atman. Heroics is not *just* a vital lie (although that is a part of it), but also a vital truth;

and that mixture, that compromise, is the Atman-project.

For Becker, development is the unfolding of the vital lie of character—the unfolding of heroics. For myself, it is the unfolding of Atman, driven by the Atman-project. Becker's analysis of development is still valid, I believe, but only if we set heroics in the true context of the Atman-project.

With that in mind, then what Becker tries to show, using existential and psychoanalytical concepts, is that heroism (the Atman-project) goes all the way back to the very earliest stages of development, and is central to the whole notion of development itself. From the beginning, he says, the child is involved in cosmocentricity (narcissism-Eros) and in death-denial (Thanatos). "The child has an idea of death by the age of three, but long before that he is already at work to fortify himself against vulnerability. This process begins naturally in the very earliest stages of the infant's life—in what is called the 'oral' stage [uroboric and typhonic]. This is the stage before the child is fully differentiated from his mother [the Great Mother], before he is fully cognizant of his own body and its functions—or, as we say technically, before his body has become an object in his phenomenological field."[25] That is, the body *is* the self at the typhonic stage, and thus is not perceived *by* the self—the body would be, at this stage, the embedded unconscious.

Becker's point about the oral-typhonic stage is just that "the mother, at this time, represents literally the child's life-world. During this period her efforts are directed to the gratification of the child's wishes, to automatic relief of his tensions and pains. The child, then, at this time, is simply 'full of himself,' an unflinchable manipulator and champion of his world. He lives suffused in his own omnipotence and magically controls everything he needs to feed that omnipotence.... His body is his narcissistic project [the Atman-project], and he uses it to try to 'swallow the world.'"[25] That, as we saw, was one of the earliest and crudest forms of the Atman-project.

We come now to the anal stage—the major topic of this section. (I will briefly discuss Becker's interpretation of this stage and then go on to discuss the overall stage itself; we will pick up Becker's thoughts again in the next section.) "The 'anal stage'," says Becker, "is another way of talking about the period when the child begins to turn his attention to his own body as an object in his phenomenological field."[25] That is, the period when the self, as verbal-mind, starts to differentiate itself from the physical body, so that the body becomes object to the self—the body is no longer the embedded-unconscious. "His narcissistic [Atman] project then becomes the mastery and possession of the world through self-control."[25] That is, the problem of heroics—the attempt to be cosmocentric and immortal—now starts to shift its focus to the body. The body becomes the focus of life and death.

And an extraordinary focus it is. Orthodox psychoanalysis has done a good job detailing all the desires—and all the terrors—of the anal stage of development. I shall never forget Erik Erikson's discussion of Peter, a four-year-old boy: "I had been told that Peter was retaining his bowel movements, first for a few days at a time, but more recently up to a week. I was urged to hurry when, in addition to a week's supply of fecal matter, Peter had incorporated and retained a large enema in his small, four-year-old body. He looked miserable, and when he thought nobody watched him he leaned his bloated abdomen against a wall for support."[108]

Through a series of thoughtful questions, Erikson discovered that Peter was absorbed with the children's story of "The Little Engine That Could," because on one page of this picture story the little engine, puffing smoke, enters a tunnel—but on the next page, it emerges *without* the funnel smoking. "You see," Peter told Erikson, "the train went into the tunnel and in the dark tunnel it *went dead!*" "Something alive," commented Erikson, "went into a dark passage and came out dead."[108] We have often commented on the primary process and paleologic thinking which dominate these early stages, and you can now start to see why they are so significant. Paleologic confuses whole and part and equates all subjects with similar predicates; thus, the tunnel and Peter's intestines were "equated" (both long, hollow, dark, etc.); so was the "alive-smoking engine" with food, and the "dead-smokeless engine" with feces. Thus, Peter believed that if he released his feces, something that was alive would come out hurt or dead—and so he held on for dear life. To put it simply, the battle of life vs. death—Eros vs. Thanatos—was occurring inside the bowels of little Peter and in an existential anguish he simply froze in terror.

But that is only a slightly exaggerated case of the normal terrors that accompany this stage. Says Becker: "The basic key to the problem of anality is that it reflects the [now budding and growing] dualism of man's condition—his self and his body. Anality and its problems arise in childhood because his body is strange and fallable and has a definite ascendency over him.... The tragedy of man's dualism [in this case, the growing differentiation between ego and body], his ludicrous situation, becomes too real. The anus and its incomprehensible, repulsive product represents not only physical determinism and boundness, but the fate as well of all that is physical: decay and death."[25] Anality is actually the child's introduction to *anicca* (impermanence, one of Buddha's three marks of existence). The Buddha's last words were: "All that is compounded will decompose. Work out your salvation with care." The child discovers this decomposition—and imagine the incredible horror: that which is decomposing is literally part of himself! And he is simply to flush it down the toilet. No wonder that every child, in this stage, awakens screaming with night terrors. No wonder that we all repress the memories in order to bolster our pretend permanence and substantiality. But, in fear and trembling, the child discovers this inherent decomposition—what poor little Peter could not "release," what he could not stand to confront, was the black stench of death, the skull that grins in at the feast. "What to do with feces?" is really, "What to do with a mortal and mutable body, when in my heart of hearts I know I'm immortal (Atman)?" There, I think, is the true crux of anality. And, as we will see, this whole trend of body-terror (along with its correlate, body-incest) reaches an extraordinary climax in the next psychosexual stage, heralded under the names of Electra and Oedipus.

Fenichel points out that this entire anal stage is shot through with "fantastic fears of body damage."[120] We will shortly return to this, but the essential point is quite clear—the overblown fears of body damage are simply a new form of *separation anxiety*. The self is starting to differentiate or *separate out* from the physical body, and until this process is completed, the self is open to body separation anxiety. The self was once *totally* identified with the body, and as long as that exclusive identification remains, the self is open to—and terrified of—body castration, those "fantastic fears of body damage." In the previous stage, the infant suffered separation anxiety whenever the Great Mother was removed, and that occurred simply because the self was once totally identified with the Mother and had not yet completed the necessary differentiation. Just so, the self now experiences separation anxiety with regard to the physical body or its appendages or its representatives (such as feces). Peter would not "separate" from his feces because it represented his body and his life. He suffered separation anxiety and would not differentiate.

But in the midst of all these death terrors and castration fears, the child has its secret wants, its Eros, its incests. It still wants to be Hero, wants to be Atman, clamors for immortality, and demands omnipotence. Psychoanalysis calls the wants and desires of the anal period "anal eroticism." But what underlies these desires? "Anal eroticism is sustained by the infantile fantasy of a magic body which would fulfill the narcissistic [Atman] wish for a self-contained and self-replenishing immortality."[57] Immortality—the denial of death: the feces threatened Peter's immortality project. "Infantile anality...is an ambivalent mixture of Eros and death, involving attachment to the anal zone of...fantasies of union with the [Great] mother and narcissistic fantasies of being both Self and Other."[57] It is, says Brown, the drive towards "symbolic retention, mastery, possession of the world," and it is based on "fantasies of human narcissism in flight from death."[57]

The point is simply that the child is seeking some sort of Unity—union with the Mother, trying to be *both* Self and Other—through the symbolic manipulation of the body. The search itself, and the context of the search, is simply for that Unity which is the ground of all grounds. Consciously or unconsciously all beings gravitate towards that Estate. And so does the child, in his own simple and even crude fashion. At this point, he seeks some kinds of substitute symbolic unions through the manipulation of his body, and also through the manipulation of language (the membership-side of this stage). This is why Ferenczi and Freud spoke of the "omnipotence of words and thoughts" which blossoms at this level;[131] why Sullivan spoke of the peculiar power of "autistic language," a language that wields immense but phantasized power;[359] and Lacan of the "forgotten language of childhood" rooted in oceanic (primitive Atman) yearnings and self-only demands.[269] All of that is simply part of the child's Eros, his incest, his struggling Atman-project, his desire to be Hero, God, the One above all.

How better to view this stage, which the Germans call the stage of stubbornness and Erikson calls the focus of autonomy?[108] To be *autonomous*! Hero! That surely is part of the child's deepest yearnings. To be autonomous—the prime-mover of his world, "the unique motor-principle!" The child shouts "No!" and "Do it by self!"[243] He is contrary in the most exquisitely stubborn fashion; he flexes his muscles of resistance and dares to defy the whole world if only he can be as absolutely autonomous, a type of miniature First Cause of himself and his world. He crashes his will against the recalcitrant otherness of the not-self, and demands to triumph absolutely. It is an intense battle, this clash between a would-be God and a world that does not comprehend his magical attempt and will not cater to it. But the attempt is made, the absolute gesture thrown out, and the wish flourishes to magically coerce and ultimately possess the world as a Zeus or Thor or Isis.

And it is doomed; the child can no more be the whole world, be the All, be Atman, through word and body manipulation than through, for example, thumb-sucking. The new substitute self is not, after all, the prime and autonomous mover of self and other. From all sides, that infantile form of the Atman-project is shaved down, so that, eventually, the next higher-order substitute—closer to real Atman—can emerge. In this way only are subtler and subtler selves created; in this way only does Atman-project give way to Atman. On the other hand, if the self refuses to surrender this low form of incest, then it will remain open to the correspondingly low form of castration and death-terror; it cannot overcome the separation anxiety of the body itself, and thus remains victimized by its own foundations.

15

Evolution Through the Egoic Levels

We have seen that the egoic stage witnesses the emergence, or in many cases the consolidation, of an extraordinary number of developmental factors. But if I could briefly summarize the overall stage, I would say that it marks the final differentiation of the mental-ego from the physical body. I will key on this aspect in the present chapter, and I will begin with the body aspects first, and then address the mental aspects.

On the body side, the essential point is that the oral and anal impulses eventually give way to the genital (phallic-clitoral), and this whole process culminates in the infamous Oedipal/Electra complex.

Now according to traditional analytic theory (which we will shortly amend), during the Oedipal phase of development every normal boy child—if, as is customary for simple parsimony, I may limit my discussion to the male sex—seeks, at least in words and symbols and phantasies, to *sexually possess the mother*. Actual masturbation is very common, and analysis of the accompanying phantasies shows unmistakably that the mother is the first object of genital love, no matter how obviously fledgling and unripe the genitality may be. Further, analytic theory maintains, the child develops a jealous rage at the father, for the simple reason that the father is now viewed as the great rival for mother's affections: he is the obstacle, the frustrator, the worm at the core of otherwise luscious phantasies. Sooner or later, however, the child imagines in his own fantastic way, that if the father discovered his secret wishes he would drastically punish the child by dismembering the offending organ: this is the castration complex, and it is said to "smash to pieces" the Oedipal desires. In order to avoid the catastrophe, the child sides with the view of the father, internalizes the parental prohibitions and taboos in the form of the super-ego, and thus abandons or represses his incestuous wishes. The Oedipal and castration complexes—what on earth are we to make of them?

As for the Oedipal complex: we have already seen that at each previous stage the child translates his world to avoid Thanatos and to present himself as cosmocentric, and that to implement this Atman-project he develops narcissistic focusing, substitute gratifications, special resistances, compensations, and defenses. To look back: we saw that at the bodyego level he translated so as to become both self and other, to make himself into his world by "swallowing the world"; at the membership stage, he attempted to gain unity by mastering the membership world and attempting to possess it in every way, thereby proving himself autonomous and cosmocentric. And now at the beginning of the egoic-syntaxical stage, he imagines he can *bodily* unite with the Great Mother and thereby gain a type of prior unity. To unite with the mothering one, who for all purposes has represented the entire world to the child, is literally a desire for union with the All, or at least a very good substitute for it. What could be more natural? Behind it all is the desire to regain Atman, the unlimited and true state of every being and every consciousness. *To unite by means of body-Eros with the Great Mother*—this is the compelling form of his incest. "The purpose of the sex act can be none other than an attempt to return to the mother's womb." Ferenczi was close—it is the true and absolute return to Atman that is desired, and only secondarily do actual regressive elements enter the picture. But the sex act, whether fantasized or actualized, does not itself achieve this *direct and lasting* union (Tantra aside for the moment), for no matter how much you may engage in sexual intercourse, you are still you. You are not the All, which is the hidden aim and desire of intercourse. Thus, genital sexuality is a substitute gratification. Sex is a symbol, a symbol for Atman.

And yet there is more. To unite with the Great Mother—one's *own* Great Mother—is literally to *conceive oneself*, to be the father or parent of oneself...a god to oneself. We call as witness Norman O. Brown: "The essence of the Oedipal complex is the project of becoming God—in Spinoza's formula, *causa sui*: in Sartre's, *entre-en-soi-pour-soi....* The Oedipal project is the quest to conquer death by becoming father of oneself."[57] And Freud, "All the instincts, the loving, the grateful, the sensual, the defiant, the self-assertive and independent—all are gratified in the wish to be the father of himself."[57] And Becker, "The Oedipal project is the flight from passivity, from obliteration, from contingency: the child wants to conquer death by becoming *father of himself*, the creator and sustainer of his own life."[25]

The project of becoming God—or rather, *the project of moving toward God-consciousness*, unity consciousness, Atman-consciousness—is precisely what lies behind the Oedipal complex: The Oedipal complex is just another form, although a very low form, of the immortal Atman-project—the desire to be one with the All, death-defying, omnipotent, eternal, expressed, in this case, through genital impulses. The genital aspects of the project are thus secondary—the child simply has a new organ through which to dramatize his immortal quest.

He can manipulate and translate the phallus, just as he did the feces—both are ultimately driven by the Atman-project.

Now, up against this Eros-incest crashes the genital castration complex, and this complex is said to shatter his incest. But since this incest is really a form of the Atman-project, what are we to make of the castration complex? Let us begin with Becker: "The horror of castration is not the horror of punishment for incestuous sexuality, the threat of the Oedipal complex; it is rather the existential anxiety of life and death finding its focus on the animal body.... Today we realize that all the talk about blood and excrement, sex and guilt, is true...because all these things reflect man's horror of his own basic animal condition, a condition that he cannot—especially as a child—understand.... This, finally, is the hopeless terror of the castration complex...".[25] The castration complex is the final and forced realization of the Buddha's First Noble Truth: composed things suffer and then fall apart.

Beyond that point of explanation, however, we part company with the existentialists and with Becker (and with orthodox psychoanalysis as well), because—after admirably humanizing the castration complex—they leave the whole affair hanging in mid-air. Becker thinks the Atman-project is *totally* impossible—there is no God, no Atman, only vital lies about God and Atman. He therefore thinks he has proven that the castration complex totally "dethrones" the chance of paradise, totally smashes to pieces the Atman-project: "It expresses the realization by the child that he is saddled with an *impossible* project; that the *casui-sui* [Atman-project] pursuit on which he is launched *cannot be achieved by body-sexual means*.... This is the tragic dethroning of the child, the ejection from paradise that the castration complex represents."[25]

In fact, however, he has simply demonstrated that the heroic Atman-project—to use his own words—"cannot be achieved by *body-sexual* means." And indeed it cannot! But it *can* be achieved by higher means, and one of the first steps (even though it is *only a step*) is to surrender the body-sexual form so as to be able to begin the transformation-upward to higher realms (mental, then subtle, then causal). The whole point of the castration complex is that by helping to differentiate and transcend body-sexual incest, it opens the self to transformation-upward into the mental realms—that is the entire point of "sublimation," and that is why psychoanalysis insists that sublimation is the *only* successful "defense mechanism".[46, 120] (Actually, sublimation is not even a defense mechanism—it is another term for transformation-upward or evolution, but the point is clear enough: transform *from* the body *to* the mind: *sublimate*). The castration complex is indeed the end of the *exclusive* body-sexual-incest form of the Atman-project, but it is not the end of the Atman-project itself. The castration complex does not shatter the Atman-project, but merely the infantile and bodily form of the Atman-project.

In short, the "successful" castration complex helps to point out the utter impossibility of gaining Atman—of gaining true Unity—via the exclusively typhonic body. That is the core of the castration complex. Of course, the castration complex can be too severe and result in the repression or dissociation of the body, not its simple differentiation (for which, see below). I certainly don't mean to recommend traumatic castration anxieties, or that all parents should threaten their children at age 5 with actual physical dismemberment. Obviously, I am using the "castration complex" in its general sense to cover all its aspects, good and bad. The point is that the *exclusively* body-genital incest must be surrendered, and this surrender is traditionally called the "castration complex" or the "weathering of the castration complex." The self has to die to the desire to reunite the bodyego with the world in an exclusively sexual fashion. Next to pleromatic fusion (uroboric incest), and hunger (typhonic incest), sexual union is the lowest of all possible forms of unity: it is a simple and primitive unity of only two bodies for only brief periods. That is a very meager union in comparison with that absolute Unity wherein *all* bodies, high or low, are perfectly One in Eternity. That is Atman-Unity, of which sexual release is but a brief glimmer and for which orgasm is but a substitute gratification. But in order for any of the higher unities to emerge (mental, then subtle, then causal, then Atmic), it is mandatory that these lower unities and incests be surrendered in their exclusivity and transformed in their aims. The self has to *die* to the desire to find Unity via sex. *And the death of that incest means that the castration complex has been successfully completed*, that Thanatos has been accepted on this level, and that transformation-upward can thus occur: sublimation.

On the other hand, if this incest is not transformed, then the individual remains open to "castration" in the very negative sense of the term—Thanatos not accepted. When psychoanalysis says that "the boy at the phallic phase has *identified with his penis*,"[120] All they mean is that this is the last point where the self is still more-or-less identified with the body. Beyond this stage, the ego and the body finally *differentiate*. But precisely because the self is identified with the emotional-sexual body at this stage, the genitals themselves become something of a prized possession (if this seems somewhat odd to you, then think of the people you know—men or women—who have never outgrown this stage. But to return to the child himself:) *Because* the boy "has identified himself with his penis," *then* he suffers genital-castration anxiety. Fenichel makes that point very clearly,[120] and I think he is quite right (that's not the whole story—there are cognitive and moral development, etc.—but it is a true part of the whole story).

"The fear that something might happen to this sensitive and prized organ is called castration anxiety."[120] Now I think it is very obvious that purely genital castration anxiety is simply one of the new forms of *separation anxiety*. This is why "its forerunners [are] oral and anal anxieties over loss of breast or feces."[120] Fenichel says the feces, the mother's breast, the bottle, and the mother herself—"all of these were once [self] but now are objects"[120]—and, as we saw, precisely because that is true, there was a *separation anxiety* connected with each, and this anxiety lasted until differentiation or dis-identification from each was complete. Likewise, until the self differentiates itself from the genital-body, it will experience *genital separation anxiety*, known as the classic genital-castration anxiety—Thanatos in its morbid and resisted forms focused on the body. "Castration anxiety in the boy in the phallic period can be compared to the fear of being eaten in the oral period, or the fear of being robbed of the body's contents in the anal period: it represents the climax of the fantastic fears of body damage."[120] All of that occurs *because* of the fantastic/exclusive *identification* with the body, played out through one of its connections with the world: oral, anal, genital. Body-incest brings body-castration and there, in a phrase, is the basic story.

On the other hand, to surrender the exclusiveness of this emotional-sexual incest, to accept its *death*, to differentiate from or dis-identify with it, is to successfully "weather the castration complex" and open oneself to sublimation into mental realms (via mental identification with the ego/superego complex, as we will see). Thus, as Thanatos outweighs Eros, as this lower translation is surrendered, the individual transforms, once again, both his mode of self and the form of his seeking (the substitute subject and the substitute object). He finally differentiates from the typhonic or emotional-sexual body and shifts his central identity to the mental ego. And into the hands of this new and higher substitute self he delivers his Atman-project.

Fusion, Differentiation, and Dissociation

I want to interrupt our story of evolution through the egoic realms to quickly discuss a very important point about development on the whole, and that is—as the sub-title of this section suggests—the difference between fusion, differentiation, and dissociation, because this "choice" is, more or less, offered at every stage of development. And the consequences of the "decision" are absolutely fateful.

There can be no doubt—to start our discussion with this egoic stage—that it is necessary and desirable that the mind and body *differentiate*; only in this way can the self rise above a confinement to simple sensations, perceptions, and impulses (the overall bodyself). As the mind and body differentiate, the self can expand through the world of the mind and not simply remain stuck in the immediateness of the present-bound body. Just as it was desirable for the body and the environment to differentiate, so is it now desirable for the ego and the body to differentiate. Psychoanalysis tells us very clearly of the dire results of a self that remains fixated to mere bodily modes (oral, anal, phallic), that cannot rise above simple bodily eroticisms, that stalls in infantile categories of bodily manipulation. For example, we saw that a self which fails to differentiate completely and cleanly from the body will try to find Atman-unity *through* bodily orifices: perhaps by compulsive over-eating (oral fixation: trying to find unity with the world by trying to eat the world), or sadistic manipulation (anal fixation: trying to find unity with the world by trying to possess the world), or by hysterical flourishes (phallic fixation: trying to find unity with the world by trying to "sexually make" the world). There is the terrible result of the Atman-project remaining *stuck*—in *fusion*—at the bodyself levels.

On the other hand, however, there is a difference between *differentiation* and *dissociation*. It is necessary and desirable that the ego and the body differentiate—it is disastrous if they dissociate or fragment. In general, wherever differentiation occurs, dissociation *can* occur. Successful development means a series of clean differentiations with little or no dissociations—but that, of course, is rare. Dissociation simply means the exiling of a structure to the submergent-unconscious; not its transcendence, but its repression.

We have, then, a continuum here, ranging from 1) fusion to 2) differentiation to 3) dissociation. In general, at any given level of development, *fusion*—or the *failure to differentiate at all*—occurs when Eros-incest is not surrendered or transformed. The person accepts that level's substitute gratifications and refuses to develop or differentiate or transcend any further. This is what psychoanalysis means when it says, "The consequence of experiencing excessive satisfactions [too much Eros-incest] at a given level is that this level is renounced only with reluctance; if, later misfortunes occur, there is always a yearning for the satisfaction formally enjoyed."[120] *And this occurs at all levels of development.* We all know of the three-year-old who continues thumb-sucking because the present situation is stressful and the earlier breast-union of pleromatic fusion was overly satisfying. But can you see that this same *type* of thing may occur at all stages of development, even into the causal? A rationalist experiences satisfaction through conceptual activity, and so tends to refuse to differentiate and dis-identify with that mental level—he thus refuses to enter the subtle, because he is afraid to let go of his rational thumb-sucking. Just so, certain forms of high-subtle meditation are so blissful that the individual might remain stuck (in *fusion*) in that realm for a prolonged period, refusing to surrender that subtle-level thumb-sucking and thus refusing entry into the causal realm. In each of these cases, the Eros-incest of that level is not surrendered, and so the self *stops* differentiating—it remains in *fusion* with that level and accepts its substitute gratifications as real.

Now where excessive Eros-incest leads to fusion, excessive Thanatos-castration leads to *dissociation*. this excessive Thanatos-castration can take the form of either excessive frustration (so that Eros is reduced) or outright terror and trauma (so that Thanatos is overblown). As psychoanalysis puts it, "If the frustration has led to repression [because Thanatos is overblown], the drives in question are thus *cut off from the rest of the personality* [they are dissociated];

they do not participate in further maturation and send up their disturbing derivatives from the unconscious into the conscious."[120] And we have already extensively covered the nature of those "disturbing derivatives": they are simply *symbols* and *symptoms*, originating in the repressed-submergent unconscious (the *dissociated* aspects of self).

I should mention that I believe no one escapes some form of body/mind dissociation at this egoic stage. The ego is indeed a transcendence of the body—but not *that* much. The ego still retains an overly close association with the exclusive body (what Aurobindo called the "physical ego") and thus tends to be overly terrified of the body itself. Only toward the centaur stage, when consciousness starts differentiating from the ego itself, can the ego and body be brought into an extensive and binding integration. Prior to that time, we can only attempt to *reduce* the amount of body/mind dissociation—but we can never eradicate it. In most normal cases, then, we can only say (and hope that) the *fusion* of mind and body is not excessive, and the *dissociation* of mind and body is not excessive—and the *differentiation* of mind and body proceeds more-or-less on schedule. And this is a procedure we will see on every major level of development, because wherever there is differentiation there *can* be dissociation....

Maternal Incest/Castration

Because I am, in this book, trying to touch bases with all the major schools of psychology, I would like in this section to connect with the Jungian view, represented by Erich Neumann. This will not, however, be just a side venture, because Neumann's thoughts tie in directly with our whole discussion. For instance:

In Neumann's view, the movement from the typhonic-body to the mental-ego is a movement from "maternal incest" to "paternal incest" (we will explain that last term in the next section). This development, according to Neumann, consists of several sub-stages (surrender, the strugglers, the killers, the dragon-fight), but on the whole it is simply the move, the transformation, from body-bound desires to mental modes and concepts.[279]

The "maternal realm", as Neumann uses the term, is the realm of "mother nature"—instinctual, emotional, biological—and it centers on the oral, anal, and genital zones of the body. "Maternal incest" can occur through any of these zones, but reaches its conclusion at the genital stage. Notice that we are here using a few terms in a very broad sense; for example, the "bodyself". The typhonic-body begins its influence in a rudimentary way with the uroboros; it becomes the dominant mode of self at the axial and image body levels; it stretches through the membership/anal phase and concludes at the early egoic stage. In a very *general* sense, then, we can refer to *all* these levels as the "body realms," even though many other processes are simultaneously occurring (cognitive development, verbal development, etc.). It is the same with the "Maternal Realms": the Great Mother began to exert influence at the uroboric stage, became absolutely significant at the axial stage, stretched into the anal/membership stage, and concluded at the early egoic/phallic stage. Therefore, Neumann uses the terms "maternal incest" and "body incest" *interchangeably*. He simply means (to use my own terms) that the "body realms" and the "great Mother realms" are roughly the same, and they *both* stretch from their early beginnings in the uroboros through their height of influence in the axial/image body stages into the anal/membership stages and finally conclude at the phallic/early-egoic stages. If you simply think of the earliest stages of development as being *dominated* by the body (the "typhonic realms") and dominated by the Mother ("maternal incest": the child seeks its unity through the "mothering one"), then Neumann's points will fall naturally into place. I will, in this section, use all of these terms very loosely and very generally, simply to join up with Neumann's extremely important conclusions on this overall transformation: body/maternal to egoic/paternal.

Neumann's point, in effect, is that as long as body-sexual incest occurs (oral, anal, or phallic—the whole "body realms"), then the self is open to "maternal castration"—castration or dissolution or traumatic disruption by the Great Mother who rules over the typhonic/body realms. For the Great Mother "threatens the ego with the danger of self-naughting, of self-loss—in other words, with death and castration."[274] And there we are on very familiar ground. "We have seen," he continues, "that the narcissistic nature of the phallus-obsessed adolescent constellated a connection between sexuality and the fear of castration."[279] Again, familiar ground. "The death of the phallus in the female is symbolically equated with castration by the Great Mother, and in psychological terms this means the [budding] ego's dissolution in the unconscious."[279] And making much the same point that the psychoanalyst Fenichel did, he states that at this maternal stage "the masculinity and ego of the hero are...identified with the phallus and sexuality."[279] Thus, the threat of matriarchal "castration *impends over an ego that has not yet broken its tie with the Great Mother*."[279] And this castration can take the specific form (at this stage only) of actual *genital*-castration fears (as well as the more general form of the castration-dissolution of the ego-mind in irrational "tantrums," hyperemotionality, and hedonistic impulses). These are my words, but Neumann's ideas: to be castrated by the Great Mother/body realms is to be dragged back from the newly emergent mental realms into the typhonic-pranic-bodily realms; that interpretation is just what Neumann has in mind.[279]

I have suggested that for development to continue past this stage, the self has to die to this body-identification, with its maternal-incest. This is why, I believe, Neumann states that "we now come to the fight with the Great Mother and her defeat. The awe-inspiring character of this dragon consists essentially in her power to seduce the ego and then to castrate and destroy it in matriarchal incest.... But when the ego is no longer prepared to remain at [the stage], it must conquer the fear...and do the very thing of which it was most afraid. It must expose itself to the annihilating force of the...Mother Dragon without letting itself be destroyed."[279] It must pass through the death (Thanatos) and separation of the maternal levels without regressing, dissolving, or repressing—it must cease fusion (incest) and start differentiating, *without* dissociating. If this is successful, then "the ego of the hero is no longer identified with the phallus and sexuality. On this [new and higher level], another part of the body erects itself symbolically as the ...'higher masculinity': the head, symbol of consciousness, with the eye for its ruling organ—and with this the ego now identifies itself."[279]

Note again: the acceptance of the death/separation of a lower level, the differentiation or dis-identification from that level, the emergence of the next higher level, and the identification with it. This occurs only after a separation anxiety is overcome and passed through (Neumann's "dragon fight"), and it heralds a higher mode of transcendence. By this means, says Neumann, "The supremacy of the Great Mother, the control she exercised through the instinctual power of the body [typhon], is superseded by the relative autonomy of the ego, of the higher [self] who has a will of his own and obeys his reason."[279]

Further, this new realm—the mental-egoic—is marked by its differentiation from the body, according to Neumann. As he puts it, "The development of ego consciousness is paralleled by a tendency to make itself independent of the body," for the ego is "the world of light and consciousness as contrasted with the earthy, body-bound world of the unconscious.... The ego and consciousness experience their own reality by distinguishing themselves from the body. This is one of the fundamental facts of the human mind."[279] Notice also that although he does not articulate it, Neumann is aware of the difference between dissociation and differentiation: "The development that has brought about the division of the two systems [mind and body] is in accord with a necessary process of psychic differentiation, but, like all differentiation, it runs the risk of becoming overdifferentiated and perverse."[279] That's dissociation.

At any rate, this new stage, the mental-egoic, is the world of concepts, will, reason, logic, and morals. It is governed, initially, by "paternal incest-castration," or what we might better call "cultural or parental incest-castration": one's desires, and one's fears, center less on the body and more on the socio-cultural persona and its *ideas*. And it is now through this higher medium that the self, swinging between the two arms of the Atman-project, carries its new incests and suffers its new deaths.

Parental Incest/Castration

We have seen that the normal mental-ego has accepted the differentiation from, or the death of, or the transcendence of, the lower levels: pleromatic, uroboric, typhonic, and membership (or the overall "body realms"). But the self is now identified with the mental-ego, and thus the death of this new structure is violently resisted. The battle of life vs. death, Eros vs. Thanatos, *switches* to this mental level, and the Atman-project begins to play itself out through this structure. The Atman-project is no longer bodily-sexual, but mental-egoic. It is no longer played with feces and phallus but with ego and persona.

We saw in chapter 5 that a distinctive feature of the mental-ego is its *internal* differentiation—the differentiation of the ego into several (necessary and useful) subpersonalities or personae, the most dominant ones being the Parent/Super-ego/Top Dog, the Child/Infra-ego/Under dog, the Adult/Calculator, the ego-ideal and the conscience. Any of these sub-personae *can*, upon emergence, de *dissociated* (instead of differentiated) and thus rendered submergent-unconscious (they become shadow, or "unconscious personalities," ruthlessly intermingled with the archaic-unconscious). Likewise, any of these sub-personalities can—and frequently do—emerge from the ground-unconscious *as* the embedded-unconscious (this is particularly true of the super-ego): a process that is—as far as it goes—natural, normal, and healthy.

Because I admire the work of Transactional Analysis, I frequently refer to the whole mental-ego (or at least its early and middle states) as the P-A-C ego. This is also an easy way to remember both the internal differentiation of the ego, and three of its most important personae (P, "Parent"; A, "Adult"; C, "Child." Incidentally, when, for example, "Parent" is capitalized, it means the "internalized Parent," not the actual, external parent). However—and this is fairly important—*I will restrict most of the discussion of the rest of this chapter to the super-ego [Parent] alone.* Please do not take this restriction of discussion for a restriction of the importance of the rest of the aspects of the ego. It is just that the super-ego is one of the most important of all sub-personae, and thus most of our theoretical points can be made with reference to the super-ego alone (and the interested reader can then apply them to the other sub-personae as needed).

In the most general terms, the super-ego is simply part and parcel of the *higher-level identification* of the mental-egoic self. In particular, the super-ego means that the child has *identified with the parents*—he has *mentally* internalized the parents to form the Parent—he has "mentally mimicked" the parents to help form a mental self.[14, 38, 51, 97] This is done on a verbal and mental level, not on a bodily and sexual level. Because the child can form *ideas* and *concepts* at this stage, he can *conceptually* or mentally identify with his mentors, the parents. This is not bodily incest, but parental/conceptual incest: a higher level of Eros.

The child's first introduction to the physical-body world is through the Great Mother—starting with birth and continuing through suckling, nursing, touching, feeling, toilet training, etc. But the child's first introduction to the mental world is through membership-language

and discourse with the *verbal* mother and father. The pre-verbal Great
Mother embodies a world of non-conceptual feelings, wishes, sensations, wants, and desires. But the *individual* and *verbal* and concept-
using mother is different: she, unlike the Great Mother she once was,
is now understood on a word-and-name basis, on a verbal and mental
level.[359] And she is soon joined by the *father figure*, another verbal and
concept-using individual. This is all more-or-less new to the child, and
hence he tends to use the new parents, the verbal parents, as *higher-
order role models*, so that the child eventually identifies with the parents as the Parent—the super-ego—and this is simply part of the new
and higher-order self.[165, 178] The child *conceptually models* the self on
the parents through *parental incest* or parental role modeling.

To say the same thing from a slightly different angle, the parents
offer the child new ways of translating reality, embodied in sets of
special conditions, and these special conditions—*as always*—simply
represent the characteristics of the new and higher level. In this case,
the special conditions offered to the child are sets of verbal, conceptual, egoic, and syntaxic patterns. The child is requested (and sometimes demanded) to put into egoic-syntaxical form that which he
previously would act out bodily or emotionally. And the parents continue to enforce these special conditions, so that the child continues
this new mode of translation until transformation itself occurs and is
more or less complete. All of this is part of what we refer to generally
as "parental incest."

In effect, this parental incest helps the child move from the body-
bound Oedipus complex to the mental-ego and super-ego. This is what
psychoanalysis means when it says that "the super-ego is heir to the
Oedipus complex,"[46] and this occurs, because "identifications replace
object-choices"[382] (which really means that mental-identifications replace bodily-sexual desires). Fenichel would put it like this: "The ego
'borrows' from its strong parents the strength that enables it to suppress the Oedipus complex. In this way the resolution of the Oedipus
complex brings about the marked and decisive 'step within the ego' [its
internal differentiation], which is so important for subsequent ego
development...".[120] For instance, according to psychoanalysis "the
change from [external] parents to [internal] superego...is a prerequi-
site of the individual's independence. Self-esteem is no longer regu-
lated by approval or rejection by external objects, but rather by the
feeling of having done or not done the right thing."[120] But all of this
simply points out "the fact that the construction of the superego takes
place on a higher level...".[120] (It is true that aspects of the superego
can be regressive, narcissistic, and archaic [it is said to be formed in
part by oral incorporation, a theory I by-and-large reject]—but the
overall point is straightforward: to say the superego is a "higher-level"
heir to the Oedipus complex is to say the mental-ego moves beyond
the typhonic body).

This whole realm of superego psychology, Neumann calls "paternal
incest/castration."[279] He uses the term "paternal" for several reasons.

One, the patriarcy *historically* and *mythologically* superseded the matriarchy.[17],[66] That *might* have been a sexist development, but the sexism is mankind's, not Neumann's—he is only reporting what happened. Two, today, we also find that—according to Fenichel— "under our cultural conditions, generally for both sexes the *fatherly* superego is decisive."[120] This, too, might be sexist and culturally induced—but even if it is, until society changes, then for most people— men and women alike—"the fatherly superego is decisive." Hence, *paternal* incest/castration, which simply means that the father parent is, for most people, the most decisive role model and authority-figure at this stage.

Nonetheless, and for various reasons, I prefer the more general term of "*parental* incest/castration", and one can simply decide in each individual case whether the mother-parent or the father-parent is the more decisive figure. Both play a significant role, and both are, to one degree or another, internalized via parental incest.[427]

I would only like to emphasize that the essential point of the super-ego or Parent is that it helps the self to differentiate from, and thus transcend, the typhonic body; and this occurs, as usual, through the emergence of a higher-order structure and the identification of the self with that structure. The parents are extremely important figures at this stage because they offer—or are supposed to offer—tangible role models of all the various and necessary personae with which the child can identify via parental incest, and this in turn helps the development of rich inner differentiation. It frequently happens that the parents do not so much force repression on the child as they fail to offer adequate role models to the child: thus the child fails to differentiate and develop his potentials out of the ground-unconscious. This lack of growth results not from something the parents did, but from something they failed to do—provide role models for parental incest.

The Egoic Atman Project: Ego-Ideal and Conscience

The egoic self—the P-A-C- ego—is indeed a new and higher-order self-embodying a new and higher-order unity. It is a little closer to Atman, it has a little more Atman-telos—but it is still *not* Atman and thus it still has its Atman-project, its attempt to be itself the shining Hero, the immortal and omnipotent One. The self has accepted (more-or-less) the death and transcendence of all the lower levels but it is now squarely *identified* with the mental-ego, the P-A-C ego, and this new substitute self is therefore ferociously guarded against death and transcendence. While being suckled by its new incests, it cringes in terror at its new deaths. A new battle of life vs. death commences, and a new form of the Atman-project rears its immortal head.

We can see this very clearly just with the superego alone (again, I am restricting my discussion of the subpersonalities of the ego to the superego or Parent only—and so I will discuss the Atman-project of the ego level in terms of the Parent alone). Now the superego is traditionally sub-divided into the ego-ideal, or all the "positive" injunctions and ideals, and the conscience, or all the "negative" injunctions and prohibitions. (I do not mean to exclude the very important works of Kohlberg; I am simply limiting my discussion to a re-interpretation of psychoanalytic concepts.) In my opinion, this whole topic can be summarized by saying that the ego-ideal is simply the Eros side of the egoic Atman-project, and the conscience is the Thanatos side of that project. They represent the positive and negative sides of the egoic form of that immortal attempt to be Hero, God, Atman—and the facts bear out just that interpretation.

We can begin with the ego-ideal: Loevinger nicely summarizes the orthodox view of the generation of the ego-ideal (as set forth by Lampl-de Groot):

> The ego ideal begins with the infant's "hallucinatory wish fulfillment" [the uroboric realms]. As the infant becomes aware of the distinction between inside and outside [the axial-body level], hallucinatory wish fulfillment is replaced by fantasies of omnipotence and grandeur [the image Atman-project of the primary process]. Following experience of his relative powerlessness, these fantasies are replaced by fantasies of his parents' omnipotence [beginning of parental incest]. After he is disillusioned in this regard also, he forms ideals and ethics. For Lampl-de Groot the entire sequence remains one of wish-fulfillment [or Eros-incest in general].[243]

That paragraph is a summary of almost a century of psychoanalytic research, and in my opinion, it simply means that the ego-ideal is basically the culmination of Eros-wish fulfillment, the positive side of the Atman-project. That is, the ego-ideal is simply the culmination and summation of the many transforming events which aimed at securing various forms of the Atman-project—beginning, according to some, as far back as the pleromatic and uroboric states. It contains—or rather, has passed through—all the earlier forms of Eros, of incest, of positive desires and thirsts and overblown wants, of all the earlier attempts to be cosmocentric and heroic. And to the extent that fixation occurred at any of these earlier levels, then these primitive incests and desires—according to psychoanalysis—live on in the ego-ideal, thereby distorting one's ideals, falsely stretching one's capacities, burdening one with impossible dreams of paradise. All in all, we can generally say that the ego-ideal can be the home of all the past attempts at cosmic perfection. That is the simplest way to understand the nature of the ego-ideal, and that is an interpretation which fits not only with psychoanalysis in particular, but also with Becker and the existentialists in general.

But that is only half the story—a true half, I believe, but a half nonetheless. Psychoanalysis looks at the ego-ideal, finds that its core is a wish for transcendent perfection *beyond personal limitations*, and—because it knows not of the transpersonal realms—concludes that the ego-ideal is a regressive wish for the *pre-personal* perfection of the pleromatic paradise.[120] And I have said that that *can* be *part* of the truth, but only part. For much of the ego-ideal is simply the *present* form of the Atman-project. It is the mold into which the adult pours his moment-to-moment intuition of real and higher Atman-consciousness. It is a small hole in the ego through which intuitions of real Perfection stream. And so, unless actual fixation has occurred, then the "idealness" of the ego-ideal is not a regressive wish for the pre-temporal perfection of the pleroma, as so many analysts seem to think.[46, 120, 122, 141] It is rather a progressive (but still somewhat limited) wish for trans-temporal release in Unity. Since the self wants transcendence, wants Atman, but since it will not accept the death or Thanatos of the present egoic level, then it is forced to accept a compromise and a substitute, and that is basically the ego-ideal—part illusion and vital lie, and part truth and reality. It contains all the Atman-intuitions that cannot at present be realized or actualized, and thus it always drives the individual to reach beyond his own present state of mediocrity, even while he fusses about with substitutes.

And so, naturally, what does this ego-ideal seek? I will not make a drawn-out argument for this—I will simply agree with Blos when he states that the ego-ideal propels people "toward the incredible feats of creativity, heroism, sacrifice, and selflessness. One dies for one's ego-ideal rather than let it die [the substitute sacrifice]. It is the most uncompromising influence on the conduct of the mature individual: its position always remains unequivocal."[45] And its position? It is simply a "search [which] extends into the limitless future that blends into eternity. Thus, the fright of the finity of time, of death itself, is rendered non-existent...".[45] Immortality and cosmocentricity—the Atman-project of the ego-ideal. The immortality project of the ego-ideal is simply everlasting perfection, and this is just the new estate of Eros in flight from death and sunyata, of Eros anxious for immortality through an everlasting chain of tomorrows. The ego-ideal, in short, is seeking to sustain and secure the self sense which is under the illusion—otherwise correct, but distorted—that it is the immortal and perfected Atman. There, I think, is the core of the ego-ideal.

If we move now to the *negative side* of the Atman-project, we can say that if the ego-ideal is the home of Eros, then Thanatos grins in as the conscience. As the roots of the ego-ideal reach down to the pleromatic and uroboric stages, so the origin of the conscience lies with the first experience of Thanatos—handed out by the uroboric other—and the consequent resistance to it.[225, 226] "Some of the experiences of unpleasure [Thanatos] later become structured as restrictions and demands of the parents [at the membership stage as "visceral ethics"], which the child obeys to retain the parents' love. At the next stage [the beginning of the egoic] some of these demands are internalized via identification [parental incest]. Finally the child accepts the restrictions and form a conscience.... The [conscience] throughout remains primarily an agency of restriction."[243] And restriction enforced by

Thanatos—the ever-present fear of death bound by the conscience and released in the dosages necessary to conform the ego to its demands (did not Freud himself finally say that this aspect of the superego was formed by Thanatos?)

Thus, for a summarizing phrase, we might say that as the ego-ideal is the culmination of all prior incests, the conscience is the culmination of all prior castrations—of all the restrictions, negations, and death-seizures. And if the castrations of the previous levels were severe, and fixations occurred, then the individual will continue, at the hands of the harsh conscience, to repress and dissociate those previous aspects of consciousness which should in fact have been integrated. Instead of differentiation, transcendence, and integration, there occurred dissociation, fixation, and repression. Instead of *sacrificing* the previous stage and accepting its death, the individual dissociated aspects of that stage as a *substitute sacrifice*. Dissociation is basically a substitute sacrifice. That is, instead of accepting the proper death of the particular previous stage, the individual offers up portions of himself as substitute sacrifices. Under the directives of the internalized Parent, the individual will repress, alienate, and dissociate any aspect of the self which, in the eyes of the internal Parent, threatens death. Thus, an individual who has a false and idealized persona will dissociate and repress any facets of his self (such as the shadow) which threaten this inflated self-image. Instead of accepting the death of the false persona, the individual substitutes the death of the shadow by repressing and dissociating it. As the ego-ideal is substitute Eros, the conscience is substitute Thanatos. There, I think, is the easiest way to re-interpret the important works of psychoanalysis on the superego, its ego-ideal and its conscience.

The Surrender of Parental Incest/Castration

Once parental incest has served its function—the creation of a higher-order self via parental incest or parental role modeling—then it must be surrendered via dis-identification and differentiation. The Mother-Parent and Father-Parent must be sacrificed, their death accepted, and their exclusive hold on consciousness broken. If the self refuses to surrender parental incest, then it is open to parental castration: the individual remains in a state of stunted conformity with parental commands. The self remains in parental *fusion*. The individual cannot stand the *separation anxiety* of leaving behind the Mother-Parent and Father-Parent, and thus the whole mental-egoic realm is *castrated* by the opinions of "mommy and daddy." The person goes through life never daring to entertain an original idea and never daring to "strike out" on his own. Fusion reigns: development stops, differentiation stops, transcendence stops.

This whole drama usually reaches a climax in adolescence. The individual, after creating several appropriate personae (via parental incest), now begins to differentiate from and dis-identify with all these personae, to the extent that he can transcend them and integrate them into the mature ego, and then *start* to transcend the ego altogether. This demands the death of the old mother-father superego (which Neumann calls the Slaying of the First Parents).[279] Naturally, this is something that the actual parents might find threatening, and the resultant tension brings hard times on all parties.[292]

Should this stage be successfully negotiated, then the individual develops the mature or integrated ego—first step on the Inward Arc— and then goes on to the trans-egoic modes of self: centauric, subtle, causal, and ultimate. The Atman-project becomes subtler and subtler, and might eventually give way entirely to Atman alone. And in the vision of that ultimate Light, the Radiant God is born.

16

Higher-Order Evolution

Since we have in the last few chapters already developed an outline of the basics of evolution (Eros/Thanatos, emergence, incest/castration, differentiation/dissociation, etc.), we can proceed quickly through the remaining stages of development. Besides, we won't have to pause to offer our re-interpretations of orthodox Western psychological models of the higher realms, because there are no orthodox Western psychological models of the higher realms.

The Centaur

In general, all of the characteristics of the centaur (intentionality, vision-image, bodymind integration) represent or reflect *higher-order unities*, new and higher forms of Atman-telos. This is why most centauric therapists (humanistic or existential), are always talking about either a "higher-level unity" or an "underlying unity"—a unity of ego, body, mind, and emotions. Rollo May: "if it be countered that this picture of the multitude of egos [postulated as ultimate by many schools of psychology] reflects the fragmentation of contemporary man, I would rejoin that any concept of fragmentation presupposes some unity *of which* it is a fragmentation.... Logically as well as psychologically we must go behind the ego-id-superego [typhon and P-A-C ego] and endeavor to understand the 'being' of whom these are expressions." [266]Carl Rogers: "Organismic sensing or experiencing is more than heightened sensory awareness of internal bodily states and of limbic [typhonic] system activities. It is the integration of this awareness with awareness of those functions represented by the neocortex. It is also the integration of the activities of the left and right cortices [vision-image]." [187]Perls *et al.* point out that most people experience the ego and the body as quite distinct or even fragmented; but, they say, "fortunately the *true underlying unity* (my

142

ital.) can be demonstrated," and they devote an entire book to just that demonstration.[292] Likewise, Lowen points out that most people dissociate body and mind, and develop a block or barrier between psyche and soma: "The block also operates," he says, "to separate and isolate the psychic realm from the somatic realm. Our consciousness tells us that each acts upon the other, but because of the block it does not extend deep enough for us to sense the *underlying unity* (my ital.)."[251]

The centaur or bodymind integration is simply the new and higher form of the Atman-project, a new and higher form of unity on the path to Unity. But to get to this new stage, one must die to the old stage: one must accept the death of the ego.

And that process entails a new *separation anxiety*: the anxiety of letting go of the ego, of dying to an exclusive identity with the egoic self-concept. By-and-large, this separation anxiety can be terrifying, especially given the present-day stage of collective evolution, where anything beyond the ego is viewed with utmost suspicion and is usually diagnosed as pre-egoic.

But at this point in evolution (to return to the individual), the ego's task is done: it has served well to advance evolution from sub-consciousness to self-consciousness, but now it must itself be abandoned to make room for superconsciousness. On the Inward Arc, one must say good-bye to this old friend. The self must differentiate from the ego, dis-identify with it, transcend it, and then integrate it with the higher and newly-emergent structures. But please remember that the ego remains intact when the self dis-identifies with it—just as the body remained intact when the ego transcended it. Transcendence does not mean deformation. One still possesses an ego—it's just that one's identity is no longer exclusively bound to it.

But for all of that to occur, one must pass through the separation anxiety of leaving the ego behind—just as earlier the ego itself had to overcome the separation anxiety of the body (castration complex) and before that the body itself had to overcome the separation anxiety of the Great Mother. Everything that the self was once unconsciously identified with must be differentiated, dis-identified with, and transcended. And it is now the ego's turn.

As long as one remains identified with the ego, as long as one operates through egoic desires and incests, then one is open to *egoic castration*. Because the ego translates with concepts and ideas, if you attack the ego's ideas, the ego experiences it as a death. Because the ego has certain power-drives and goals, if you frustrate those goals, the ego experiences it as death.[252] All of that is nothing more than a form of egoic castration. As long as there is ego and egoic incest, then there is egoic death and castration.

If the self can sustain egoic separation anxiety, then it can differentiate from the ego, transcend it, and integrate it. If not—if the self remains in love with the substitute gratifications and incests of the ego—then differentiation halts, growth halts, transcendence halts. Egoic *fusion* reigns.

It is very rare, however, given the "level" of present-day society, for any individual to evolve past the mature ego stage. Because the average mode of the self sense in society at large seems to be early, middle, or late egoic, then past that point the force of society as "pacer of transformation" tends to drop off. Thus, individuals who grow *beyond* the egoic stages have to do so either on their own exceptional talents or through special professional assistance. By the latter, I do not mean a "doctor for mental illness," but a guide for self-actualization: in general, the existential-humanistic therapist (and beyond that, the spiritual Masters).

The job of the humanistic therapist (who, as we saw, tends to address the centauric realms) is to help the consenting ego begin its transformation-upward to the centaur level itself. And this means that the centaur-level therapist will start by giving the individual a new way to *translate* reality. The therapist will pit his existential translations against the client's egoic (or personic) translations until the ego can *transform* as centaur. That is, the therapist acts as a *pacer of transformation*, replacing the now "fizzled-out" forces of the society and the parents. The therapist strategically frustrates and disrupts the old egoic translations and incests, while encouraging and teaching the new and higher centauric translations.[426] When the client can genuinely and freely adopt the new centaur translations, then transformation is more-or-less complete, and "therapy" is for most purposes over.[292]

It is not that in this process the individual has simply created, out of the plastic of his psychic programming, a self-fabricated reality. True transformation—on any level—is not a form of brain-washing, hypnosis, or propaganda. It is rather a form of emergence, of remembrance, of recollection. The therapist, in translating reality *from* the centaur level, *elicits* the same level of self in the client (if all goes well, that is). The therapist engages the language of the client's higher self, and *lives* that language or form to the client until the client lives it himself. The therapist simply assists in the *emergence* (via remembrance) of the centauric level from the ground-unconscious.

As we earlier explained for *all* cases, the existential-centauric therapist assists in this tranformation by imposing *special conditions* upon the client, and these special conditions act as *symbols of transformation* to the client. And any of the characteristics of the centaur will work in this regard: the therapist (depending upon his or her particular school) might use intentionality, or vision-image, or living in the present, or bodymind union exercises, and so on. I think the literature on the whole Third Force (humanistic/existential) is so familiar that I needn't chronicle the details. The general point is that the centaur therapist is trying to help the client develop new and subtler forms of incest-Eros, new and subtler desires and motivations (pre-eminently, the motivation of self-actualization). This drive to self-actualization, consciously engaged, is simply the new form of incest: no longer body-incest of sex and hedonism, no longer ego-incest of linear goals and drives and conceptual wishes, but the centaur-incest of desiring one's own self-actualization beyond conventional modes of being (beyond the biosocial bands).

And that new incest, which rises out of the remains of the death of the ego, is not only one which is *self-actualizing*, but also one which creates authentic *meaning* in life.[64] That creation of meaning—according to the existentialists—is simply part of intentionality, which is why Rollo May devoted an entire book to demonstrating that *"Intentionality* [is] *the structure which gives meaning to experience."*[265] And he quotes Husserl in support: "Meaning is an intention of the mind." Thus, the world without meaning, the existentialist points out, is simply a world without the higher-order intentionality, a world where one does not *intend* one's total life, join in and wish one's life, and thus *create* life's meaning in the same act.[181] To intend, or reach out to a thing, is also to point to, or *mean* that thing, and that is why the existentialists always equate intentionality with meaning. That is, "My life is meaningless" actually says "I don't mean my life," and *that* says "I do not intend or wish my own being." According to the existentialists, if intentionality does not *emerge* in my life, then *meaning* does not emerge in my life.[265]

For the existentialists, this is no mere theorizing without substance, for not only have they spotted the disease (lack of meaning in life, or lack of self-actualizing Eros), they have spotted the cause as well. They have pinpointed *why* I won't allow intentionality to emerge from the ground-unconscious, or why I won't intend my life and find meaning in it. And it is what we have been talking about all along: it is the fear of death....

Death. It is Thanatos, Shiva, and Sunyata, and as it registers its new presence, I freeze in its new embrace. I am faced, in fact, with existential terror on this new level, with dread, angst, and "sickness unto death."[233] And that terror does not just freeze the lower levels of my self—it does not just freeze my "maternal incest" or my "parental incest" or my "egoic incest"; it freezes my *overall* centauric intentionality, my wish to life *on the whole*.[25]

Because I am afraid of the death of the total bodymind, I have to be *careful* in life—I have to hold back, inhibit, and freeze my entire being.[25, 36] I thus freeze out, at the same time and for the same reason, intentionality and vision-image: there is no *vision* of my life and its meaning on the whole, so that I am left only with old egoic agitations and linear abstractions. They have gone flat in their appeal, yet I fear to move on. I freeze on this new level because I am faced with the death of this new level. I have found a higher self only to see it threatened globally by the skull of death which grins in again. There is now the possibility of new and higher Eros (self-actualization), but it necessarily brings in its wake the terror of new and subtler Thanatos—

the castration of the total bodymind. I have found a total self, only to
face total death. It is then impossible for me to orient meaningfully to
life's future because I am terrified of life's present....²²⁸

And so Maslow found that the greatest barrier to self-actualization
was the "Jonah Syndrome," which in its most general form is the
"fear of greatness." But why this fear of greatness, of full potential
and self-actualization? The real answer, Maslow says, is that "we are
just not strong enough to endure more!" Self-actualization and full
meaning in life, full openness to life, is just too much. As Maslow
puts it, "It is just too shaking and wearing. So often people in...ec-
static moments say, 'It's too much,' or 'I can't stand it,' or 'I could,
die'.... Delirious happiness cannot be borne for long." The Jonah
Syndrome, at root, is nothing more than the "fear of being torn apart,
of losing control, of being shattered and disintegrated, even of being
killed by the experience."²⁵, ²⁶³ So notice, the *fear of death* recoils as a
fear of life. This obviously occurred in some minor forms on all previous levels (as the castrations of those levels), but here we are faced,
for the first time, with the life and death of the total bodymind, and
this fear of death can conspire to freeze the potentials of this level, the
potentials for self-actualization and the possibilities of fundamental
meaning to existence.

I am sorry to have to treat this extraordinary topic so summarily,
because it is truly important. I can only say, by way of summary, that
the job of the existential therapist is to help the individual confront
centauric castration by helping him to *ground* himself in the present
so that, from this present-centered "courage to be,"³⁷⁷ he can then
start to *intend* and *mean* his future and thus find meaning in it. Self-
actualization.⁶⁴, ¹³¹, ²²⁸ For when all the egoic incests start to die, when
all egoic substitute gratifications go flat, what then? When all egoic
goals have been met, when history runs out of meanings for the soul,
what then? Without social, egoic, or personic substitutes, what then?
In T.S. Eliot's moving words,

"What shall I do now? What shall I do?
I shall rush out as I am, and walk the street
With my hair down, so. What shall we do tomorrow?
What shall we ever do?"
        The hot water at ten
And if it rains, a closed car at four.
And we shall play a game of chess,
Pressing lidless eyes and waiting for a knock upon
        the door.

As all the egoic drives wind down and go flat in their appeal, the
soul is naturally drawn into a reflection on life, on self, on being—and
the problem of *meaning* and *self-actualization* tends inexorably to
emerge, so that one's total bodymind or centaur is drawn into the
dilemma. According to the existentialists, one must face this dilemma
and move through it (not around it) so as to resurrect a vision-image
of one's own life and an intentionality and meaning for it. For the

existentialists tell us that the *meaning* of life is the same thing as the *wishing* for life, and one can summon the courage to wish one's life only by facing one's death.

All in all, the existentialist serves the ego's death and the centaur's emergence. The centaur is the new and higher self; its Eros is simply intentionality and the drive to self-actualization. Its Thanatos is simply the global anxiety of death—but here, for the first time, the self starts consciously and seriously to reflect on and acknowledge death *in general*. The centaur does not—as centaur cannot—accept its own death; but it is the first self-sense strong enough to openly face and confront death. And this is precisely why "The inauthentic person [of the typhonic or egoic realms] experiences anxiety less frequently and less intensely. He does not have the vivid awareness of lonely and unexpected death which Heidegger attributes to authenticity."[228] And part of the job of the centaur-level therapist is to help one confront this new fear with the "courage to be," and find a vision-image in the midst of that atmosphere of lonely and unexpected death.

Beyond that, there is only one way to transcend the death-seizure of the centaur, and that is to transcend the centaur itself: to differentiate from it, dis-identify with it. And that means one has to die to centauric incest. Odd as it initially sounds, one has to go *beyond* "meaning in my life" (because one is starting to go beyond "my"); one has to give up intentionality and "self-actualization" (because one has to give up "self"); one has to let go of self-autonomy (because "not I, but Christ" will soon motivate consciousness).

The centaur is indeed the new and higher self of this stage—but it is still a substitute self, still a mixture of truth and illusion, still imagining itself to be Atman and still under sway of the Atman-project. All we have said about the centaur being a higher-order self is true—but it is still not Atman and, therefore, is still playing itself the swaggering Hero. Nowhere is this form of the Atman-project seen more clearly than in the notion of "autonomy": to be self-sufficient, content to oneself, a miniature god, self-idol in the face of eternity. This is really nothing but the most sophisticated attempt of the separate subject to *remain* a separate subject—playing out its isolated tendencies, puffing up its limited potentials, assuming in its temporal character to be the Omnipotent and Autonomous God, taking *aseity* unto itself.

The centaur—like every previous structure—does indeed perform a necessary but *intermediate* function, and once the centaur has been actualized, it should be transcended, not glorified, and certainly not worshipped. The Eros of the centaur should eventually be surrendered; if this does not occur, then one remains in *fusion* with that level, stuck in its incests. Differentiation stops, development stops, transcendence stops, and one settles for the substitute gratification of isolated "autonomy," an autonomy *based* on the primal intuition of Autonomous Atman but displaced and perverted to the isolated and mortal organism. The whole point of the centaur—which is indeed a relatively strong and capable structure—is to *create a self strong enough to die,* not to create a self strong enough to brag about it, let alone become a humanistic encounter group leader forever.

If one can stand to differentiate from all that—if one can stand this new and demanding *separation anxiety*, stand to surrender centauric incest, stand to go "beyond self-actualization" and "autonomy"— stand, in fact, to let go *personal life on the whole*—then one is open to the transpersonal realms of the subtle and causal planes.

Subtle and Causal Evolution

I will treat the subtle and causal realms very briefly and succinctly, both because we have already covered many of the points, and because the essential points should be fairly obvious by now. There is simply a series of higher-order differentiations and unities, with new incests, new castrations, new identities and new substitute selves, until at the summit there is no self, only Self, and the Atman-project collapses back into Atman.

To start with the subtle: Through the *special conditions* imposed by the Guru or Master, the subtle realm begins to emerge from the ground-unconscious. Centauric translation winds down; subtle-level transformation begins. Eventually, the self *identifies* with this Archetypal structure—through *subtle incest* or subtle Eros—and then operates *as* that structure by dis-identifying with the centaur (and body and mind). Subtle incest, subtle Eros, then continues to operate from that subtle self: it takes the form of blissful love, direct incestuous union with the Guru and his or her lineage, ishtadeva union, sahasrara bliss-light, and so on. Incest in the higher realms of the subtle (beyond sahasrara) involves revelations of sound (nada), audible illumination, and ecstatic release from gross mortality in Radiant Presence. The soul starts to become "one with God," and that oneness or identification is effected via subtle incest *with* and *as* the Archetypal-Deity form.

That, briefly, is subtle incest—and it brings with it subtle castration. The most common form of subtle castration is the relentless fear of loosing Light, on the one hand, and the actual obliteration of the self by Light, on the other. The obliteration of the self by Light-Bliss is not the same as the identification or re-absorption of the self into the Light (which is what is supposed to happen). Subtle castration involves a disruption and destruction of the self, not its graceful transcendence and integration.

In subtle level development, the self is supposed to be re-absorbed by the yidam/ishtadeva/guru, which is actually one's own highest Archetype and thus involves not the loss or a lessening of consciousness but an intensification and expansion of consciousness. However, the subtle energies can invade and disrupt the self (subtle dissociation), and that is one form of subtle castration, usually brought on by a too rapid rise in subtle incest. This seems to happen frequently in kundalini yoga—the yogi pushes it too hard, sublimating gross incest into subtle incest, and is innundated by his own Archetypal energies.

The subtle self is an extraordinarily high-order self, close to Atman, but still not yet Atman. However, so subtle is the substitute self at this stage that it is almost always mistaken for Atman itself— and this makes it probably the most difficult form of the Atman-project to break. The individual will have to give up his subtle incest— his sahasrara bliss and light and his nad-sound ecstacy—if he is to break this *fusion* and pass into the causal. Should he be able to pass through the *separation anxiety* of the subtle, then he is open to the transcendence of the subtle, which leads, in due course, to the causal.

In the causal, the last major form of the ground-unconscious has emerged in and as consciousness, and thus *all* forms are reduced to, and re-absorbed by, Consciousness as Such. All forms are reduced to Archetype (in the subtle), which reduces to final-God (in the low causal), which reduces to Formless Consciousness (in the high causal). Now this fall into Formlessness is actually causal incest, and the extraordinarily subtle tension that develops between Form and the Formless—this is causal castration. That is, in nirvikalpa or jnana samadhi, there develops an extremely subtle tension (if that's the right word) between the Manifest and the Unmanifest. The fall into the Unmanifest, the Love of Release in Emptiness, is causal incest; and around that causal incest develops the subtle feeling that the Manifest realm detracts from Release—that the Manifest castrates Formless Radiance. This subtle tension is the last knot to uncoil from around the Heart.

If the individual can surrender causal incest—his exclusive love affair with the Void—then the ultimate state is resurrected as the only Real, final in all directions, where Form and Formless are each other. This state cannot be seen, because it is everything seen, and so remains Unshown. It cannot be heard, because it is everything heard, and so remains Unspeakable. It cannot be known, because it is everything known, and so remains Great Mystery.

As unknowable, unobstruced, unqualified Consciousness, it shines forth in completion from moment to moment, like an infinite series of ever-newly-perfected states, forever changing in its play, forever the same in its fullness. It appears to be the end limit of evolution, but is actually the prior reality of every stage of evolution, first to last, endlessly. In just this way, it is always and perfectly unattainable, simply because it is always already the case, timeless and eternal. It is just that, as all attempts to attain it, even in the causal realm, are finally undone, it is understood to have been fully present from the start, never lost and never regained, never forgotten and never remembered, but always already the case prior to any of that (which is why it is said that ordinary beings do not lack it and Buddhas do not possess it).

As infinite, all-pervading and all-embracing Consciousness, it is both One and Many, Only and All, Source and Suchness, Cause and Condition, such that all things are only a gesture of this One, and all forms a play upon it. As Infinity, it demands wonder; as God, it demands worship; as Truth, it demands wisdom; and as one's true Self it demands identity.

In its being, it has no obstructions, and this no trace continues forever. Bliss beyond bliss beyond bliss, it cannot be felt. Light beyond light beyond light, it cannot be detected. Only obvious, it is not even suspected. Only present, it shines even now.

17

Schizophrenia and Mysticism

Schizophrenia and mysticism have always been looked upon in a way similar to madness and genius—they seem to be both closely akin and somehow drastically different. But the similarity between schizophrenia and mysticism has lead to two general climates of belief about these two mental states. Those who look upon schizophrenia as an illness, as a sickness, as pure pathology of the worst sort, tend likewise to view all mysticism in a similar light (given their similarities). If the mystic-sages aren't purely pathological, then they are at least halfway there. "The psychiatrist," says a recent report from the Group for the Advancement of Psychiatry (GAP), "will find mystical phenomena of interest because they can demonstrate forms of behavior intermediate between normality and frank psychosis; a form of ego regression in the service of defense against internal or external stress...".[167] I have frequently agreed with, and often argued for, the fact that true regression can and does occur; that some who call themselves mystics are actually caught in some form of regression; and that some true mystics occasionally reactivate regressive complexes on their way to mature unity states. That, however, should not stop us from clearly and decisively differentiating schizophrenia and mysticism *per se*. Thus, as a blanket psychological statement on the nature of transcendence and mysticism, that GAP attitude is of quite limited help.

The second general attitude on schizophrenia and mysticism seems a little closer to the truth, but occasionally suffers from being as dogmatic and over-encompassing as the first attitude. This group tends to view schizophrenia as being, not pathological, but *super*-healthy. These researchers, whose views I otherwise hold in the very highest esteem (such as R.D. Laing[239] and Norman O. Brown[58]), are sympathetic to the notion that transcendent states are ultra-real (a point with which I agree), and since schizophrenia and mysticism seem so similar, the schizophrenic must also be an example of ultra-health. As Brown put it, "It is not schizophrenia but normality that is split-minded; in schizophrenia the false boundaries are disintegrating.... Schizophrenics are suffering from the truth.... The schizophrenic world is one of mystical participation; an 'indescribable extension of inner sense'; 'uncanny feelings of reference'; occult psychosomatic influences and powers...".[58]

My own opinion lies somewhere in between these two camps, and is based on the all-important distinctions between *pre* and *trans* which we outlined in chapter 7. In reference to Figs. 2 and 3, and based on the phenomenological reports now available on the schizophrenic experience itself, the typical schizophrenic episode usually involves the following factors:

1. The precipitating event is frequently some extremely stressful situation or relentless dilemma.[114] Prior to this, the individual may have had great difficulty in establishing social relations, have a fairly weak ego (as persona), and tend to isolationism.[6] On the other hand, the individual may simply be hit with the true dukhka or suffering inherent in samsara, and be temporarily overwhelmed by the painful insight.[239] Whatever the trigger (and I am not excluding biochemical factors—those are extremely important, and biochemical research into brain-based processes constitutes a psychiatric breakthrough of the first magnitude—I am not discussing those factors here since that would require several extra chapters and would not fundamentally alter the conclusions we will reach)—whatever the trigger, the egoic/personic translations break down or are greatly impaired (and the double-bind theory of schizophrenia would relate directly to this disruption of egoic translation or meta-programming).[23]

2. The disruption of the editing and filtering functions of egoic translation (secondary process, reality principle, syntaxical structuring, etc.), leaves the individual open to and unprotected from *both the lower and the higher* levels of consciousness. In my opinion, a *dual process* is thus set in motion: the self begins to regress to the lower levels of consciousness while, at the same time, it is opened to flooding by aspects of the higher realms (particularly the subtle). Put differently, as the individual moves into the subconscious, the superconscious moves into him. As he regresses to the lower, he is invaded by the higher. He is hit by the submergent-unconscious as well as the emergent-unconscious. I personally see no other way to account for the phenomenology of the schizophrenic break. Those who see schizophrenia as all regression totally overlook its real religious dimension, and those who see it as all super-spiritual and super-healthy just fly by the evidence of actual psychic fragmentation and regression.

At any rate, as egoic translation begins to fail, extreme anxiety usually results.[75] As regression starts, and egoic syntax disrupts, the individual is opened to mythic-thinking and magical references characteristic of the mythic-membership realms.[6] Mythic-thinking, as we saw, confuses part and whole, members and classes—and that is *the* defining characteristic of schizophrenic thinking.[6, 7, 23] For instance, a schizophrenic might say, "Last night I crawled into a bottle but couldn't get the cork in," when all he is reporting is that he had difficulty sleeping because he was cold. The mythic-logic runs like this: the bed with its covers or blanket belongs to the class of "containers"—that is, objects that can contain other objects. A bottle also belongs to this class, and since mythic-thinking cannot distinguish between members of a class, "getting into bed" and "getting into a bottle" are the *same thing* (not symbolic). In the same way, "covers" and "corks" are the same. "Can't get the cork in" means "the covers kept falling off"—and that is why he was cold and could not sleep: the cork kept falling out of the bottle. At Bateson would say, he is having trouble with logical types.

If regression goes even slightly past mythic-thinking, the individual is left open to florid pre-verbal phantasy and the primary process. That is, he hallucinates—usually audible, occasionally visual.[6, 114, 217]

3. The twist to the story comes: in my opinion, as the egoic translations begin to fail and the self is drawn into pre-egoic realms, it is also open to invasion (castration) from the trans-egoic realms. The individual's awareness is therefore often flooded with highly intense intuitions, frequently religious in nature (actual and valid spiritual insights, not just regressive phantasies). "Creative experience, religious conversion, and other 'peak experiences' may involve much of the...form of inner experience which can accompany the acute psychotic reaction."[114] That fact, it seems to me, just cannot be overlooked.

Frequently, however, the individual cannot coordinate these insights logically—if he reports something as simple as getting into bed as "crawling into a bottle", just imagine how he might describe a vision-image of Christ! On top of that, these insights tend to be very "autistic", self-oriented, secretive: he understands them, but nobody else can. This seems to be related to the fact that since this regressive side of schizophrenia tends to move into levels that are prior to or *pre*-to role comprehension, the individual thinks that he, and he alone, is (for example) Christ. He cannot take or admit the role of others, and so he cannot see that everybody is Christ. He intuits vividly and strongly his Atman-nature (an influx from higher levels), but he intuits it from only a primitive and narcissistic level. Here is a conversation between a mystic and an institutionalized schizophrenic, which perfectly points up what I am talking about:
Baba Ram Dass is speaking—

> He [the hospitalized schizophrenic] was producing voluminous amounts of material, reading Greek, which he had never been able to read. He was doing a number of phenomenal things which the doctors saw as pathological—the fact that he could steal, lie, and cheat and tell that he was Christ. He escaped from the hospital a number of times, a very creative fellow. My reading of his materials showed me that he was tuned in on some of the greatest truths in the world that have been enunciated by some of the highest beings. He was experiencing

these directly, but he was caught in a feeling that this was happening *only to him*.... And, therefore, he got into a messy predicament of saying, "I've been given this, and you haven't...". I said, "Do you think you're Christ? the Christ in pure consciousness?" He says, "Yes." I say, "Well, I think I am too." And he looks at me and he says, "No, you don't understand." I say, "That's why they lock you up, you see."[114]

4. Van Dussen, in some very important work based on Swedenborg, has phenomenologically distinguished two major forms of these hallucinations.[381] I can't really describe how he does it—too complicated—but for what it's worth I find his methods and conclusions valid. Basically, he simply "talks" to these hallucinations, via the patient, and does "biographical sketches" of them. And two types essentially emerge. The "lower ones" are generally malevolent, they "look like Freud's id," they are "anti-spiritual," and they "talk endlessly" (i.e., are verbal structures). Most importantly, they "reside in a lower but still unconscious area of the mind, the personal memory" and are "somehow bound to and limited within the patient's own experiences." The individual is hallucinating his own shadow. But the "higher order are purely visual and use no words at all [they are transverbal and subtle-realm]." They "look most like Carl Jung's archetypes." These hallucinations, that is, stem from purely subtle, transpersonal, and archetypal levels—and to *that* degree are real, not hallucinatory.

5. Finally, the individual may regress into actual uroboric and prepersonal structures, completely confusing self and other, inside and outside; time evaporates into pre-temporality, and the self system all but collapses. This is not an intuition of the trans-temporal Eternal Now—just the plain and simple inability to cognize temporal sequences, as Arieti's poor patients made so obviously clear.[6, 7]

Overall, schizophrenia shows us that, in search of unity—driven by the Atman-project—the individual can regressively move to any number of archaic or infantile unity structures, ranging from parental through maternal to uroboric to pleromatic. Erich Fromm seems to be perfectly aware of this phenomenon and its implications, and although he does not state the specific stages in detail, the following quote shows that he is quite cognizant of what is involved: "Man can strive to find this *regressive unity* at several levels, which are at the same time several levels of pathology and irrationality.

> He can be possessed by the passion to return to the womb, to mother earth, to death [pleromatic incest]. If this aim is all-consuming and unchecked, the result is suicide or insanity [pleromatic castration]. A less dangerous and pathological form of a regressive search for unity is the aim of remaining tied to the mother's breast [maternal incest], or to mother's hand, or to the father's command [parental incest]. Another form of regressive

orientation lies in destructiveness, in the aim of over-
coming separateness by the passion to destroy everything and everybody [what we call "substitute sacrifices"]. One can seek it by the wish to eat up and incorporate everything and everybody, that is, by experiencing the world and everything in it as food [oral fixa-
tion].[148]

Fromm, in that short quote, gives an example each of regressive
unity sought through pleromatic incest, maternal incest, parental
incest, and alimentary-uroboric incest—the whole spectrum. Yet with
all of that, Fromm is perfectly aware that the satori-mystical state is a
totally different type of unity: for mystical unity is "not the regressive
unity found by going back to the pre-individual, preconscious harmony of paradise [pleromatic-uroboric subconsciousness], but unity
on a new level: that unity which can be arrived at only after man has
experienced his separateness, after he has gone through the stage of
alienation from himself and his world, and has been fully born. This
new unity has as a premise the full development of man's reason,
leading to a stage in which reason no longer separates man from his
immediate, intuitive grasp of reality."[148] That fact is now so clear that
I do not see how it can be ignored any longer, and the facile equation
of the mystic with the psychotic can be done only by demonstrating
one's ignorance of the subtleties involved.

One final point, and an extremely significant one at that: the individual may or may not "return" to normal egoic reality after the
schizophrenic episode. If he does not, he tends simply to remain lost,
stuck, forsaken in the confusion of pre-verbal or even pre-personal
fragments. Most "chronic" schizophrenia is just that. It is almost
entirely pre-verbal, with little or no trans-verbal elements. The classic
"schizophrenic break", however, possesses that peculiar mixture of
both pre and trans that would allow Laing to write, "When a person
goes man, a profound transposition of his position in relation to all
domains of being occurs. His center of experience moves from ego to
Self. Mundane time becomes merely anecdotal, only the Eternal mat-
ters. The madman is, however, confused. He muddles ego with self,
inner with outer, natural and supernatural.... An exile from the scene
of being as we know it, he is an alien, a stranger, signaling to us from
the void in which he is foundering."[114]

If this individual does "return," and fairly completely, he is usually much better adjusted—he feels more capable, more open to the
world and less defended. But in *neither* case—remaining schizophrenic
or returning healed—does anything resembling "enlightenment" or
"moksha" occur. "There is nothing in the reports of recovered schizophrenics to suggest that once having freed themselves from the pathological patterns of their pre-morbid living they continue to explore
those inner experiences that had previously overwhelmed them. Unlike
the mystic, whose inner experiences are consciously chosen over a
period of time and developed within the cultural context, the schizophrenic's experience of his deepest feelings is sudden and occurs in the

denial of his social functioning [it is not trans-biosocial but pre-biosocial]. The flight into psychosis, if successful, restores his capacity to function as a productive member of society, but it does not necessarily prepare him for the life-long process of movement between inner [and transpersonal] experience and social functioning."[386]

The "successful" schizophrenic episode (where one returns "healed") seems to me a precise example of true regression in service of the ego. It is, as many researchers are now suggesting, a creative type of psychic re-adjustment and growth, a type of death and rebirth experience.[49, 217, 239, 347] Recovered schizophrenics tend to speak of their "old selves" as totally inadequate, maladjusted, fragmented, or even incapable of simple living. One woman spoke of her "breakdown" this way: "Something has happened to me—I do not know what. All that was my former self has crumbled and fallen together and a creature has emerged of whom I know nothing." But that former self which "has crumbled" was actually "a pitiful creature who could not cope with life as she found it—nor could she escape it—nor adjust herself to it. So she became mad, and died in anguish…".[386]

After five days of intense suffering, madness, and a literal death of her old self, this woman emerged with what she called a "new self," at relative peace with the world and her own being. *Not a transcendent self, not an enlightened self*, but a fairly well-adjusted self. A "healthy ego," as psychoanalysis would say.

My own feeling is that in these types of episodes, *one* of the things that occurs (again, I don't want to exclude biochemical factors, nor, on the other hand, do I want to deny that many phenomena incorrectly diagnosed as schizophrenia are really the beginnings of kundalini rising towards the subtle realms—the Sannella-Bentov interpretation) is that the individual regresses to a deep psychological structure that was traumatized during its construction in infancy or early childhood. Foremost among these, it seems to me, is the bodyself stage, the stage where self and not-self were first differentiated, the stage where consciousness is *supposed* to become firmly seated in the body, which, from that point on, will then act as a firm base of self-operations in the gross realm. R.D. Laing feels that a failure to seat consciousness in the body leads, during subsequent development, to an exaggerated split or dissociation between mind and body and the fabrication of a "false-self" system.[238, 289] Not only do I agree with his general points, I think my presentation of developmental sequences bears out that agreement. In particular, we might note the following:

In my opinion, the two "danger" points for schizophrenic etiology are the emergence of the bodyself stage and the emergence of the mental-egoic stage. A disruption of the bodyself stage tends to prevent the complete seating of consciousness in the body, so that a weak image-body becomes the base of subsequent personality construction, and helps lead to the "false-self" system. Essentially this occurs, I believe, with the emergence of the mental-egoic stage: because the personality is not firmly seated in a strong body-image, then as the ego begins to differentiate from the body, it is fated from the start to experience the body "incorrectly," as part of the "other"; and further, it will then necessarily fall prey (during the castration complex stages) to a more violent form of dissociation of mind and body than is usual, leaving the person with a "false self" dissociated from the body. Thus, according to Laing, the schizophrenic tends to experience his "mind" as being "self" while the body is felt to be "other."[238]

I would add, however, a small point to Laing: once the false self is created in a dissociation from the body, then the stage is set for what is usually the most dramatic aspect of schizophrenia. We have seen that, in general, at any point after the emergence of the ego, the subtle *can* emerge. Thus, from adolescence onwards, one is potentially open to the natural emergence of the subtle. The point is that, in the schizo- phrenic, if and when the subtle emerges, it is received only by the false self system. It does not meet a strong ego or centaur, but the tenuous- ly anchored false self. And *that*, I believe, results in the classic schizo- phrenic-break-with-religious-insight. The subtle floods the false self, forces regression to lower structures with simultaneous invasion from higher realms. And notice that statistically[200] the late twenties is the most common age of the schizophrenic break—the same age that the subtle can start to emerge. I am suggesting it is a breakthrough of the subtle and a breakdown of the self.

To return to our story: in the course of the severe break, the indi- vidual regresses to a deep structure (bodyself or otherwise) that was "traumatized" during its construction in infancy or early childhood. He literally regresses to that point,[6, 7] and then, as it were, re-builds the personality, ground up, from that point. Or one may say, after re-contacting or "re-living" that deep complex or deep structure dis- turbance, then the upper layers of consciousness spontaneously re- shuffle or re-build themselves around the newly refurbished deep structure. That is a true growth experience, a true regression in service of ego. This view is well expressed by Anton Boisen: "We may there- fore draw the conclusion that such [schizophrenic] disturbances are not necessarily evils but, like fever or inflammation in the physical organism, they are attempts by regression to lower levels of mental life to assimilate certain hitherto unassimilated masses of life experi- ence."[49]

All in all, the best that can be said of the schizophrenic break (not chronic schizophrenia) is that it is a true regression in the service of ego, followed by a progressive evolution to a healthier ego. It might also leave the individual, the new ego, with profound insights. Gen- erally, however, this movement is not desired and happens against one's will, depriving the individual of access to the structures of logic, syntax, membership, and ego. And the individual does not end up enlightened or in true unity consciousness, whatever else the outcome.

In the true mystic path of progressive evolution, none of the above holds, except the acknowledged fact that the mystic is exploring and mastering some of the same higher realms that overpower the schizophrenic. The mystic *seeks* progressive evolution. He trains for it. It takes most of a lifetime—with luck—to reach permanent, mature, transcendent and unity structures. At the same time, he maintains potential *access* to ego, logic, membership, syntax, etc. He follows a carefully mapped out path under close supervision. He is not contacting past and infantile experiences, but present and prior depths of reality.

I would like to end this chapter by pointing to the clinical work of Cooper, Laing, and Esterson, for it seems to me that in their writings as well as in their actual clinical work, they have done an unmatched job of advancing our phenomenological understanding of schizophrenia and its relationship to normality and sanity (the last two are not the same). I would simply like to present the diagram that Cooper uses to summarize the results of their entire orientation (see Fig. 4).[87]

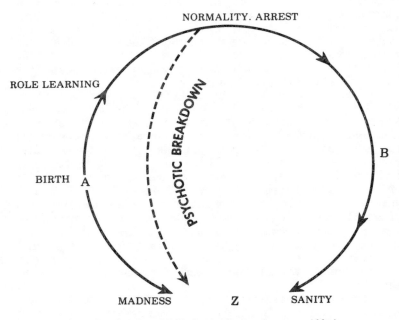

Fig. 4. Cooper's Life Cycle: Sanity, Arrest, and Madness

The reader will note the similarity between Fig. 4 and the basic model we have been presenting here (compare Fig. 4 with Fig. 3). The point A, which Cooper labels "birth," is analogous to our axial level, our bodyself stage. His "normality" is our ego-persona. The movement B is our Inward Arc, and the "psychotic breakdown" is our regression. All of the points in Cooper's figure beneath the "birth line" are (for us) either pre-personal (on the left) or trans-personal (on the right). Cooper's own explanation of this diagram is as follows:

From the moment of birth most people progress through the social learning situations of family and school until they achieve social normality. Most people are developmentally arrested in this state of normality. Some others break down during this progress and regress to what is called madness in the diagram. Others, very few, manage to slip through the state of inertia or arrest [ego/persona] represented by alienated statistical normality and progress [evolve] to some extent on the way (B) to sanity [the trans-personal for us], retaining an awareness of the criteria of social normality [i.e., retaining access to all lower levels, as we have frequently pointed out] so that they may avoid invalidation (this is always a dicey game). One should note that normality is "far out" at an opposite pole not only to madness but also to sanity [a point we have been at pains to emphasize]. Sanity approaches madness but an all-important gap, a difference, always remains. This is the omega point (Z).[87]

As for "sanity" as represented on his diagram, collaborator R.D. Laing puts it thus: "True sanity entails in one way or another the dissolution of the normal ego, that false self competently adjusted to our alienated social reality: the emergence of the 'inner' archetypal mediators of divine power, and through this death a rebirth, and the eventual re-establishment of a new kind of ego-functioning, the ego now being the servant of the Divine, no longer its betrayer."[114]

Finally, notice the omega point: whatever the final decision on the nature of the omega point, one thing is absolutely, finally, and undeniably certain: it exists. And that alone supports what one day will, I trust, be a simple truism: to Return to the Divine, one doesn't regress to infancy. Mysticism is not regression in service of the ego, but evolution in transcendence of the ego.

18

Involution

According to Hinduism, the relation of Brahman to the manifest universe actually consists of two major "movements": evolution and involution.[13] We have already examined evolution, which is the movement of the world towards Brahman-Atman. Involution is, more or less, the opposite of that—it is the movement whereby Brahman throws itself outward to create the manifest worlds, a process of *kenosis* or self-emptying which, at the same time, is a process of pure act and pure creativity. As evolution is a movement from the lower to the higher, involution is a movement from the higher to the lower—a movement which "enfolds" and "involves" the higher levels of being with the lower. It is a movement "down" the great Chain of Being. And this movement of involution is what we will briefly examine in this chapter (see Figs. 5 and 6).

I should warn the reader that at this point we are, as it were, driving in reverse—at least compared with the story of evolution that has, up to this time, occupied our attention. Heretofore, we have been talking of the generation of successively higher structures of consciousness, moving forward on the path of ascent. But now we will be telling the reverse side of the story—we will be discussing the prior descent and enfolding and involution of the higher modes of being down and into the lower modes. To understand this process, the reader must, so to speak, now learn to walk backwards.

For, according to the perennial philosophy, *in order* for evolution—which is the unfolding of higher structures—to occur at all, those higher structures must, *in some sense*, be present from the start: they must be enfolded, as *potential*, in the lower modes. If not, then evolution is nothing but creation *ex nihilo*, out of nothing. And, as theologians have long known, out of nothing you get nothing—*ex nihilo nihil fit*. And the story of involution is simply the story of how the higher modes came to be lost in the lower—how they came to be enwrapped and enfolded in the lower states. Involution, or the enfolding of the higher in the lower, is the pre-condition of evolution, or the unfolding of the higher states from the lower.

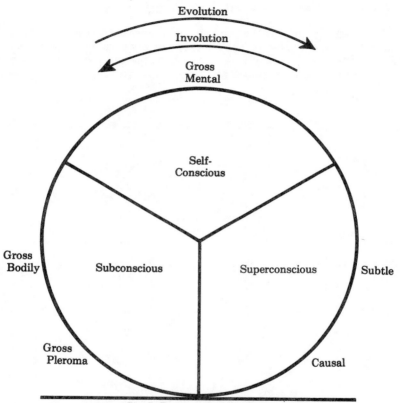

Fig. 5. Evolution and Involution

At the extreme point of involution—which is simply the *pleroma* or the material world—all of the higher and highest states of being lie enfolded as *undifferentiated potential*. The highest and the lowest, the infinite and the finite, spirit, mind, and matter—all are enfolded as undifferentiated and unconscious potential: *and that is the ground-unconscious*. Evolution is simply the unfolding of that enfolded potential—all the various modes of being can then eventually emerge from the ground-unconscious, starting with the lowest (pleroma) and ending with the highest (Atman). At each stage in this process, the fusion of lower and higher is replaced by the integration of lower and higher, a process that itself cannot occur until the lower and higher are differentiated and dis-identified. At the end of evolution, *all* of the struc-

tures enfolded in the ground-unconscious have emerged in consciousness, which drains the ground-unconscious and leaves only Atman, or
Consciousness as such.

The Tibetan Book of the Dead

Something happened to you before you were born. You may think
of this metaphorically, or symbolically, or mythically—or you may
take it literally, but something definitely happened to you before you
were born. In this chapter I will present one version of that extraordinary story.

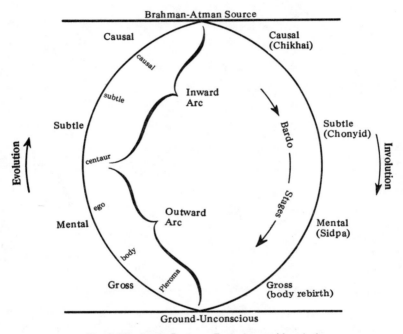

Fig. 6. The Bardo Passage—Evolution and Involution

The Tibetan Book of the Dead is one of several spiritual documents
which purport to tell of the "events" prior to birth (or rebirth). It
reports of the events which are said to occur from the moment of physical death until the moment of physical rebirth in a new body—a series
of events said to take up to a 49-day period. The Tibetan title of the
book is *Bardo Thotrol*, (most often in classical works it is spelled
Bardo Thodol) and Bardo means "gap," "transition state," "intermediate state," or as I prefer, "in between." The 49-day period is the
period "in between" death and rebirth.

But the actual birth event—delivery from the womb—is not the only type of birth. As the Buddhist sage Ippen put it, "Every moment is the last moment and every moment is a re-birth."[367] That is, birth and death are also occurring moment to moment, every moment, now. At each moment the entire universe and all its inhabitants spring into existence, and at each moment they are all reduced to their prior ground. At each moment they are born; at each moment they die. Since bardo is simply the state "in between" death and rebirth, it follows that there is a real bardo between this moment and the next. The bardo state, that is, occurs moment to moment with the rise and fall of the worlds.

Thus, there are two major bardos or "in betweens"—one occurs as a series of temporal events lasting up to 49 days after physical death, and the other occurs *now*, moment to moment. And the Tibetan tradition adds one simple and crucial point: *these two bardos are the same.* What happened to you before you were born is what is happening to you now, moment to moment. To understand one is to understand the other, which is why the Tibetans absolutely insist that the Book of the Dead is a precise manual on how to conduct one's *life*. We will briefly describe the events of the Bardo state as it is said to occur in the 49-day period following death, and then we will apply that understanding to the bardo state of moment-to-moment existence.

Something happened to you before you were born, and this is what it was:

Stage One: the Chikhai

The events of the 49-day Bardo period are divided into three major stages, the *Chikhai*, the *Chonyid*, and the *Sidpa* (in that order). Immediately following physical death, the soul enters the Chikhai, which is simply the state of the immaculate and luminous Dharmakaya, the ultimate Consciousness, the Brahman-Atman. This ultimate state is *given*, as a gift, to all individuals: they are plunged straight into ultimate reality and exist *as* the ultimate Dharmakaya. "At this moment," says the *Bardo Thotrol*, "the first glimpsing of the Bardo of the Clear Light of Reality, which is the Infallible Mind of the Dharmakaya, *is experienced by all sentient beings.*"[110] Or, to put it a different way, the Thotrol tells us that "Thine own consciousness, shining, void, and inseparable from the Great Body of Radiance, hath no birth, nor death, and is the Immutable Light—Buddha Amitabha. Knowing this is sufficient. Recognizing the voidness of thine own intellect to be Buddhahood...is to keep thyself in the Divine Mind."[110] In short, immediately following physical death, the soul is absorbed in and as the ultimate-causal body (if we may treat them together).

Interspersed with this brief summary of the *Bardo Thotrol*, I will add my commentaries on involution and on the nature of the Atman-project in involution. And we begin by noting that at the start of the Bardo experience, the soul is elevated to the utter heights of Being, to the ultimate state of Oneness—that is, he starts his Bardo career *at the top*. But, at the top is usually not where he remains, and the Thotrol tells us why. In Evans-Wentz's words, "In the realm of the Clear Light [the highest Chikhai stage] the mentality of a person...momentarily enjoys a condition of balance, of perfect equilibrium, and of [ultimate] oneness. Owing to unfamiliarity with such a state, which is an ecstatic state of non-ego, of [causal] consciousness, the...average human being lacks the power to function in it; karmic propensities becloud the consciousness-principle with thoughts of personality, of individualized being, of dualism, and, losing equilibrium, the conscious-principle falls away from the Clear Light."[110]

The soul falls away from the ultimate Oneness because "karmic propensities cloud consciousness"—"karmic propensities" means seeking, grasping, desiring; means, in fact, *Eros*. And as this Eros-seeking develops, the state of perfect Oneness starts to "break down" (illusorily). Or, from a different angle, because the individual cannot stand the intensity of pure Oneness ("owing to unfamiliarity with such a state"), he *contracts* away from it, tries to "dilute it," tries to extricate himself from Perfect Intensity in Atman. Contracting in the face of infinity, he turns instead to forms of seeking, desire, karma, and grasping, trying to "search out" a state of equilibrium. Contraction and Eros—these karmic propensities couple and conspire to drive the soul away from pure consciousness and downwards into multiplicity, into less intense and less real states of being. But at this point, let us simply remember the general role of 1) Eros and 2) contraction; and let us also note that right here the soul is starting to move from the highest state into lower states, which means that involution itself has just started.

According to the *Thotrol*, this whole buildup of karmic propensities, of Eros and seeking and contraction, occurs over and over again throughout all the various stages of the Bardo realm. With each successive contraction, the soul falls further away from the Source, a pattern that is repeated until contraction and Eros and karma wear themselves out and are exhausted as forces of involution. There is the essential message of the *Bardo Thotrol*. As Lama Kazi Dawa-Samdup explains, at the beginning of the Bardo, there is the first Clear Light "of ecstasy of greatest intensity. The succeeding stage is less intense. A ball set bouncing reaches its greatest height at the first bound; the second bound is lower, and each succeeding is still lower until the ball comes to rest."[110]

The ball, as it were, is the self in *involution*, which is driven by contraction and Eros, or "karmic propensities" to seek, grasp, and thirst, and it simply bounces itself out into more diluted and less energetic states. On the first bounce (already briefly examined) it goes through the ultimate-causal realm, on the second (as we will soon see) it bounces through the subtle realm, and on the third it bounces out into the gross realm of the physical body and subsequent rebirth. As Trungpa explains the general principle, "Some basic tendency of grasping [Eros/contraction] begins to develop in the state of luminosity..., then the energy builds up blindly and finally falls down into different levels of diluted energy, so to speak, from the absolute energy of the luminosity."[132] So that finally, according to the *Thotrol*, "the force of karma having spent itself, the consciousness-principle comes to rest"[110] — in the basement. Contraction-and-Eros finally wind down, the ball stops bouncing, transformation-downnward ceases, and the soul is reborn pleromatic and body-bound.

To return, however, to the *beginning* of this involution story, we simply note that, due to an individual's seeking and grasping and contracting, the prior rest in the Fullness of the Causal/Dharmakaya is abandoned. And has to be abandoned, because in the Dharmakaya there is only One, and seeking requires two (a seeking-subject and a sought-after object). Thus, stabilization fails and transformation-downward eventually ensues. With that, the individual enters the next stage of the In Between: the subtle realm.

Stage Two: the Chonyid

The Chonyid is the period of the appearance of the peaceful and wrathful deities — that is to say, the subtle realm, the Sambhogakaya. When the Clear Light of the causal realm is resisted and contracted against, then that Reality is *transformed* into the primordial seed forms of the peaceful deities (ishtadevas of the subtle sphere), and these in turn, if resisted and denied, are *transformed* into the wrathful deities.

The peaceful deities appear first: through seven successive substages, there appear various forms of the tathagatas, dakinis, and vidyadharas, all accompanied by the most dazzlingly brilliant colors and awe-inspiring supra-human sounds. One after another, the divine visions, lights, and subtle luminous sounds cascade through awareness. They are presented, *given*, to the individual openly, freely, fully, and completely: visions of God in almost painful intensity and brilliance.

Now, how the individual handles these divine visions and sounds (nada) is of the utmost significance, because each divine scenario is accompanied by a much less intense vision, by a region of relative dullness and blunted illuminations. These concomitant dull and blunted visions represent the first glimmerings of the world of samsara, of the six realms of egoic grasping, of the dim world of duality and fragmentation and primitive forms of low-level unity.

According to the Thotrol, most individuals simply *recoil* in the face of these divine illuminations — they *contract* into less intense and more manageable forms of experience. Fleeing divine illumination, they glide towards the fragmented — and thus less intense — realm of duality and multiplicity. But it's not just that they recoil against divinity — it is that they are *attracted* to the lower realms, drawn to them, and find satisfaction in them. The Thotrol says they are actually

"attracted to the impure lights." As we have put it, these lower realms
are *substitute gratifications*. The individual thinks that they are just
what he wants, these lower realms of denseness. But just because
these realms are indeed dimmer and less intense, they eventually
prove to be worlds without bliss, without illumination, shot through
with pain and suffering. How ironic: as a substitute for God, individuals create and latch onto Hell, known as samsara, maya, dismay.
In Christian theology it is said that the flames of Hell are God's love
(Agape) denied.

Thus the message is repeated over and over again in the Chonyid
stage: abide in the lights of the Five Wisdoms and subtle tathagatas,
look not at the duller lights of samsara, of the six realms, of safe illu-
sions and egoic dullness. As but one example:

> Thereupon, because of the power of bad karma, the
> glorious blue light of the Wisdom of the Dharmadhatu
> will produce in thee fear and terror, and thou wilt wish
> to flee from it. Thou wilt begat a fondness for the dull
> white light of the devas [one of the lower realms].
> At this stage, thou must not be awed by the divine
> blue light which will appear shining, dazzling, and glor-
> ious; and be not startled by it. That is the light of the
> Tathagata called the Light of the Wisom of the Dhar-
> madhatu.
> Be not fond of the dull white light of the devas. Be not
> attached to it; be not weak. If thou be attached to it,
> thou wilt wander into the abodes of the devas and be
> drawn into the whirl of the Six Lokas.[110]

The point is this: "If thou are frightened by the pure radiances of
Wisdom and attracted by the impure lights of the Six Lokas [lower
realms], then thou wilt assume a body in any of the Six Lokas and
suffer samsaric miseries; and thou wilt never be emancipated from the
Ocean of Samsara, wherein thou wilt be whirled round and round and
made to taste the sufferings thereof."[110]

But here is what is happening: in effect, we are seeing the primal
and original form of the Atman-project in its negative and contracting
aspects. In this second stage (the Chonyid), there is already some sort
of boundary in awareness, there is already some sort of subject-object
duality superimposed upon the original Wholeness and Oneness of
the Chikhai Dharmakaya. So now there is boundary—and wherever
there is boundary, there is the Atman-project. The individual, through
Eros and contraction, has illusorily split his own ultimate and non-
dual Consciousness into two major fragments: into a 1) subjective-self
which now witnesses, and 2) an objective display of illuminations
which are witnessed (divine illuminations, true, but "objective and
external" nonetheless). At the beginning of the Bardo state—when
the soul was "at the top"—the soul *was* all of that, he did not watch
it from afar. He simply *was* Oneness, with no subject-object split, in
the primal state of Unity disclosed in the Chikhai. But now he has

split that Oneness into a subjective-self, on the one side, and an objective-display on the other. There is now boundary, now Atman-project, now Eros, now Thanatos. All of that comes crashing into existence with the first Boundary.

Because the soul is now no longer the All, it feels, for the first time, a *lack*, and thus a *desire* (Eros). And the only way the soul will not suffer this lack is when the soul *recovers* that Original Oneness as Brahman-Atman. At the very base of its being, therefore, the soul desires this state of Oneness—nothing less than that will satisfy it. *This is the original Atman-desire and Atman-telos.* Dante saw it clearly: "The desire for perfection is that desire which always makes every pleasure appear incomplete, for there is no joy or pleasure so great in this life that it can quench the thirst in our Soul."³⁵² Even Freud intuited this, although he not surprisingly messed it up with his sexual obsessions: "What appears as...an untiring impulsion toward further perfection can easily be understood as a result of the instinctual repression upon which is based all that is most precious in human civilization. The repressed instinct [actually, repressed Atman consciousness] never ceases to strive [Eros] for complete satisfaction [ananda-bliss], which would consist in the repetition [satori] of a primary experience of satisfaction [unity consciousness as the One]. No substitutive or reactive formations and no sublimations will suffice to remove the repressed instinct's persisting tension."¹³⁹ This is also St. Augustine's *corr irrequitum*, and this is the message of Plato's *Symposium*: "This becoming one instead of two was the very expression of mankind's ancient need. And the reason is that human nature was originally One and we were a whole, and the desire and pursuit of the whole is called love."

The only way the soul—now in the subtle Chonyid stage—can recover that Oneness is to *re-unite* the subjective self with the objective and divine display of illuminations which are now cascading past in *front* of it. And this is precisely what the Thotrol recommends; over and over again it almost pleads with the soul at this stage: *"If all objective phenomenon shining forth be understood to be nothing but the emanations of one's own Consciousness, Buddhahood will be obtained at that very instant of recognition."*¹¹⁰

Yet to re-unite the subject and object is to *die* to the *subject*, or relax the exclusive contraction of consciousness around the separate self sense. And the subject, the separate self sense, is horrified of this death, this Thanatos, this Sunyata. That is precisely why the subject becomes so terrified of the divine-illuminations and why it fears so much to re-unite with God: it means death. The pure radiances threaten literal death and dissolution—they are manifestations of Shiva and Sunyata.

Here, then, is the origination of that fundamental dilemma which I have often mentioned: the great dynamic of the self is to recapture or return to the original Oneness. But to *actually* return to that Oneness means a death and dissolution of the self, and this death is precisely what is now avoided or resisted. And there is the dilemma—the self wants that Unity, but seeks it in a way that absolutely prevents it.

That is where the Atman-project steps in. Since real, immediate, and undiluted Unity is not now possible for the separate self sense (because that demands death), then the soul must seek some sort of *substitute* for the lost Unity. And this substitute, in order to work, *must present as fulfilled* the wish for prior Unity. And since the substitute obviously is not real, not true Unity, not actual Atman, then it can only be symbolic or pretend or relative: it is a half-truth, known as the Atman-project. Each level of the spectrum is thus constructed as a symbolic substitute for lost unity, so that ultimately each level of the spectrum is (prior to enlightenment) a substitute for Atman-consciousness.

Remember that we are now discussing *involution*, not evolution. The Atman-project is at work in both because substitutes are at work in both, but the directions are obviously reversed. We saw that *evolution* was indeed a series of substitute gratifications and substitute selves and substitute unities—but in evolution each substitute was of a higher-order, was closer to the Source, was more Real or, if you will, was less substitutive. And that "upward-movement" or transformation-upward occurred precisely because the self accepted the *death* and Thanatos of each lower unity so that higher unities could emerge in consciousness. Evolution continued as long as the self could (eventually) accept the death of its present structure, dis-identify with it, and transcend it to higher structures, more unified, less substitutive. And this emergence of higher-order unities is driven by that original Atman-telos—in Christian terms, Agape.

But in *involution* that is precisely what does *not* occur. The self does not at any stage accept death and Thanatos, it does not operate with Agape but with contraction, not Atman-telos but Atman-restraint. These forces (Agape, contraction, Eros, Thanatos) can be displayed as follows:

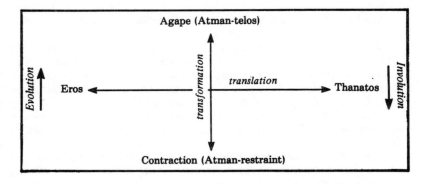

In *evolution*, as each higher stage emerged (through Agape), the self then identified with it, and *while* identified with it, the self's Eros did indeed fight and deny that level's Thanatos: the self would not accept the death of its present level, and so it created all sorts of death-denials and immortality projects for that particular level. Eventually, however, the Eros of that stage wound down, and Thanatos was finally accepted—the self "died" to that level, dis-identified with it, and transcended it to a higher-order level. Evolution continued as long as Agape and Thanatos eventually overcame Eros and contraction.

In involution, just the opposite occurs: Eros and contraction win out over Agape and Thanatos. Each substitute self is thus of a lower order; each bounce of the ball is lower and lower and lower.

Eros and Thanatos are basically forces of translation—they rage across the face of any present level, they battle horizontally for the soul's fate. But Agape and contraction are best thought of as forces of transformation—they pull, in opposite directions, for the self to change levels altogether. As long as Eros wins out over Thanatos on a given level, then the translations of that level continue more-or-less undisturbed. But when Thanatos outweighs Eros, then translation fails, and the self system begins transformation, or vertical change of level. And if *Agape exceeds contraction, then the transformation is upward*: the Atman-project moves closer and closer to Atman itself—that is evolution. But if *contraction exceeds Agape, then the transformation is downward*: the Atman-project moves further and further away from Atman—that is involution. The Atman-project is involved in both because substitutes are involved in both; the directions are different for each because the forces of transformation are reversed.

If we return now to the soul in the subtle realm—the Chonyid stage—I think much of this will become clear. At the Chonyid stage, the soul has passed out of the ultimate-causal realm (the Chikhai), and into the subtle realm of divine and archetypal illuminations (Chonyid). But the soul did not just leave the ultimate Oneness of the previous stage, just like that! As we said, in order to sustain the extraordinary loss of the One, the soul has to arrange various *compensations*. And since the One was (illusorily) lost because the subject-object duality was superimposed upon It, then these compensations and substitutes can be played out through both the subjective fragment and the objective fragment of awareness (the two wings of the Atman-project).

To take the objective side first: Since the soul no longer *is* the One, it has only visions or pictures of that Oneness, and these "objective visions" are all it has left of an awareness that once *was* the One itself. In place of direct, formless, and immediate union with the One, the soul substitutes mere visions or forms of the One, and these archetypal forms actually operate to separate the soul from the Oneness itself. They hold open the split between subject and object. But notice: these subtle forms are part of the soul's substitute gratifications; it latches onto them instead of onto the Real One and unity with It. Instead of being the All (in the causal Chikhai), the soul is suckled by *forms of* the All (in the subtle Chonyid). And these (archetypal) forms and visions are, according to the Thotrol, nothing other than the peaceful deities, the ishtadevas, the subtle illuminations and sounds which now cascade through awareness. Instead of being God, the individual listens to and perceives reduced versions of God, known as nada, ishtadeva, subtle sound and light. The ultimate One, as the Thotrol says, is *transformed* (downward) into the subtle divinities, and these dancing visions, archetypal and primordial, now act as substitute gratifications for the substitute self, consolation prizes for Paradise Lost. They are substitute objects. The soul no longer *is* God, but merely has a vision *of* God.

But that is not the only substitute gratification, for there is the subjective side of the Atman-project as well. Since the soul no longer *is* the non-dual Dharmakaya of Oneness, it is transformed into a watcher-principle, a subjective tendency, a constricted mode of awareness that no longer is the All but, now cut off from the whole, merely stands back to watch *aspects* of the whole *appear* objectively. *In place* of the Atman-Self the soul settles for a *separate self* which, contracting inward on itself, appears set apart from the subtle realm at large. But remember the condition of a substitute self—it must pretend to fulfill the desire for Atman-consciousness, the desire to be cosmocentric and "in charge" of, or at least central to, the universe. And this the soul arranges by *focusing* its prior Unity consciousness onto itself, and placing this focused self in the very center of its focused universe. Instead of *being* the Universe at large, the soul then merely *seems* central to the Universe at large.

This is what we mean when we say that a substitute self *presents as fulfilled* the wish to be cosmocentric, to be Atman, to be the Source. It is a self which substitutes for the illusorily lost Atman and pretends to itself, in symbolic form, to be that lost Atman. Since 1) the self wants to recapture Atman-consciousness, but 2) since it is terrified of the necessary death and transcendence involved, then 3) it arranges a compensation and a substitute: it takes the intuition of Atman-consciousness that always arises moment-to-moment and subverts it to itself. It is *seeking* Atman in ways that *prevent* it and force symbolic *substitutes*. Remember the quote from Hubert Benoit? How can the soul live without Atman? "He arrives at it, essentially, through the play of his imagination, through the faculty which his mentality possesses of recreating a *subjective world whose unique motor principle this time he is*. The man would never resign himself to not being the unique motive-power of the real universe [i.e., not being Atman] if he had not this consoling faculty of *creating a universe for himself*, a universe which he creates all alone."

And yet, we heard Benoit add, "Man only seeks to deify himself in the temporal sphere because he is ignorant of his real divine essence. Amnesic, he suffers from illusorily feeling himself abandoned by God (while he is in reality God himself), and he fusses about in the temporal sphere in search of affirmations to support his divinity which he cannot find there."

Thus, in place of Atman-consciousness, which is always his true and prior estate, though one he has illusorily abandoned, he "fusses about" in search of substitutes which will pretend (convincingly) to present him as cosmocentric, deified, unique immortal, one without a second—a search based on the prior intuition of his Real Self, which is indeed infinite and eternal, but an intuition perverted by its application to his separate self, which is absolutely finite and mortal. In place of unity consciousness, the individual, on the one side, takes as a substitute self an inward-subjective world, and, on the other, he creates a "world-out-there" as a substitute object, and he places this substitute self squarely in the middle of this substitute world (so as to appear cosmocentric). The inward-self and outward-world are both symbolic substitutes for lost Unity, which was neither subjective nor objective but simply Whole. These are the substitute gratifications with which he consoles himself at the loss of Oneness, and through which he now engages the drama of his separate self sense, the play of his desires, and the search for Atman-substitutes targeting on his individuality.

And—to return to the story of the Bardo state—the soul, now in the subtle realm (the Chonyid), has both a substitute self and a substitute world. The separate self, imagining itself cosmocentric and invulnerable, settles back now to watch the divine display of subtle visions and lights and archetypal ecstasies which now flood its own awareness. And these substitute gratifications do indeed gratify. But not for long. However divine and archetypal this realm, it is still only a substitute, and the soul eventually starts to grow agitated with its pacifiers.

If it could, at this point, *accept the death and transcendence* of the separate self, it would immediately revert to and as the One. The Bardo Thotrol is very clear about that point. But the soul is in flight from death and sacrifice, and thus the peaceful deities begin to *transform* into the wrathful deities. "Therefore," says the Thotrol, "after the cessation of the dawning of the Peaceful and Knowledge-Holding Deities, who come to welcome one, the 58 flame-enhaloed, wrathful, blood-drinking deities come to dawn, who are *only the Peaceful Deities in changed aspect* [transformation]."[110]

Because the soul is now operating in the subtle realm, with subtle Eros and subtle-incest, it is open to subtle-castration. Thanatos, Shiva, and King Death—these now crash onto the scene with blood-drinking fury—literally. And this is something the soul hadn't bargained for! The soul thought that it was getting all sweetness and light when it rejected the One and took as a substitute the less intense realm of the subtle-deities. But *wherever* there is other there is fear; there is now other because there is now boundary. Divine other is simply divine terror. And through the subtle realm come marching 58 blood-drinking terrors to prove it.

The soul—because of its subtle-incest—is open to subtle castration. Now in evolution, the self progresses upward by *passing through* the castration-terror and separation-anxiety, *accepting* the death of the particular level, and thus transcending that level via Agape. Not so in involution. The self does *not* accept the death of its present structure—what it does, in effect, is simply pass out from terror. As the Bardo Thotrol puts it, the self simply "swoons" or "blanks out". In more modern terms, it represses the whole affair, the entire subtle realm, peaceful and wrathful, and renders it all unconscious. The soul falls into a swoon—goes blank—falls unconscious—and then "awakens" in the next lower bardo, even though it arranged the whole drama itself and dictated the entire course of events.

Thus, the Atman-project of the subtle level eventually fails miserably its soothing mission: the substitute self of the subtle realm is not, after all, immune to death and the flame-enhaloed, wrathful, blood-drinking fate of all separate selves and substitute subjects. The substitute self does *not* promise immortality and everlasting perfection; it is not, after all, the prime and autonomous mover of self and other; it is not cosmocentric, heroic, God-like. And so when real Death and Thanatos threatens, the subtle self contracts and then passes out in terror, and awakens to find itself in the next bardo. Translation fails, and transformation ensues. And since contraction outweighs Agape, the transformation is downward. Involution continues.

Stage Three: the Sidpa

Thus the individual is tossed—by his efforts to find a substitute for Atman—into the sidpa stage, which is the realm of the gross-reflecting mind, the realm where the mind starts to turn towards the gross, physical world in search of its substitutes. In this realm, the soul experiences an intense incest/castration battle, represented in the Bardo Thotrol by a terrifying judgement from the Lord of Life (Eros) and the Lord of Death (Thanatos). And what is the form of incest of this level? In the words of the Thotrol, "O nobly born, at this time thou wilt see visions of males and females in union. If [about] to be born as a male, the feeling of being a male dawneth upon the knower, and a feeling of intense hatred towards the father and of jealousy and attraction towards to mother is begotten [if female, the opposite]."[110]

And there we are, about to enter the lowest of all realms—pleromatic and typhonic, with body-sexual incest and body-sexual castration, with Oedipus and Electra, with the pleasure principle and Freud and all. The substitute self is now gross-reflecting, tending towards body-bound modes, typhonic and uroboric, and its substitute gratifications are reduced to simple hedonistic pleasure and sexual release. According to the Thotrol, if—in this vision of the male/female union—the soul tries to separate them, then it winds up reborn with that couple as parents. Its simple Atman-project is reduced to trying to be cosmocentric by separating the parents, heroically stealing the female from the male by coming between them—which it does, literally, and—terrified of the impending crises—it goes once again into a swoon, passes out, represses the whole Sidpa realm, and emerging from the mother's womb, wakes up in the gross realm, merged with the pleroma, forgetful of the whole affair.

Amnesia and the In Between

But look at all that the soul has passed through *in order* to be born! From the ultimate Oneness, the clear light of the omnipresent Dharmakaya, through the subtle Sambhogakaya, the divine and illuminative bliss, through the gross-reflecting mental realm of the Sidpa stage, and then into the gross body and pleromatic rebirth. Through all of that. And the individual *was* all of that. In the Bardo experience, he started out as God and ended up as typhon. And he can't remember a single thing that happened In Between....

Here is what happens: we saw that at each stage of involution, the soul constructs a substitute self and a substitute world. The causal (if we had treated it separately), the subtle, the mental and the bodily—all were created as substitute formations to present the self as death-less, god-like, immortal and cosmocentric. But the substitutes eventually failed at each stage, and the self—terrified of its own dissolution—did not accept the death of its substitutes but merely *contracted* and then passed out in terror. "The passing from one Bardo to another," says Evens-Wentz, "is analogous to the process of birth; the knower wakes up out of one swoon or trance state and then another, until the third [and last] Bardo ends...".[110] The individual, therefore, "is represented as retrograding [what we call involution or transformation-downward], step by step, into lower and lower states of consciousness."[110] *Looking for Wholeness in ways that prevent it, the individual is driven to create ever tighter and narrower and more restricted modes of identity.* Looking for Atman in ways that forestall it, the individual is driven to create substitutes that contain ever less consciousness and ever less Atman. Thus is created the spectrum of consciousness.

But since each of these "steps down" is accompanied by a swoon of forgetfulness, the entire sequence is rendered unconscious—*rendered unconscious*—not destroyed, not removed, not vacated, but rendered unconscious. Which means: all of the higher levels are *present*, but they are simply forgotten (or, if you wish, it would be proper in involution to speak of the higher realms as being repressed, or forcefully screened out of awareness).

And, very simply, the result of that entire sequence of forgetting is the *ground-unconscious*. Thus, enfolded and enwrapped in the ground-unconscious of the newborn lie all the higher states of being. They were put there by involution, and they exist there as *undifferentiated potential*. Development or evolution is simply the unfolding of these enfolded structures, beginning with the lowest and proceeding to the highest: body to mind to subtle to causal.

We already saw that in evolution each of these structures emerges as a *substitute* gratification, and is abandoned when it ceases to gratify. And we can see now that each of them emerges as a substitute in evolution because each was *created* as substitute in involution. The self can climb back up this involved chain of substitutes only by tasting them, finding them lacking, accepting their death, and thus transcending them (all of which the self in involution refused to do). But the self will evolve up the chain of being only to the point at which it will accept the substitute gratifications as satisfactory (bodily substitutes, or mental substitutes, or subtle ones, or causal ones). At that particular level, its incest settles in, it accepts its substitutes as real, its Eros wins out over Thanatos, it will not undergo the separation anxiety of transcending and dying to that level, and so evolution stops cold (for this lifetime). The self has, in this life, gotten as close as it can to the Source (while still imagining it *is* the Source). In the Bardo state after its physical death, it will then *involve* as far as it has *evolved*, and a highly evolved being will escape involution altogether: at the first stage of the Clear Light, this soul will remain One *as* the Clear Light—it will not contract in the face of God nor recoil from the embrace of eternity; and, refusing to create any substitute subjects or substitute objects, it will never again be reborn as a separate self (although it might choose to be reborn as tulku, as avatar, or as bodhisattva—final enlightenment awaits only those who vow not to "step off" until all are liberated).

But to return to the newborn: because all of the deep structures of the various levels—gross, mental, subtle, causal—*already* exist as potentials in the ground-unconscious, they do not have to be created, just remembered. They were *en*folded through swooning and forgetting, and now they *un*fold through awakening and remembering. As the deep structures are themselves remembered (via Agape), their surface structures are filled-in by the events that transpire in *this* realm and *this* lifetime. As we said, deep structures are remembered, surface structures are learned (there are naturally a few exceptions—specific past-incarnation memories are an example of remembered surface structures).

Now this unfolding or manifesting of successively higher modes *appears* to the psychologist as the emergence of the higher "from" the lower—and many try to so define it: the ego is said to come *from* the id, the mind is said to come *from* conditioned body reflexes, the soul is said to come *from* the instincts, man is said to come *from* amoebas. In fact, the higher comes *after* the lower, and *separates itself out of* the lower, but it does not come *from* the lower. It is now common knowledge that at each stage in development or evolution, elements emerge that *cannot* be accounted for solely in terms of the stages that preceded it. Piaget himself has made that very clear;[297] so has Polanyi.[298] One cannot logically, ontologically, psychologically, or metaphysically derive the higher from the lower. The higher modes can emerge because, and only because, they were enfolded, as potential, in the lower modes to begin with, and they simply crystallize out and differentiate from the lower modes as evolution proceeds. This is exactly what Aurobindo means when he says: "Since this Consciousness [ultimate Brahman-Atman] is creatrix of the world, it must be not only state of knowledge, but power of knowledge, and not only a will to light and vision, but a will to power and works. And since mind, too, is created out of it [Atman], mind must be a *development by limitation* out of this primal faculty and this...supreme consciousness [that "development by limitation" is precisely involution] and must therefore be capable of resolving itself back into it through a *reverse development by expansion* [and that is evolution]."[306] Evolution, then, is a remembrance of involution—a rediscovery of the higher modes which were enwrapped in the lower ones during the soul's flight from God.

Thus evolution—wherever it appears—manifests itself as a series of transcendences, of ascents, of emergences—and emergences of higher-order *wholes*. For to remember is really to re-member, or join again in unity, and that is just why evolution consists of a series of ever-higher wholes until there is only Wholeness. Evolution is holistic because it is nature's remembrance of God.

And here, finally, is the other meaning of the Bardo, of the In Between, and if you feel that "reincarnation" or "rebirth" is unacceptable, then this might be easier to accept (although they both are really *exactly* the same): not only did the whole involutionary series occur prior to one's birth, one re-enacts the entire series moment to moment. In this moment and this moment and this, an individual *is* Buddha, is Atman, is the Dharmakaya—*but*, in this moment and this moment and this, he ends up as John Doe, as a separate self, as an isolated body apparently bounded by other isolated bodies. At the beginning of *this* and every moment, each individual *is* God as the Clear Light; but by the *end* of this same moment—in a flash, in the twinkling of an eye—he winds up as an isolated ego. And what happens In Between the beginning and ending of *this* moment is identical to what happened In Between death and rebirth as described by the Thotrol.

This moment-to-moment phenomenon we call "microgeny"—the micro-genetic involution of the spectrum of consciousness.[412] Each moment, the individual passes through the entire Bardo sequence—ultimate to causal to subtle to mental to gross—and he remembers only to the extent he has *evolved*. If an individual has evolved to the subtle realm, then he will remember the gross, mental, and subtle aspects of consciousness, but he will not remember the causal and ultimate aspects *of this moment's experience*: they remain in the emergent unconscious, awaiting emergence via remembrance. Evolution is simply the interception of micro-involution at higher and higher stages: the more evolved a person is, the less involved he is.

The soul's duty in this life is to remember. The Buddhist *smriti* and *sati-patthana*, the Hindu *smara*, the Sufi *zikr*, Plato's recollection,

Christ's *anamnesis*: all of those terms are precisely translated as re-membrance. "It is precisely a failure to remember," says Coomara-swamy, "that drags down from the heights the soul that has walked with God and had some vision of the truths, but cannot retain it."[84] But there, of course, is the exact message of the Thotrol. No wonder Neumann concluded that "Man's task in the world is to remember with his conscious mind what was knowledge before the advent of consciousness."[279] Likewise, "The Saddik finds that which has been lost since birth and restores it to men."[279]

And so, the soul that finally remembers all this, and sees it how-ever vaguely, can only pause to wonder: How could I have forgotten? How could I have renounced that State which is the only Real? How could my soul have sunk to such that misery alone embraced it? But to see this now, to remember only God in all that passes and mark the grace of that very Self outside of which is nothing—how could the mark be ever missed? How could the mark be missed....

At that final remembrance, the impact of only God in absolute Mystery and radical Unknowing dismantles once and for all the At-man-project. There is no longer the Atman-project, for there is only Atman, radical, radiant, all-pervading, perfectly ecstatic in its release, perfectly ordinary in its operation, perfectly obvious in its way. But Atman is Unseen. Atman is Unknown. Atman is Unspoken. Prior to all that arises, It is not other than all that arises, so it can be seen after all: Dogen Zenji—

This slowly drifting cloud is pitiful!
What dreamwalkers we all are!
Awakened, the one great truth:
Black rain on the temple roof.

For all the eons we have searched for this. For all the eons we have wanted this. But for all the eons there was only this: Black rain on the temple roof....

And because there is always only Atman, the Atman-project never occurred.

Appendix—Reference Tables

Reference Tables

As a type of survey and summary of the various stages of the ascent of consciousness, I have compiled several reference tables, included herein. There are a few disclaimers, however, that I must put forward. Although I have placed side-by-side such items as cognitive development, moral development, and ego development, I do not at all mean to equate them. As a general comparison, however, I have decided not to try to separate all the various threads of psychological development. As I mentioned at the beginning of this book, that task is in many ways beyond our present-day knowledge. It is fairly obvious that, for example, intellectual development is independent of psychosexual development. Loevinger, for one, thinks ego development is independent of psychosexual development.[248] Kohlberg has shown that intellectual development is necessary but not sufficient for moral development.[229] And so it goes, with all sorts of various developmental threads running parallel, independent, and/or correlative with all sorts of other developmental threads. I naturally have my own thoughts on the matter, but that is an entire study in itself, and one which will have to await further advances in developmental studies and research.

No, what I am doing here is simply setting out all the various stages of various developmental schemes suggested by respectable researchers, so that the general trend—which is the ascent of consciousness—can be seen at a glance. This will not only help us see the general ascent of consciousness on the whole, it will also help us direct further research into the higher stages of evolution and self-development. I should mention that the table correlations of Western researchers was helped significantly by the works of Loevinger,[248] Arieti,[7] Di Leo,[97] Jones,[204] and Roberts.[321]

As a typical example of the data that the tables represent, let us take Maslow's hierarchy of needs,[321] which several researchers have suggested can also serve as a developmental sequence.[243] It runs as follows: the infant must first satisfy its simple *physiological needs*, such as hunger—which is our alimentary uroboros. As the infant bodyego emerges from its fusion-state with the environment, it is then faced with the *safety needs*, the need to secure itself as a stable being in the face of the Great Other. As the self-system eventually evolves into membership cognition and membership awareness, it is faced with the *need for belonging* (and love)—that is, the need to belong to a membership-group larger than one's bodyself. As the self-system eventually matures to the middle and late egoic stages, as the ego itself clearly emerges, then so do the self-esteem needs (a point Carl Rogers has also made).[187] As the individual evolves to the mature centaur level, then the *self-actualization needs* tend to emerge (as we saw in chapter 7). Finally, "beyond self-actualization" is the *need for transcendence*—into the transpersonal realms, subtle and causal. All of that is summarized on Table 4 by a simple listing of Maslow's stages next to our corresponding ones.

TABLE 1.				
Approximate mode of self sense	Kabalah[338]	Aurobindo[11,12]	Grof[166] (approximate correlations)	Green and Green[163]
Pleromatic Uroboric Axial-body	malkuth	Subconscient physical	Somatic Aesthetic	1 Physical
Pranic-body Image-body	yesod	vital emotional		2. Emotional
Membership-cognition Early egoic/personic Middle egoic/personic Late egoic/personic	hod netzach	Will Reasoning mind Physical ego Idea-mind	Psychodynamic Freudian COEX systems	3 Mental
Mature ego Biosocial Centaur	tipareth	Higher mental-body	Existential/death-rebirth	4 Intuitional
Low subtle	geburah chesed	Illumined mind	Psychic/astral events	
High subtle		Intuitive mind	Archetypal/deity/illumination	Level 5
Low causal High causal	binah chokmah	Overmind Supermind	Universal Mind Supracosmic Void	Level 6
Ultimate	kether	Brahman/ Paramatman	Ultimate	Level 7

TABLE 2.

Approximate mode of self sense	Loevinger[243] (ego levels)	Buddhist Vijnanas[362] (levels of consciousness)	Erikson[108] (psychosocial stages)
Pleromatic	Presocial		
Uroboric	Symbiotic	Five vijnanas (five senses)	Trust vs. Mistrust
Axial-body			
Pranic-body	Impulsive		
Image-body			
Membership	Self-protective		Autonomy vs. shame and doubt
Early egoic/personic	Conformist		Initiative vs. guilt
Middle egoic/personic	Conscientious-conformist	Manovijnana (gross-mind)	Industry vs. inferiority
Late egoic/personic	Conscientious		Identity vs. role confusion
Mature ego	Individualistic		Intimacy vs. isolation
Biosocial Bands	Autonomous		Generativity vs. stagnation
Centaur/existential	Integrated		Integrity vs. despair
Low subtle		Manas (subtle mind)	
High subtle			
Low causal		Tainted alaya-vijnana (collective psyche)	
High causal			
Ultimate		Cittamatra	

TABLE 3.

Approximate mode of self sense	Kohlberg[229] (moral development)	Psychosynthesis[10]	Piaget[297] (cognitive development)
Pleromatic / Uroboric	1. Punishment and obediance	Lower collective unconscious	Sensori-motor
Axial-body / Pranic-body		Lower unconscious	
Image-body	2. Instrumental hedonism		Pre-conceptual pre-operational
Membership-cognition	3. "Good boy-nice girl" conformity		Intuitive pre-operational
Early egoic/personic			
Middle egoic/personic	4. Law and order	The conscious self (with middle unconscious)	Concrete operational
Late egoic/personic	5. Social contract		
Mature ego / Biosocial Bands / Centaur	6. Universalism		Formal operational
Low subtle / High subtle		The higher unconscious	
Low causal		The higher collective unconscious	
High causal / Ultimate		The transpersonal Seif	

TABLE 4.

Approximate mode of self sense	Ferenczi (F),[121] Ausubel (A)[14] (ego stages)	Fromm (F),[146] Riesman (R)[318] (ego types)	Maslow[262,263] (needs hierarchy)
Pleromatic	Unconditional omnipotence (F)		
Uroboric-alimentary	Magical-hallucinatory omnipotence (F) Ego omnipotence (A)	Symbiosis (F)	Physiological
Axial-body Pranic-body	Omnipotence by magic gestures (F)		Beginning of Safety
Image-body	Animism (F) Crisis of ego devaluation (A)	Anomy (R)	
Membership-cognition	Magic words and thoughts (F) Beginning of satellization (A)	Tradition-directed conformity (R)	Safety
Early egoic/personic	Satellization (A)	Conformity (F)	Belongingness
Middle egoic/personic	Crisis of desatellization (A)	Other-directed conformity (R)	
Late egoic/personic Mature Ego Biosocial Bands	Desatellization (A)	Inner-directed conformity (R)	Self-esteem
Centaur/existential		Autonomy (F) Autonomy (R)	Self-actualization
Low Subtle High Subtle Low Causal High Causal Ultimate			Transcendence

TABLE 5.

Approximate mode of self sense	Sullivan, Grant, and Grant[358, 243] (levels of integration)	Bubba Free John[60] (stages of life)	Broughton[53, 243] (natural epistemology)
Pleromatic			
Uroboric		1. Physical body	
Axial-body	1. Self vs. not-self		0. Inside vs. outside
Pranic-body	2. Crude manipulation, impulsive, differentiation of objects and people	2. Emotional body	
Image-body			
Membership	3. "Cons"—exploitative		
Early egoic/personic	3. "Conformists"	3. Lower-mental Will-power	1. Big-person mind vs. little-person body
Middle egoic/personic	4. Awakening conflict, individuation of response, (neurotic subtype of this level is our persona)	Verbal-mind	2. Mind and body differentiated
Late egoic/personic	5. Start of dis-identification with all roles	Gross-mind	3. & 4. Persona is differentiated from true ego
Mature ego	6. Separation of self from roles		5. Ego differentiated from observer
Biosocial Bands			
Centaur/existential	7. Integration of all lower levels	4. Higher mental-body being	6. Integrated
Low subtle		Lower psychic	
High subtle		5. Cosmic gnosis Higher subtle/psychic	
Low causal		Supra-mental	
High causal		6. Atmic (Brahman= Atman)	
Ultimate		7. Nirvanic	

TABLE 6.

Approximate mode of self sense	Vedanta Hinduism[94]	Buddhist Skandhas[379]	Battista[24]	Welwood (W)[392] Smith (S)[352]	Arieti[7]
Pleromatic	annamayakosa				instincts
Uroboric					
Axial-body		1. body form	sensation	body (S)	sensorimotor exoceptual
Pranic-body	pranamayakosa	2. sensation / 3. perception	perception / emotion	felt meaning (W)	proto-emotions
Image-body		3. emotion/ impulses			phantasmic endoceptual
Membership-cognition		4. cognition verbal	cognition		language paleologic
Early egoic/personic					
Middle egoic/personic	manomayakosa	5. stream of self-consciousness			conceptual
Late egoic/personic			self-aware	mind (S)	
Mature ego				personal ground (W)	
Biosocial Bands					
Centaur/existential					
Low Subtle	vijnanamayakosa				
High Subtle			unition	soul (S)	
Low Causal	anandamayakosa			transpersonal ground (W)	
High Causal					
Ultimate	Brahman-Atman		absolute	spirit (S) open ground (W)	

TABLE 7.

Approximate mode of self sense	7 Kundalini chakras and the 7 higher Shabd "chakras"	Tiller[271] (substance hierarchy)
Pleromatic Uroboric	1. Hunger, materialistic, pleromatic, food	Physical
Axial-body Pranic-body Image-body	2. Emotional-sexual drives	Etheric Astral
Membership	3. Power: safety *within* membership-world	M-1 (or lower mind)
Early egoic/personic	4. Love and belongingness of early ego within membership-world	
Middle egoic/personic	5. Fully verbal self; concrete operational and verbal knowledge	
Late egoic/personic Mature ego Biosocial Bands	6. Formal operational and conceptual knowledge; (*beginning* of psychic)	M-2 (or intellectual mind)
Centaur/existential	6. Integration of lower six chakras	
Low subtle	6. Opening of ajna/psychic chakra	
High subtle	7. Sahasrara Realm of the 7 higher Shabd "chakras" beyond the sahasrara	M-3 (or spiritual mind)
Low causal	Culmination of higher chakras in final-God	
High causal	Transcendence of all chakric coils, high or low	Spirit
Ultimate		

Bibliography

1. Allport, G. W. *Personality: a psychological interpretation.* New York: Holt, Rinehart, Winston, 1937
2. ____. *Pattern and growth in personality.* New York: Holt, Rinehart, Winston, 1961
3. Anderson, R. "A holographic model of transpersonal consciousness." *J. Transpersonal Psychol,* vol 9, no. 2, 1977
4. Angyal, A. *Neurosis and treatment: a holistic theory.* New York: Wiley, 1965
5. Aquinas, T. *Summa theologiae.* 2 vols. Garden City: Doubleday, 1969
6. Arieti, S. *Interpretation of schizophrenia.* New York: Brunner, 1955
7. ____. *The intra-psychic self.* New York: Basic Books, 1967
8. ____. *Creativity: the magic synthesis.* New York: Basic Books, 1976
9. Arlow, J.A., and Brenner, C. *Psychoanalytic concepts and the structural theory.* New York, International Universities Press, 1964
10. Assagioli, R. *Psychosynthesis.* New York: Viking, 1965
11. Aurobindo *The life divine.* Pondicherry: Centenary Library, XVIII, XIX
12. ____. *The synthesis of yoga.* Pondicherry: Centenary Library, XX, XXI
13. ____. *The essential Aurobindo.* McDermott, R. (ed.) New York: Schocken, 1973
14. Ausubel, D. *Ego development and the personality disorders.* New York: Grune and Stratton, 1952
15. Avalon, A. *The serpent power.* New York: Dover, 1974
16. Baba Ram Dass. *Be here now.* San Cristobal: Lama Foundation, 1971
17. Bachofen, J. *Das mutterecht.* Basel, 1948. 2 vols.
18. Bak. "The phallic woman: the ubiquitous fantasy in perversions." *Psychoanalytic Study of the Child,* 1968
19. Bakan, D. *The duality of human existence.* Chicago: Rand McNally, 1966
20. Baldwin, J. M. *Thought and things.* New York: Arno, 1975
21. Bandura, A. *Social learning theory.* Englewood Cliffs: Prentice Hall, 1977
22. Barfield, O. "The rediscovery of meaning." Adventures of the Mind, *Sat. Evening Post,* vol. 1. New York: Knopf, 1961

23. Bateson, G. *Steps to an ecology of mind.* New York: Ballantine, 1972
24. Battista, J. "The holographic model, holistic paradigm, information theory and consciousness." *Re-Vision,* vol. 1, no. 3/4, 1978
25. Becker, E. *The denial of death.* New York: Free Press, 1973
26. ____. *Escape from evil.* New York: Free Press, 1975
27. Benoit, H. *The supreme doctrine.* New York: Viking, 1955
28. Berdyaev, N. *The destiny of man.* New York: Harper, 1960
29. Berger, R. and Luckmann, T. *The social construction of reality.* New York: Doubleday, 1972
30. Bergson, H. *Introduction to metaphysics.* New York, 1949
31. ____. *Time and free will.* New York: Harper, 1960
32. Berne, E. *Games people play.* New York: Grove, 1967
33. ____. *What do you say after you say hello?* New York: Bantam, 1974
34. Bertalanffy, L. von. "The mind-body problem: a new view." *Psychosomatic Medicine,* vol. 26, no. 1, 1964
35. Bharati, A. *The tantric tradition.* Garden City: Anchor, 1965
36. Binswanger, L. *Being-in-the-world.* New York: Basic Books, 1963
37. Blakney, R. B. (trans). *Meister Eckhart.* New York: Harper, 1941
38. Blanck, G. and Blanck, R. *Ego psychology: theory and practice.* New York: Columbia Univ. Press, 1974
39. Blanco, M. *The unconscious as infinite sets.* London: Duckworth, 1975
40. Blavatsky, H. P. *The secret doctrine.* London: Theosophical Publishing House, 1966
41. Blofeld, J. *Zen teaching of Huang Po.* New York: Grove, 1958
42. ____. *Zen teaching of Hui Hai.* London: Rider, 1969
43. ____. *The tantric mysticism of Tibet.* New York: Dutton, 1970
44. Bloom, C. M. *Language development.* Cambridge: M.I.T., 1970
45. Blos, P. "The genealogy of the ego ideal." *Psychoanalytic Study of the Child,* vol. 29, 1974
46. Blum, G. *Psychoanalytic theories of personality.* New York: McGraw-Hill, 1953
47. Blyth, R.H. *Zen and zen classics, vols. 1-5.* Tokyo: Hokuseido, 1960 1964, 1970, 1966, 1962
48. Boehme, J. *Six theosophic points.* Ann Arbor: Univ. of Michigan, 1970
49. Boisen, A. *The exploration of the inner world.* New York: Harper, 1962
50. Boss, M. *Psychoanalysis and daseinanalysis.* New York: Basic Books, 1963
51. Bower, T. *Development in infancy.* San Francisco: Freeman, 1974
52. Broad, C. D. *The mind and its place in nature.* New Jersey: Littlefield, Adams, 1960
53. Broughton, J. "The development of natural epistemology in adolescence and early adulthood." Unpublished doctoral dissertation, Harvard, 1975
54. Brown, D. "A model for the levels of concentrative meditation." *Int. J. Clin. Exp. Hypnosis,* vol. 25, 1977
55. Brown, G. "The farther reaches of Gestalt therapy." *Synthesis 1.*
56. Brown, G. S. *Laws of form.* New York: Julian, 1972
57. Brown, N.O. *Life against death.* Middletown: Wesleyan, 1959
58. ____. *Love's body.* New York: Vintage, 1966
59. Bubba Free John. *The paradox of instruction.* San Francisco: Dawn Horse, 1977
60. ____. *The enlightenment of the whole body.* Middletown: Dawn Horse, 1978
61. Buber, M. *I and thou.* New York: Scribners, 1958

62. Bucke, R. *Cosmic consciousness.* New York: Dutton, 1923
63. Buddhagosa. *The path of purity.* Pali Text Society, 1923
64. Bugental, J. *The search for authenticity.* New York: Holt, Rinehart, Winston, 1965
65. Burke, K. "The rhetoric of Hitler's 'battle.'" *The philosophy of literary form.* New York: Vintage, 1957
66. Campbell, J. *The masks of God, vols. 1-4.* New York: Viking, 1959, 1962, 1964, 1968
67. Canetti, E. *Of fear and freedom.* New York: Farrar Strauss, 1950
68. Capra, F. *The tao of physics.* Berkeley, Shambhala, 1975
69. Cassirer, E. *The philosophy of symbolic forms.* New Haven: Yale, 1953-1957. 3 vols
70. Castaneda, C. *Journey to Ixtlan.* New York: Simon and Schuster, 1972
71. Chang, G.C.C. *Hundred thousand songs of Milarepa.* New York: Harper, 1970
72. ———. *Practice of zen.* New York: Harper, 1970
73. ———. *The Buddhist teaching of totality.* Pennsylvania: Univ. of Penn., 1971
74 ———. *Teachings of Tibetan yoga.* New Jersey: Citadel, 1974
75. Chapman, J. "The early symptoms of schizophrenia." *British Journal of Psychiatry,* vol. 112, 1966
76. Chaudhuri, H. *Philosophy of meditation.* New York: Philosophical Library, 1965
77. Childe, C. *Man makes himself.* New York: Mentor, 1957
78. Chomsky, N. *Syntactic structures.* The Hague: Mouton, 1957
79. ———. *Language and mind.* New York: Harcourt, 1972
80. Conze, E. *Buddhist meditation.* New York: Harper, 1956
81. ———. *Buddhist wisdom books.* London: Allen and Unwin, 1970
82. Cooley, C. H. *Human nature and the social order.* New York: Scribners, 1902
83. Coomaraswamy, A. K. *Hinduism and Buddhism.* New York: Philosophical Library, 1943
84. ———. "Recollection, Indian and Platonic." Supplement to JAOS, no. 3, 1944
85. ———. *Time and eternity.* Ascona: Artibus Asial, 1947
86. ———. *The dance of Shiva.* New York: Noonday, 1957
87. Cooper, D.*Psychiatry and anti-psychiatry.* New York: Ballantine, 1971
88. Corsini, R. *Current personality theories.* Itasca: Peacock, 1977
89. Dasgupta, S. B. *An introduction to tantric Buddhism.* Berkeley: Shambhala, 1974
90. Davidson, J. "The physiology of meditation and mystical states of consciousness." *Perspectives Biology Medicine,* Spring, 1976
91. Dean, S. (ed.) *Psychiatry and mysticism.* Chicago: Nelson Hall, 1975
92. Deikman, A. "De-automatization and the mystic experience." *Psychiatry,* vol. 29, 1966
93. Desoille, R. *The waking dream in psychotherapy.* Paris: Presses Universitaires de France, 1945
94. Deutsche, E. *Advaita vedanta.* Honolulu: East-West Center, 1969
95. Dewey, J. and Bently, A. F. *Knowing and the known.* Boston: Beacon, 1949
96. Dewey, J. and Tufts, J. *Ethics.* New York: Holt, Rinehart, Winston, 1908
97. DiLeo, J. *Child development.* New York: Brunner/Mazel. 1977

98. Duncan, H. *Symbols in society*. New York: Oxford Univ., 1968
99. Edgerton, F. (trans). *The Bhagavad Gita*. New York: Harper, 1964
100. Edinger, E. F. *Ego and archetype*. Baltimore: Penguin, 1972
101. Ehrmann, J. (ed.) *Structuralism*. New York: Anchor, 1970
102. Eisendrath, C. *The unifying moment*. Cambridge: Harvard, 1971
103. Eliade, M. *The myth of eternal return*. New York: Pantheon, 1954
104. ____. *The sacred and the profane*. New York: Harvest, 1959
105. ____. *Shamanism*. New York: Pantheon, 1964
106. ____. *Images and symbols*. New York: Sheed and Ward, 1969
107. Eliot, C. *Hinduism and Buddhism*. vols. 1-3. New York: Barnes and Noble, 1968
108. Erikson, E. *Childhood and society*. New York: Norton, 1963
109. ____. *Insight and responsibility*. New York: Norton, 1964
110. Evans, Wentz, W. *The Tibetan book of the dead*. London: Oxford Univ., 1968
111. ____. *The Tibetan book of the great liberation*. London: Oxford Univ., 1968
112. ____. *Tibetan yoga and secret doctrines*. London: Oxford Univ., 1971
113. Fadiman, J., and Frager, R. *Personality and personal growth*. New York: Harper, 1976
114. ____, and Kewman, D. (ed.) *Exploring madness*. Calif.: Brooks/Cole, 1973
115. Fagan, J., and Sheperd, I. (ed.) *Gestalt therapy*. New York: Harper, 1970
116. Fairbairn, W. *Psychoanalytic studies of the personality*. London: Tavistock, 1952
117. ____. *An object-relations theory of the personality*. New York: Basic Books, 1954
118. Farber, L. *The ways of the will*. New York: Basic Books, 1966
119. Federn, P. *Ego psychology and the psychoses*. New York: Basic Books, 1952
120. Fenichel, O. *The psychoanalytic theory of neurosis*. New York: Norton, 1945
121. Ferenczi, S. "Stages in the development of the sense of reality." In *Sex and psychoanalysis*. Boston: Gorham, 1956
122. ____. *Thalassa*. New York: *The Psychoanalytic Quarterly*, 1938
123. ____. *Further contributions to the theory and technique of psychoanalysis*. New York: Basic Books, 1952
124. Festinger, L. *Theory of cognitive dissonance*. New York: Peterson, 1957
125. Feuerstein, G. A. *Introduction to the Bhagavad Gita*. London: Rider, 1974
126. ____. *Textbook of yoga*. London: Rider, 1975
127. Fingarette, H. *The self in transformation*. New York: Basic Books, 1963
128. Flugel, J. *Man, morals and society*. New York: International Universities Press, 1945
129. Foulkes, D. *A grammar of dreams*. New York: Basic Books, 1978
130. Frank, J. "Nature and function of belief systems: humanism and transcendental religion." *American Psychologist*, vol. 32, 1977
131. Frankl, V. *Man's search for meaning*. New York: Washington Square, 1963
132. Freemantle, F., and Trungpa, C. *The Tibetan book of the dead*. Berkeley: Shambhala, 1975

Bibliography

133. Fremantle, A. *The Protestant mystics.* New York: Mentor, 1965
134. Freud, A. *The ego and the mechanisms of defense.* New York: International Universities Press, 1946

Freud, S. *The standard edition of the complete psychological works of Sigmund Freud.* 24 volumes, translated and edited by James Strachey. London: Hogarth Press and the Institute of Psycho-analysis, 1953-1964

135. ____. *The interpretation of dreams.* Standard Edition, vols. 4 and 5.
136. ____. *Three essays on the theory of sexuality.* Standard Edition, vol. 7
137. ____. *Totem and taboo.* Standard Edition, vol. 13
138. ____. "On narcissism: an introduction." Standard Edition, vol. 14
139. ____. *Beyond the pleasure principle.* Standard Edition, vol. 18
140. ____. *The ego and the id.* Standard Edition, vol. 19
141. ____. *Civilization and its discontents.* Standard Edition, vol. 20
142. ____. *New introductory lectures.* Standard Edition, vol. 22
143. ____. *An outline of psychoanalysis.* Standard Edition, vol. 23
144. ____. *A general introduction to psychoanalysis.* New York: Pocket Books, 1971
145. Frey-Rohn, L. *From Freud to Jung.* New York: Delta, 1974
146. Fromm, E. *Escape from freedom.* New York: Farrar, Straus, and Giroux, 1941
147. ____. *Psychoanalysis and religion.* New York: Bantam, 1967
148. ____. Suzuki, D. T., and De Martino, R. *Zen Buddhism and psychoanalysis.* New York: Harper, 1970
149. Gardner, H. *The quest for mind.* New York: Vintage, 1972
150. Gebser, J. *Ursprung and gegenwart.* Stuttgart: Deutsche Verlags-Ansalt, 1966
151. ____. "Foundations of the aperspective world." *Main Currents*, vol. 29, no. 2, 1972
152. Geertz, C. *The interpretation of cultures.* New York: Basic Books, 1973
153. Gendlin, E. *Experiencing and the creation of meaning.* New York: Free Press, 1962
154. Giovacchini, P. "Psychoanalysis." In Corsini, R., reference note #88
155. Glasser, W. *Reality therapy.* New York: Harper, 1965
156. Globus, G. *et al.* (eds). *Consciousness and the brain.* Plenum, 1976
157. Goble, F. *The third force.* New York: Pocket, 1974
158. Goffman, E. *The presentation of self in everyday life.* Garden City: Anchor, 1959
159. Goldstein, K. *The organism.* New York: American Book, 1939
160. Goleman, D. *The varieties of the meditative experience.* New York: Dutton, 1977
161. Govinda, L. *Foundations of Tibetan mysticism.* New York: Weiser, 1973
162. Gowan, J. *Trance, art, and creativity.* Northridge, CA; 1975
163. Green, E., and Green, A. *Beyond biofeedback.* New York: Delacourte, 1977
164. Greenacre, P. "Certain relationships between fetishism and faulty development of the body image." *Psychoanalytic Study of the Child,* vol. 8, 1953
165. Greenson, R. *The technique and practice of psychoanalysis.* New York: International Universities Press, 1976
166. Grof, S. *Realms of the human unconscious.* New York: Viking, 1975

167. Group for the Advancement of Psychiatry. *Mysticism: spiritual quest psychic disorder?* New York: Group for the Advancement of Psychiatry, 1976

168. Guénon, R. *Man and his becoming according to the Vedanta.* London: Luzac, 1945

169. Guenther, H. *Buddhist philosophy in theory and practice.* Baltimore: Penguin, 1971

170. ———. *Treasures on the Tibetan middle way.* Berkeley: Shambhala, 1971

171. ———. *Philosophy and psychology in the abhidharma.* Berkeley: Shambhala, 1974

172. ———. trans. *The life and teaching of Naropa.* London: Oxford Univ., 1963.

173. ———. and Trungpa, C. *The dawn of tantra.* Berkeley: Shambhala, 1975

174. Hakeda, Y.S., trans. *The awakening of faith.* New York: Columbia Univ., 1967

175. Hall, C. *A primer of Jungian psychology.* New York: Mentor, 1973

176. Hall, R. "The psycho-philosophy of history." *Main Currents,* vol. 29, no. 2, 1972

177. Harrington, A. *The immortalist.* New York: Random House, 1969

178. Harris, T. *I'm o.k. — you're o.k.* New York: Avon, 1969

179. Hartmann, H. *Ego psychology and the problem of adaptation.* New York: International Universities Press, 1958

180. Hartshorne, C. *The logic of perfection.* Illinois: Open Court, 1973

181. Heard, G. *The ascent of humanity.* London: Jonathan Cape, 1929

182. Heidegger, M. *Existence and being.* Chicago: Henry Regney, 1950

183. ———. *Being and time.* New York: Harper, 1962

184. ———. *Discourse on thinking.* New York: Harper

185. Hixon, L. *Coming home.* Garden City: Anchor, 1978

186. Hocart, A. *Social origins.* London: Watts, 1954

187. Holdstock, T., and Rogers, C. "Person-centered theory." In Corsini, R., reference note #88

188. Hood, R. "Conceptual criticisms of regressive explanations of mysticisms," *Rev. Religious Res.,* vol. 17, 1976

189. Hook, S. (ed.) *Dimensions of mind.* New York: Collier, 1973

190. Horney, K. *The neurotic personality of our time.* New York: Norton, 1968

191. Hume, R., trans. *The thirteen principle Upanishads.* London: Oxford, 1974

192. Husserl, E. *Ideas.* New York: Macmillan, 1931

193. Huxley, A. *The perennial philosophy.* New York: Harper, 1970

194. Jacobi, J. *The psychology of C. G. Jung.* London: Routledge and Kegan Paul, 1968

195. Jacobson, E. *The self and the object world.* New York: International Universities Press, 1964

196. Jakobson, R. *Child language aphasia and phonological universals.* Quoted in Gardner, reference note #149

197. James, W. *The principles of psychology,* vols. 1-2. New York: Dover, 1950

198. ———. *Varieties of religious experience.* New York: Collier, 1961

199. Jantsch, E., and Waddington, C. (eds). *Evolution and consciousness.* Addison-Wesley, 1976

200. Jaynes, J. *The origin of consciousness in the breakdown of the bicameral mind.* Boston: Houghton Mifflin, 1976
201. John of the Cross, St. *Dark night of the soul.* Garden City: Doubleday, 1959
202. ____. *Ascent of Mount Carmel.* Garden City: Doubleday, 1958
203. Jonas, H. *The gnostic religion.* Boston: Beacon, 1963
204. Jones, R. M. *Contemporary educational psychology: selected essays.* New York: Harper, 1967
    Jung, C.G. *The collected works of C.G. Jung,* Adler, G., Fordham, M. and Read, H., eds.; Hull, R.F.C., trans. Bolligen Series XX, Princeton: Princeton Univ. Press
205. ____. *Symbols of transformation,* collected works 5
206. ____. *Psychological types,* collected works 6
207. ____. *Two essays on analytical psychology,* collected works 7
208. ____. *The psychological foundations of belief in spirits,* collected works 8
209. ____. *The structure and dynamics of the psyche,* collected works 8
210. ____. *The archetypes and the collective unconscious,* collected works 9, part 1
211. ____. *Aion — researches into the phenomenology of the self,* collected works 9, part 2
212. ____. *Mysterium coniunctionis,* collected works 14
213. ____. *The portable Jung.* Campbell, J., ed. New York: Viking, 1972
214. ____. *The basic writings of C. G. Jung.* DeLaszlo, V.S., ed. New York: Modern Library, 1959
215. Kadloubovsky, E., and Palmer, G., trans. *Writings from the "Philokalia" on prayer of the heart.* London: Farber and Farber, 1954
216. Kahn, H. I. *The soul whence and whither.* New York: Sufi Order, 1977
217. Kaplan, B. (ed). *The inner world of mental illness.* New York: Harper, 1964
218. Kaplan, L. *Oneness and separateness.* New York: Simon and Schuster, 1978
219. Kaplan, P. "An excursion into the 'undiscovered country.'" *Rediscovery of the body.* Garfield, C. (ed). New York: Dell, 1977
220. Kapleau, P. *The three pillars of Zen.* Boston: Beacon, 1965
221. Keleman, S. *Your body speaks its mind.* New York: Simon and Schuster, 1975
222. Kierkegaard, S. *The concept of the dread.* Princeton: Princeton Univ., 1944
223. ____. *Fear and trembling and the sickness unto death.* New York: Anchor, 1954
224. Klein, G. S. *Psychoanalytic theory: an exploration of essentials.* New York: International Universities Press, 1976
225. Klein, M. *The psychoanalysis of children.* New York, 1960
226. ____. *New directions in psychoanalysis.* London: Tavistock, 1971
227. Kluckhohn, C., and Murray, H. *Personality: in nature, society, and culture.* New York: Knopf, 1965
228. Kobasa, S. and Maddi, S. "Existential personality theory." In Corsini, R., reference note #88
229. Kohlberg, L. "Development of moral character and moral ideology." In Hoffman, M. and Hoffman, L. (eds). *Review of Child Development Research,* vol. 1, 1964

230.   _____. "From is to ought." In Mischel, T. (ed). *Cognitive development and epistemology*. New York: Academic Press, 1971
231.   Krishna, Gopi. *The secret of yoga*. New York: Harper, 1972
232.   Krishnamurti, J. *The first and last freedom*. Wheaton, Quest, 1968
233.   _____. *Commentaries on living*. Series 1-3. Wheaton, Quest, 1968
234.   Kuhn, T. *The structure of scientific revolutions*. Chicago: Univ. of Chicago Press, 1962
235.   La Barre, W. *The human animal*. Chicago: Univ of Chicago Press, 1954
236.   Lacan, J. *Language of the self*. Baltimore: John Hopkins, 1968
237.   _____. "The insistence of the letter in the unconscious." In Ehrmann, J., reference note #101
238.   Laing, R. D. *The divided self*. Baltimore: Penguin, 1965
239.   _____. *The politics of experience*. New York: Ballantine, 1967
240.   Lévi-Strauss, C. *Structural anthropology*. New York: Basic Books, 1963
241.   Lifton, R. *Revolutionary immortality*. New York: Vintage, 1968
242.   Lilly, J. *The center of the cyclone*. New York: Julian, 1972
243.   Loevinger, J. *Ego development*. San Francisco: Jossey-Bass, 1976
244.   Loewald, H. "The superego and the ego-ideal. II: Superego and time." *International Journal of Psychoanalysis*, vol. 43, 1962
245.   _____. "On motivation and instinct theory." *Psychoanalytic Study of the Child*, vol. 26, 1971
246.   _____. *Psychoanalysis and the history of the individual*. New Haven: Yale, 1978
247.   Lonergan, B. *Insight, a study of human understanding*. New York: Philosophical Library, 1970
248.   Longchenpa, *Kindly bent to ease us*. cols. 1-2. Guenther, H., trans. Emeryville: Dharma Press, 1975
249.   Lowen, A. *The betrayal of the body*. New York: Macmillan, 1967
250.   _____. *The language of the body*. New York: Macmillan, 1967
251.   _____. *Depression and the body*. Baltimore: Penguin, 1973
252.   Luk, C. *Ch'an and Zen teaching*, Series 1-3. London: Rider, 1960, 1961, 1962
253.   _____. *The secrets of Chinese meditation*. New York: Weiser, 1971
254.   _____. *Practical Buddhism*. London: Rider, 1972
255.   _____, trans. *The Surangama Sutra*. London: Rider, 1969
256.   _____, trans. *The Vimalakirti Nirdessa Sutra*. Berkeley: Shambhala, 1972
257.   Maddi, S. *Personality theories*. Homewood: Dorsev Press. 1968
258.   Maezumi, H.T., and Glassman, B.T. (eds). *Zen writings series*. vols. 1-5, 1976-1978. Los Angeles: Center Publications
259.   Mahrer, A. *Experiencing*. New York: Brunner/Mazel, 1978
260.   Marcel, G. *Philosophy of existence*. New York: Philosophical Library, 1949
261.   Marcuse, H. *Eros and civilization*. Boston: Beacon, 1955
262.   Maslow, A. *Toward a psychology of being*. New York: Van Nostrand Reinhold, 1968
263.   _____. *The farther reaches of human nature*. New York: Viking, 1971
264.   Masters, R., and Houston, J. *The varieties of psychedelic experience*. New York: Delta, 1967
265.   May, R. *Love and will*. New York: Norton, 1969
266.   _____, ed. *Existential psychology*. New York: Random House, 1969

267. Mead, G.H. *Mind, self, and society*. Chicago: Univ. of Chicago Press, 1934
268. Mead, G. R. S. *Apollonius of Tyana*. New Hyde Park, N.Y.: University Books, 1966
269. Miel, J. "Jacques Lacan and the structure of the unconscious." In Ehrmann, J., reference note #101
270. Mishra, R. S. *Yoga sutras*. Garden City: Anchor, 1973
271. Mitchell, E. *Psychic exploration*. White, J., ed. New York: Capricorn, 1976
272. Muktananda. *The play of consciousness*. Camp Meeker, CA: SYDA Foundation, 1974
273. Murphy, G. *Personality: a biosocial approach to origins and structure*. New York: Harper, 1947
274. Murti, T. R. V. *The central philosophy of Buddhism*. London: Allen and Unwin, 1960
275. Musès, C. and Young, A. (ed). *Consciousness and reality*. New York: Discus, 1974
276. Naranjo, C. and Ornstein, R. *On the psychology of meditation*. New York: Viking, 1973
277. Needham, J. *Science and civilization in China*, vol. 2. London: Cambridge Univ. Press, 1956
278. Nelson, M. (ed). *The narcissistic condition*. New York: Human Sciences, 1977
279. Neumann, E. *The origins and history of consciousness*. Princeton: Princeton University Press, 1973
280. Nikhilananda, S. *The gospel of Sri Ramakrishna*. New York: Ramakrishna Center, 1973
281. Nishida, K. *Intelligibility and the philosophy of nothingness*. Honolulu: East-West Press, 1958
282. Northrop, F. *The meeting of east and west*. New York: Collier, 1968
283. Nyanaponika Thera. *The heart of Buddhist meditation*. London: Rider, 1972
284. Ogilvy, J. *Many dimensional man*. New York: Oxford Univ. Press. 1977
285. Ornstein, R. *The psychology of consciousness*. San Francisco: Freeman, 1972
286. Ouspensky, P. D. *In search of the miraculous*. New York: Harcourt Brace, 1949
287. ———. *The fourth way*. New York: Knopf
288. Pelletier, K. *Toward a science of consciousness*. New York: Delta, 1978
289. ———, and Garfield, C. *Consciousness: east and west*. New York: Harper, 1976
290. Penfield, W. *The mystery of the mind*. Princeton: Princeton Univ. Press, 1978
291. Perls, F. *Gestalt therapy verbatim*. Lafayette, CA: Real People Press 1969
292. ———, Hefferline, R., and Goodman, P. *Gestalt therapy*. New York: Delta, 1951
293. Piaget, J. *The child's conception of the world*. London: Humanities Press, 1951
294. ———. *The origins of intelligence*. New York: International Universities Press, 1952
295. ———. *The construction of reality in the child*. New York: Basic Books, 1954
296. ———. *Structuralism*. New York: Basic Books, 1970

297. ____. *The essential Piaget.* Gruber, H., and Voneche, J., eds. New York: Basic Books, 1977
298. Polanyi, M. *Personal knowledge.* Chicago: Univ. of Chicago Press, 1958
299. Pope, K., and Singer, J. *The stream of consciousness.* New York: Plenum, 1978
300. Pribram, K. *Languages of the brain.* Englewood Cliffs: Prentice Hall, 1971
301. Price, A.F., and Wong Moul-lam, trans. *The Diamond Sutra and the Sutra of Hui-Neng.* Berkeley: Shambhala, 1969
302. Prince, R., and Savage, C. "Mystical states and the concept of regression." *Psychedelic Review,* vol. 8, 1966
303. Progoff, I. *The death and rebirth of psychology.* New York: Julian, 1956
304. Pursglove, P. (ed). *Recognitions in gestalt therapy.* New York: Harper, 1968
305. Putney, S. and Putney, G. *The adjusted American.* New York: Harper, 1966
306. Radhakrishnan, S. and Moore, C. *A source book in Indian philosophy.* Princeton: Princeton Univ. Press, 1957
307. Rahner, K. and Vorgrimler, H. *Theological dictionary.* New York: Herder and Herder, 1968
308. Ramana Maharshi, Sri. *Talks with Sri Ramana Maharshi,* 3 vols. Tiruvannamalai: Sri Ramanasramam, 1972
309. ____. *The collected works of Sri Ramana Maharshi.* Osborne, A., ed. London: Rider, 1959
310. ____. *The teachings of Bhagavan Sri Ramana Maharshi in His Own Words.* Osborne, A., ed. London: Rider, 1962
311. Rank, O. *Beyond psychology.* New York: Dover, 1958
312. ____. *Psychology and the soul.* New York: Perpetua, 1961
313. Rapaport, D. *Organization and pathology of thought.* New York: Columbia Univ. Press, 1951
314. Reich, W. *The function of the orgasm.* New York: Orgone Press, 1942
315. ____. *Character analysis.* New York: Farrar, Strauss, and Giroux, 1949
316. Ricoeur, P. *Freud and philosophy.* New Haven: Yale, 1970
317. Rieker, H. *The yoga of light.* California: Dawn Horse, 1974
318. Riesman, D. *The lonely crowd.* New York: Doubleday, 1954
319. Rimm, D. C., and Masters, J. *Behavior therapy.* New York: Academic Press, 1975
320. Ring, K. "A transpersonal view of consciousness." *Journal of Transpersonal Psychology,* vol. 9, no. 1, 1977
321. Roberts, T. *Beyond self-actualization.* Re-Vision Journal, vol. 1, no. 1, 1978
322. Rogers, C. *On becoming a person.* Boston: Houghton Mifflin, 1961
323. Roheim, G. *Gates of the dream.* New York, 1945
324. ____. *Magic and schizophrenia.* New York, 1955
325. Rossi, I. (ed). *The unconscious in culture.* New York: Dutton, 1974
326. Ruesch, J. and Bateson, G. *Communication.* New York: Norton, 1968
327. Rycroft, C. *A critical dictionary of psychoanalysis.* New Jersey: Little-field, Adams, 1973
328. Sahukar, M. *Sai Baba: the saint of Shirdi.* San Francisco: Dawn Horse, 1977
329. Saraswati, S. *Dynamics of yoga.* India: Bihar School of Yoga, 1973
330. ____. *Tantra of kundalini yoga.* India: Bihar School of Yoga, 1973
331. Sartre, J. *Existential psychoanalysis.* Chicago: Gateway, 1966

332. Sasaki, R. and Miura, I. *Zen dust.* New York: Harcourt Brace, 1966
333. Satprem. *Sri Aurobindo or the adventure of consciousness.* New York: Harper, 1968
334. Schachtel, E. *Metamorphosis.* New York: Basic Books, 1959
335. Schafer, R. *A new language for psychoanalysis.* New Haven: Yale, 1976
336. _____. *Language and insight.* New Haven: Yale, 1978
337. Schaff, A. *Language and cognition.* New York: McGraw-Hill, 1973
338. Schaya, L. *The universal meaning of the Kabalah.* Baltimore: Penguin, 1973
339. Schilder, P. *The image and appearance of the human body.* New York: International Universities Press, 1950
340. Schloegl, I. *The zen teaching of Rinzai.* Berkeley: Shambhala, 1976
341. Schuon, F. *Logic and transcendence.* New York: Harper, 1975
342. _____. *The transcendent unity of religions.* New York: Harper, 1975
343. Selman, R. "The relation of role taking to the development of moral judgement in children." *Child Development,* 1971
344. Sgam. Po. Pa. *Jewel ornament of liberation.* Guenther, H., trans. London: Rider, 1970
345. Shibayama, Z. *Zen comments on the Mumonkan.* New York: Harper, 1974
346. Silverman, J. "A paradigm for the study of altered states of consciousness." *British Journal of Psychiatry,* vol. 114, 1968
347. _____. "When schizophrenia helps." *Psychology Today,* Sept. 1970
348. Singh, K. *Naam or word.* Delhi: Ruhani Satsang, 1972
349. _____. *The crown of life.* Delhi: Ruhani Satsang, 1973
350. _____. *Surat shabd yoga.* Berkeley: Images Press, 1975
351. Sivananda. *Kundalini yoga.* India: The Divine Life Society, 1971
352. Smith, H. *Forgotten truth.* New York: Harper, 1976
353. Smith, M. "Perspectives on selfhood." *American Psychologist,* vol. 33, no. 12, 1978
354. Smuts, J. *Holism and evolution.* New York: Macmillan, 1926
355. Snellgrove, D. *The hevajra tantra.* Part 1. London: Oxford Univ. Press, 1955
356. Stiskin, N. *Looking-glass god.* Autumn Press, 1972
357. Straus, A. (ed). *George Herbert Mead on social psychology.* Chicago: Univ. of Chicago Press, 1964
358. Sullivan, C., Grant, M.Q., and Grant, J. D. "The development of interpersonal maturity." *Psychiatry,* vol. 20, 1957
359. Sullivan, H. S. *The interpersonal theory of psychiatry.* New York: Norton, 1953
360. Suzuki, D. T. *Studies in Zen.* New York: Delta, 1955
361. _____. *Manual of Zen Buddhism.* New York: Grove, 1960
362. _____. *Studies in the Lankavatara Sutra.* London: Routledge and Kegan-Paul, 1968
363. _____. *Mysticism: Christian and Buddhist.* New York: Macmillan, 1969
364. _____. *Essays in Zen Buddhism,* 1st, 2nd, and 3rd Series. London: Rider, 1970
365. _____. *The Zen doctrine of no-mind.* London: Rider, 1970
366. _____. *Zen and Japanese culture.* Princeton: Princeton Univ. Press, 1970
367. _____. *Living by Zen.* London: Rider, 1972 .
368. Suzuki, S. *Zen mind, beginner's mind.* New York: Weatherhill, 1970
369. Swearer, D. (ed). *Secrets of the lotus.* New York: Macmillan, 1971
370. Taimni, I. K. *The science of yoga.* Wheaton: Quest, 1975

371. Takakusu, J. *The essentials of Buddhist philosophy.* Honolulu: Univ. of Hawaii, 1956
372. Tart, C., ed. *Altered states of consciousness.* Garden City: Anchor, 1969
373. ____. ed. *Transpersonal psychologies.* New York: Harper, 1975
374. Tattwananda, S. (trans). *The quintessence of vedanta of Acharya Sankara.* Calcutta: Sri Ramakrishna Ashrama, 1970
375. Teilhard de Chardin. *The future of man.* New York: Harper, 1964
377. Tillich, P. *The courage to be.* New Haven: Yale, 1952
378. Trungpa, C. *Cutting through spiritual materialism.* Berkeley: Shambhala, 1973
379. ____. *The myth of freedom.* Berkeley: Shambhala, 1976
380. Vaughan, F. *Awakening intuition.* Garden City: Anchor, 1979
381. Van Dussen, W. *The natural depth in man.* New York: Harper, 1972
382. Waelder, R. *Basic theory of psychoanalysis.* New York: International Universities Press, 1960
383. Walsh, R. *Towards an ecology of brain.* New York: Spectrum, 1979
384. ____, and Shapiro, D. (eds). *Beyond health and normality.* New York: Van Nostrand Reinhold, 1978
385. ____, and Vaughan, F., eds. *Beyond ego psychology.* Los Angeles: Tarcher.
386. Wapnick, K. "Mysticism and schizophrenia." *Journal of Transpersonal Psychology*, vol. 1, 1969
387. Warren, H. (trans). *Buddhism in translation.* New York: Athenum, 1970
388. Washburn, M. "Observations relevant to a unified theory of meditation." *Journal of Transpersonal Psychology*, vol 10, no 1, 1978
389. Watts, A. *The way of Zen.* New York: Vintage, 1957
390. ____. *Psychotherapy east and west.* New York: Ballantine, 1969
391. Wei Wu Wei. *Posthumous pieces.* Hong Kong: Hong Kong Univ. Press, 1968
392. Welwood, J. "Meditation and the unconscious." *Journal of Transpersonal Psychology*, vol. 9, no. 1, 1977
393. Werner, H. *Comparative psychology of mental development.* New York: International Universities Press, 1957
394. ____. "The concept of development from a comparative and organismic point of view." Harris, ed. *The concept of development.* Minneapolis: Univ. of Minnesota, 1957
395. Wescott, R. *The divine animal.* New York: Funk and Wagnalls, 1969
396. White, J., ed. *The highest state of consciousness.* New York: Anchor, 1972
397. ____, ed. *What is meditation?* New York: Anchor, 1972
398. ____, ed. *Kundalini, evolution, and enlightenment.* New York: Anchor, 1979
399. ____, and Krippner, S., eds. *Future science.* New York: Anchor, 1979
400. Whitehead, A. N. *Modes of thought.* New York: Macmillan, 1966
401. ____. *Adventures of ideas.* New York: Macmillan, 1967
402. ____. *Science and the modern world.* New York: Macmillan, 1967
403. Whorf, B. L. *Language thought and reality.* Cambridge: M.I.T. Press, 1956

404. Whyte, L. L. *The next development in man.* New York: Mento, 1950
405. Wilber, K. "The spectrum of consciousness." *Main Currents,* vol. 31, no. 2, 1974
406. _____. "The perennial psychology." *Human Dimensions,* vol. 4, no. 2, vol. 7, no. 2, 1975
407. _____. "Psychologia Perennis." *Journal of Transpersonal Psychology,* vol. 7, no. 2, 1975
408. _____. "The ultimate state of consciousness." *Journal of Altered States of Consciousness,* vol. 2, no. 3, 1975-6.
409. _____. "The eternal moment." *Science of Mind,* June 1976
410. _____. *The spectrum of consciousness.* Wheaton: Quest: 1977
411. _____. "On dreaming: the other side of you." *Foundation for Human Understanding,* vol. 1, no. 1, 1978
412. _____. "Microgeny." *Re-Vision,* vol. 1, no. 3/4, 1978
413. _____. "Projection." *Foundation for Human Understanding,* vol. 1, no. 2, 1978
414. _____. "Some remarks on the papers delivered at the spirtual/transpersonal symposium." Annual meeting of the American Psychological Association, Toronto, 1978
415. _____. "Transpersonal developmental psychology." *Re-Vision,* vol. 1, no. 1, 1978
416. _____. "The transpersonal dynamic of evolution." *Re-Vision,* vol. 1, no. 2, 1978
417. _____. "Where it was, I shall become." In Walsh and Shapiro, reference note #384
418. _____. "A working synthesis of transactional analysis and gestalt therapy." *Psychotherapy: Theory, Research, and Practice,* vol. 15, no. 1, 1978
419. _____. "Are the chakras real?" In White, J., reference note #398
420. _____. "Development and transcendence." *American Theosophist,* May 1, 1979
421. _____. "A developmental view of consciousness." *Journal of Transpersonal Psychology,* vol. 11, no. 1, 1979
422. _____. "Eye to eye—science and transpersonal psychology." *Re-Vision,* vol. 2, no. 1, 1979
423. _____. "Heroes and cults." *Vision Mound,* vol. 2, no. 8, 1979
424. _____. "Into the transpersonal." *Re-Vision,* vol. 2, no. 1, 1979
425. _____. "The master-student relationship." *Foundation for Human Understanding,* vol. 2, no. 1, 1979
426. _____. *No boundary.* Los Angeles: Center Publications, 1979
427. __ *Up from eden.* In submission.
428. Wittgenstein, L. *Philosophical investigations.* Oxford: Blackwell, 1953
429. _____. *Tractatus Logico Philosophicus.* London: Routledge and Kegan Paul, 1969
430. Woods, J. H. *The yoga system of Patanjali.* Delhi: Banarsidass, 1977
431. Yampolsky, P., trans. *The Zen Master Hakuin.* New York: Columbia Univ. Press, 1971
432. Yankelovich, K., and Barrett, W. *Ego and instinct.* New York: Vintage, 1971
433. Yogananda, P. *The science of religion.* Los Angeles: Self-Realization Fellowship, 1974
434. Yogeshwarand Saraswati. *Science of soul.* India: Yoga Niketan, 1972

435. Young, J. Z. *Programs of the brain.* Oxford: Oxford Univ. Press, 1978
436. Zilboorg, G. "Fear of death." *Psychoanalytic Quarterly*, vol. 12, 1943
437. Zimmer, H. *Philosophies of India.* London: Routledge and Kegan Paul, 1969

Index